FROM THE PAGES OF
NARRATIVE OF SOJOURNER TRUTH

It is now asked to accord a modicum of honor to a woman who labored forty long and weary years a slave; to whom the paths of literature and science were forever closed; one who bore the double burdens of poverty and the ban of caste, yet who, despite all these disabilities, has acquired fame, and gained hosts of friends among the noblest and best of the dominant race. (page 3)

When he had tied her hands together before her, he gave her the most cruel whipping she was ever tortured with. He whipped her till the flesh was deeply lacerated, and the blood streamed from her wounds. (page 19)

'Oh, I do not want money or clothes now, I only want my son.' (page 37)

She informed Mrs. Whiting, the woman of the house where she was stopping, that her name was no longer Isabella, but SOJOURNER; and that she was going east. And to her inquiry, 'What are you going east for?' her answer was, 'The Spirit calls me there, and I must go.' (page 73)

Her mission was not merely to travel east, but to 'lecture,' as she designated it; 'testifying of the hope that was in her'—exhorting the people to embrace Jesus, and refrain from sin. (page 74)

'What we give to the poor, we lend to the Lord.' (page 92)

"'Don't let her speak, Mrs. Gage, it will ruin us. Every newspaper in the land will have our cause mixed with abolition and niggers, and we shall be utterly denounced.'" (page 99)

"Ar'n't I a woman? Look at me! Look at my arm! [And she bared her right arm to the shoulder, showing her tremendous muscular power.] I have plowed, and planted, and gathered into barns, and no man could head me—and ar'n't I a woman?"   (page 100)

She sang with the strong barbaric accent of the native African, and with those indescribable upward turns and those deep gutturals which give such a wild, peculiar power to the negro singing—but above all, with such an overwhelming energy of personal appropriation that the hymn seemed to be fused in the furnace of her feelings and come out recrystallized as a production of her own.   (page 119)

"I told him that I had never heard of him before he was talked of for president. He smilingly replied, 'I had heard of you many times before that.'"   (page 131)

"She is a crazy, ignorant, repelling negress, and her guardians would do a Christian act to restrict her entirely to private life." (page 149)

"'With all your opportunities for readin' and writin',' you don't take hold and do anything. My God, I wonder what you are in the world for!'"   (page 176)

She had not courage to chide people for using spirituous liquors while indulging in the use of tobacco, herself. Accordingly she discontinued the habit. She was told it would affect her health. She said, "I'll quit if I die." She did quit and *lived!*   (page 227)

"I am pleading for my people,
    A poor, down-trodden race,
Who dwell in freedom's boasted land,
    With no abiding place.

"Yet those oppressors, steeped in guilt—
    I still would have them live;
For I have learned of Jesus
    To suffer and forgive."   (page 261)

NARRATIVE OF SOJOURNER TRUTH

with "Book of Life" and "A Memorial Chapter"

With an Introduction and Notes
by Imani Perry

GEORGE STADE
CONSULTING EDITORIAL DIRECTOR

𝒥𝓑
BARNES & NOBLE CLASSICS
NEW YORK

BARNES & NOBLE CLASSICS
NEW YORK

Published by Barnes & Noble Books
122 Fifth Avenue
New York, NY 10011

www.barnesandnoble.com/classics

Narrative of Sojourner Truth was first published in 1850. The present text of the
Narrative and the "Book of Life" is that of the Memorial Edition of 1878.
The text of "A Memorial Chapter" is taken from the 1884 edition.

Published in 2005 by Barnes & Noble Classics with new Introduction,
Notes, Biography, Chronology, Inspired By,
Comments & Questions, and For Further Reading.

Narrative of Sojourner Truth
ISBN-13: 978-1-59308-293-2
ISBN-10: 1-59308-293-2
LC Control Number 2005920892

Produced and published in conjunction with:
Fine Creative Media, Inc.
322 Eighth Avenue
New York, NY 10001

Michael J. Fine, President and Publisher

Printed in the United States of America

QM

3 5 7 9 10 8 6 4 2

Around the year 1797, the woman who would later be known as Sojourner Truth was born on a Dutch slave-holding farm in Ulster County, New York, and named Isabella. Her parents were slaves, and Isabella's twelve brothers and sisters were separated from the family when they were sold to other households. As she later recounted in her autobiography, the *Narrative of Sojourner Truth*, Dutch-speaking Isabella was often whipped and beaten during her years of servitude, particularly by her second master for her initial inability to speak English. After being sold several times and having an offer of freedom rescinded by her owners, she fled to a neighboring house with her daughter, Sophia. The family helped secure her emancipation, but only through legal action did she save another of her children, Peter, from servitude in the slave-holding state of Alabama.

Following her emancipation, Isabella moved to New York City and worked as a domestic servant while also preaching her Methodist faith. More than six feet tall, she was as physically imposing as she was eloquent, and her reputation as a gifted speaker spread quickly. In 1843 she left the city to become a preacher. She changed her name to Sojourner Truth and traveled extensively around the Northeast, preaching in homes and churches. During an inspiring stay at the Northampton Association of Education and Industry, Truth met emancipation activists David Ruggles, William Lloyd Garrison, and Frederick Douglass. With their encouragement and her own determination, she joined forces with other abolitionists and began lecturing about her history as a slave.

Having never learned to read and write, Truth asked a friend from the Northampton Association, Olive Gilbert, to transcribe her life story. In 1850 it was published as the *Narrative of Sojourner Truth*. It sold steadily at meetings everywhere Truth traveled. The next year, her fame increased even more dramatically when she gave her famous "Ar'n't (or Ain't) I a Woman?" speech at the Woman's Rights Convention in Akron, Ohio. An 1863 *Atlantic Monthly* article by *Uncle Tom's Cabin* author Harriet Beecher Stowe also acquainted the greater public with Truth's remarkable story.

A tireless lecturer and aid worker, Truth did relief work for freed slaves in Washington, D.C., during and after the Civil War. Abraham Lincoln, as well as two other presidents, invited her to the White House and commended her abolitionist and equal-rights activism. A visionary, Truth dreamed of creating a territory in the western United States where freed slaves could live, work, and own property unencumbered by servitude. Until age and ill health forced her to retire, Truth also lectured on suffrage, temperance, and capital punishment. She died in Battle Creek, Michigan, in 1883.

TABLE OF CONTENTS

THE WORLD OF SOJOURNER TRUTH
AND HER *NARRATIVE*

c.1797   The woman who will later be known as Sojourner Truth is born in Ulster County, New York, and named Isabella. Her parents, Elizabeth (Betsey or Mau Mau Bett) and James (also called Bomefree) are slaves for a Dutch family named Hardenbergh. Isabella and her twelve siblings are also enslaved from birth; the family is split up when many of the children are sold to other homes. Despite their unhappy living conditions, Isabella's mother finds time to tell her children stories, perhaps inspiring Isabella's narrative eloquence.

1799   The New York State legislature passes An Act for the Gradual Abolition of Slavery.

1806   Following the death of Mr. Hardenbergh, Isabella is sold to the Nealy (also spelled Neely) family for $100. She has been raised speaking only Dutch, and her new owner abuses her when she cannot understand English.

1807   Great Britain abolishes the slave trade.

1808   Isabella is sold again, this time to the Scriver (or Schriver) family.

1810   Isabella is sold to the Dumont family, with whom she lives for more than fifteen years. She gives birth to several children who become property of the Dumonts as well. Isabella is more than six feet tall; her master brags that she is stronger than his male slaves.

1814   Isabella's romantic relationship with a man named Robert, enslaved by another family, is destroyed by his master's violent disapproval. Francis Scott Key writes "The Star Spangled Banner."

1815   Isabella marries a man named Thomas, also owned by the Dumonts. They will raise five children together.

1817   The New York legislature passes a law granting freedom to slaves born before July 4, 1799, although certain tenets of the law mean not all will be freed until 1827. Henry David Thoreau is born. The American Colonization Society is founded, supporting the return of African Americans to Africa.

1820   The U.S. Congress passes the Missouri Compromise, an attempt to settle the North-South conflict over whether slavery will be allowed in new states admitted to the Union.

1822   Ulysses S. Grant is born. In an effort to prevent free black sailors from mixing with local slaves and spreading ideas about insurrection, South Carolina passes the Negro Seamen Act, requiring the imprisonment of black sailors while in port. Liberia is founded for the repatriation of former American slaves.

1823   The Monroe Doctrine declares the United States will not interfere in European affairs but also will not tolerate foreign intervention in the Western Hemisphere.

1826   John Dumont, who has promised Isabella he will free her a year earlier than required by law, rescinds his promise. She flees with her youngest child, Sophia, to the home of Isaac Van Wagener (also given as Wagenen). He pays off the Dumonts when Mr. Dumont comes to retrieve her, and Isabella works for the family for about a year. During that time, against New York State law, the Dumonts sell her son, Peter, to people who then illegally turn him over to a family living in Alabama, still a slave state. Quakers give Isabella the funds to hire a lawyer to sue for Peter's return.

1827   Isabella is emancipated and, following a common practice for freed slaves, takes Van Wagener as her own last name. She begins her deep spiritual involvement with the Pentecostal wing of the Methodist Church.

1828   Isabella wins her court case, and her son Peter is returned to her.

1829   Having suffered so much turmoil in the Hudson Valley, Isabella decides to move with Peter to New York City. While working as a domestic servant for the Latourette family, Isabella begins preaching. She also encounters two siblings from whom she had been separated as a child. David Walker, a free black, publishes *Appeal to the Coloured Citizens of the World*, a radical abolitionist tract.

1831 Virginia slave Nat Turner leads a rebellion that ends with the death of more than fifty whites; after his capture, he is tried and hanged. William Lloyd Garrison begins publication of the abolitionist paper *The Liberator* in Boston.

1832 Isabella becomes a follower of radical white preacher Robert Matthews, known as the Prophet Matthias. She attends his communal meetings in Sing Sing, New York, at which he prophesies the end of the world. The sect, the Matthias Kingdom, ends in disgrace with the trial of its leader for murder and child abuse. Isabella is also charged with attempting to poison the Folger family, fellow Matthias Kingdom members; she is found not guilty. William Lloyd Garrison helps found the New England Anti-Slavery Society.

1833 The American Anti-Slavery Society is founded.

1835 Isabella sues the Folgers for slander and prevails. She then returns to New York City, where she works as a domestic servant for the next eight years. Few details are known of her life during this time. Samuel Clemens, better known as Mark Twain, is born.

1836 Davy Crockett dies in the battle of the Alamo in Texas. The U.S. House of Representatives passes the first of several gag rules that table without discussion anti-slavery proposals.

1838 Frederick Bailey escapes from slavery in Maryland and heads north, where he changes his name to Frederick Douglass.

1839 A slave mutiny takes place on the slave ship *Amistad*. George D. Weed publishes a passionate anti-slavery tract, *Slavery as It Is*.

1843 Isabella feels called upon by God to adopt the name "Sojourner," to which she appends the last name "Truth." She leaves New York City to travel and preach throughout New England. Residing for a time in Northampton, Massachusetts, she joins the Northampton Association of Education and Industry, a utopian community dedicated to equality and justice; the organization's members include abolitionists David Ruggles, William Lloyd Garrison, and Frederick Douglass.

1844   Truth delivers her first public anti-slavery speech in Northampton. She begins lecturing about her life in the hope of abolishing slavery and securing equal rights for women. John Quincy Adams heads a successful fight in the House of Representatives to end the gag rule on anti-slavery debates.

1845   *The Narrative of the Life of Frederick Douglass* is published; it will become the most influential slave narrative in American history.

1848   Gold is discovered in California.

1849   Thoreau publishes "Civil Disobedience" under the title "Resistance to Civil Government."

1850   Truth's rhetorical gifts impel her to put her story in print; since she is illiterate, she engages Olive Gilbert to transcribe her life story, and the first edition of the *Narrative of Sojourner Truth* is published. On the lecture circuit, Truth gains an ever-wider audience and sells copies of her *Narrative*. Congress passes new compromises on slavery, which include the admission of California as a free state and the prohibition of slavery in Washington, D.C., but allow other territories considering statehood to determine for themselves whether to allow slavery. A stricter Fugitive Slave Law allows for the capture of runaway slaves after they have reached free states, and imposes penalties on anyone who helps a slave escape. More than 3 million black slaves live in the southern states.

1851   The Woman's Rights Convention in Akron, Ohio, serves as the podium for one of Truth's most famous speeches, "Ar'n't (or Ain't) I a Woman?"

1852   *Uncle Tom's Cabin*, by Harriet Beecher Stowe, is published.

1854   Under the principle of popular sovereignty, the Kansas-Nebraska Act is passed, allowing citizens of those two states to decide whether to allow slavery.

1855   Walt Whitman's *Leaves of Grass* is published.

1856   Truth moves her home base from Northampton to Battle Creek, Michigan.

1857   The United States Supreme Court decides the case of *Dred Scott vs. Sandford*. Scott and his wife had sued for their freedom on the basis of seven years of living in a free state and then a free territory. The court declares the Scotts to still be slaves and announces that the Missouri Compromise of 1820 guaranteeing that slavery would not expand into the new western territories is unconstitutional.

1859   Abolitionist John Brown seizes the Federal Armory in Harper's Ferry, Virginia (now West Virginia); he is captured by Robert E. Lee and hanged.

1861   The Civil War begins. Truth's grandson, James Caldwell, serves the Union Army in the all-black 54th Massachusetts Regiment. Truth lectures, preaches, and helps locate jobs and shelter for newly freed slaves in Washington, D.C. Harriet Jacobs's *Incidents in the Life of a Slave Girl* is published.

1863   President Abraham Lincoln introduces the Emancipation Proclamation. Harriet Beecher Stowe writes about Truth in the *Atlantic Monthly* article "Sojourner Truth: The Libyan Sibyl."

1864   Truth's good works, including gathering supplies for black volunteer regiments, lead to an invitation to Lincoln's White House; he is the first of several presidents who will host the tireless activist.

1865   The Civil War ends on April 9. The Thirteenth Amendment to the U.S. Constitution, abolishing slavery, is passed. In Washington, D.C., a new federal law desegregates streetcars. Truth has two drivers fired for refusing to allow her to ride; she sues another for assault and battery for forcibly removing her from a streetcar. She works for the newly formed Freedman's Bureau.

1868   The Fourteenth Amendment granting citizenship to former slaves and ensuring that all citizens have equal protection under the law is passed.

1870   Truth supports the creation of a western region to be owned and operated by freed slaves. The Fifteenth Amendment grants suffrage to black men.

1872   Truth attempts to vote in Battle Creek, Michigan, but is denied.

1875   Truth republishes her *Narrative* along with the "Book of Life," her scrapbook, which is edited by Frances Titus.

1883   The Supreme Court rules that the Fourteenth Amendment
       does not apply to privately owned locations, such as restau-
       rants and hotels. This distinction eventually leads to segre-
       gationist "Jim Crow" laws. Following many years of
       vigorous equal-rights lectures and speeches, Sojourner Truth
       dies in Battle Creek on November 26.

INTRODUCTION

"I sell the shadow to support the substance."

—Sojourner Truth

These words graced the photographs Sojourner Truth sold of herself. In her elderly years, profits from their sale served as one of her few means of support. The word "shadow" was a nineteenth-century colloquialism for a photographic portrait. But for Truth, shadow would have more than one meaning. As a figure of great historical significance, Truth dwells in the shadows of the lore surrounding her. She was throughout her life illiterate, and therefore the only written record she leaves is a second-hand transcription of her words and ideas—records that were vulnerable to the interpretation of the transcriber, so much so that it often becomes difficult to surmise what Truth actually said. Despite this, there is much that we do know to be true about Sojourner Truth, and the works included herein, the *Narrative of Sojourner Truth* and the "Book of Life," give us great insight into the character, legacy, and substance of one of the heroines of the nineteenth century.

The reader of the *Narrative* should remember that in many ways it is a biography rather than an autobiography. The *Narrative* was written by Olive Gilbert, sitting at Truth's proverbial knee, and treats Truth's life from her birth until her forties. Gilbert was a woman Truth met while a member of the Northampton Association of Education and Industry (1843–1846), a progressive intentional community in Northampton, Massachusetts. Intentional communities were comprised of people who chose to live cooperatively, according to shared ideals that were often rooted in a set of theological or philosophical beliefs. The members of the Northampton Association operated a collectively owned silk mill and believed in equal rights for women and African Americans; they were advocates of abolition.

The *Narrative* was first published in 1850 at Truth's own expense and predated her celebrity as an abolitionist, although she had delivered her first antislavery lecture six years earlier. While the *Narrative* speaks little of her abolitionism, it reveals much of her life's mission. Sojourner Truth first and foremost was a woman who lived an evangelical life. It is through her vision of Godly purpose that she came, later in life, to abolitionism. Indeed, one of her most famous, and well verified, comments was one in which religion dramatically dovetailed with abolitionism. At an antislavery meeting in Faneuil Hall in Boston, Massachusetts, Truth listened to Frederick Douglass, who, despondent at the persistence and growth of antebellum slavery, advocated taking up arms in defense of the enslaved. Truth's poignant response to his fervor was, "Frederick, is God dead?"—thus silencing the brilliant and famous abolitionist with her pious conviction.

Sojourner Truth was unlettered, while Douglass was learned. She was a northerner, while Douglass was a Maryland native. This contrast was symbolic of Truth's life. Her *Narrative*, a tale of New York slavery, lay outside the mainstream of slave narratives. Until she moved to New York City, she had never lived in a black community. Her native tongue was Dutch. But Truth's testimony of northern slavery in her *Narrative*, which revealed slavery as a national legacy and problem, was dramatically verified by the passage of a stricter Fugitive Slave Law in the same year as the book's publication. The Fugitive Slave Law dictated that those suspected of being runaway slaves could be arrested without a warrant and turned over to a claimant on nothing more than the sworn testimony of the owner. A person suspected of being a slave could neither ask for a jury trial nor testify on his or her own behalf. Federal marshals who did not arrest an alleged runaway could be fined $1,000. The law not only endangered the formerly enslaved, but all black people. Moreover, the law discouraged those who might assist runaways by providing that any person aiding a runaway in any manner was subject to six months imprisonment and a $1,000 fine. And one who captured a fugitive slave was entitled to a fee, thereby encouraging the kidnapping of free blacks for sale to slave traders. The law signaled a move toward the nationalization of slavery. This was ironic, given that most northern states had either already begun the process of emancipation or formally abolished slavery two generations prior. Nevertheless, the political power wielded by the South protected the peculiar institution and extended its power around the nation.

Truth's *Narrative* thus emerges at the precipice of transformations that would lead to the Civil War. As she developed as an abolitionist, the nation careened toward dissolution. In 1857 the Supreme Court ruled in *Dred Scott vs. Sandford* that slaves had no rights as citizens. For Dred Scott this meant that living in a free state, where his master had moved his household, did not guarantee Scott and his wife their freedom. The court moreover declared that a black man had no rights a white man was bound to respect, and that the government could not outlaw slavery in new territories, as had been provided in the Missouri Compromise of 1820 and subsequent laws. The decision virtually guaranteed that the nation would have to contend violently with slavery as a national question. Sojourner Truth's life unfolds in the midst of this transformative period in history.

Truth's critical work before the Civil War and after as an abolitionist minister, and later as an advocate for the freed people, necessitates that we include the "Book of Life" in this volume, in order to provide as full an account of her importance as possible. The "Book of Life" is Truth's scrapbook, published in 1875 with editorial comments by Frances Titus, Truth's helper in her final home of Battle Creek, Michigan. The work is a motley assortment of newspaper clippings and articles about Truth, along with the many signatures she collected as she traveled, from prominent abolitionist activists, reformers, and suffragists. While the "Book of Life" fails to have a narrative structure, it is useful for any student of Truth; it shows us what was important to her, what she collected, saved, and hoped to keep as a record of her time as a champion for African Americans, women, and the Gospel.

Sojourner Truth was born in 1797 and named Isabella by her parents, Elizabeth (also known as Mau Mau Bett) and James (also known as Bomefree, which means "tree" in the Low Dutch they spoke, because his build was tall and straight). Isabella was born in the village of Hurley, in Ulster County, New York, 7 miles west of the Hudson River, 90 miles north of New York City, and 60 miles south of Albany. Like most of the town's citizens, the family's master, Colonel Johannis Hardenbergh, was Dutch, and Isabella spoke Low Dutch exclusively until she was sold to the English-speaking Nealys (or Neelys) at age nine for $100. The Nealys were infuriated by her inability to speak English and beat her mercilessly, emotionally scarring her for life. After a couple of years she was sold again, to a bar owner named Scriver (or Schriver). With this master, Isabella suffered less cruelty and eventually learned English, which she would speak with a Dutch accent and grammatical inflections for the rest of her life. Our knowledge of Isabella's Dutch language has provided historians with evidence regarding how unlikely are many of the quotations attributed to her. The illustrious author of *Uncle Tom's Cabin*, Harriet Beecher Stowe, wrote about her in an essay called "Sojourner Truth: The Libyan Sibyl" for the *Atlantic Monthly* in 1863. In it, Stowe describes Truth's 1853 visit to Andover, Massachusetts. Though the piece is laudatory, it is clear Stowe takes a great deal of poetic license. She describes her subject as deceased though Truth would live twenty years past the essay's date of publication, and she has Truth speak in a southern dialect, which Truth, in her Low Dutch language, would be neither very familiar with nor fluent in. For Stowe, as for many of her white contemporaries, southern black dialect was used as a marker of the subject's inferior status. It also indicates Stowe's use of Truth as a vehicle for a political argument, rather than an authentic biographical subject. Stowe was apparently less concerned with reporting Truth's words and life with accuracy, and more concerned with the imagined effect her characterization would have upon her readers. The middle- and upper-class readership of Stowe's article might include some abolitionists but would include few individuals who did not maintain stereotypical images of blacks, given the prevailing racial ideology of the mid-nineteenth century. Stowe's sentimental and condescending article celebrated an image of Truth that was consistent with dominant images of black women as simple and unfeminine.

Truth's resilience despite ritual misrepresentations of her likely came from the toughness and transcendence she developed while enslaved. In 1810 she was sold for the final time, to John and Sally

Dumont. The Dumonts considered her a hardworking and capable slave, but she suffered regular physical and sexual abuse at the hands of her mistress, Sally Dumont. She remained their slave for sixteen years until she freed herself by simply walking out. Truth's self-liberation is but one witness to her legacy, and but one element of her history as a woman of religion and purpose. She would become a minister, a reformer, a litigant, and an icon—all roles that followed from her self-determined liberation.

The Minister

Isabella became Sojourner through what would be her second conversion experience. Though she describes learning to believe in God at her mother's informal instruction, she is "converted" by way of a traditional conversion narrative that is particular to the concerns of a black person in the slave-holding United States. The first conversion took her from slavery to freedom, and the second from congregant to minister. "Conversion to freedom" experiences were not uncommon in slave narratives. For example, Frederick Douglass's conversions, depicted in his *Narrative*, published to great acclaim five years earlier than Truth's, find Douglass coming first through literacy, then through the chiasmus of degradation and self-protection in response to a slave-breaker's violence ("You have seen how a man was made a slave; you shall see how a slave was made a man"), and finally through mobility in his escape from slavery. In contrast, Isabella experiences a classic religious conversion, more consistent in many ways with a figure like her contemporary, African Methodist Episcopal preacher Jarena Lee (born in 1783) of Cape May, New Jersey, who authored *The Life and Religious Experience of Jarena Lee* (1836), the first spiritual autobiography by an African American woman. However, Isabella, in the process of becoming Sojourner, described her religious conversion and her emancipation in a fashion that demonstrates how they were inextricably linked for her in one unified concept of freedom. Religious historian Albert Raboteau noted in his film documentary *Africans in America, Part 3: 1791–1831*, that it is characteristic of African-American women's nineteenth-century conversion narratives that the conversion is protracted, that there is a struggle before reaching conversion, and that the conversion empowers the congregant to transcend social prohibitions. For Isabella, becoming Sojourner Truth was a conversion that allowed her to transcend slavery, racism, and sexism in order to become a symbol of racial and gender emancipation, both figurative and literal. Her legal freedom was just the first step.

In 1799, about two years after Isabella's birth, New York State began a process of gradual emancipation. A 1799 statute provided freedom to children born after 1799 when they attained age twenty-five for females and twenty-eight for males. An 1817 legislative decree stated that slaves born before 1799 would be emancipated on July 4, 1827, at which point slavery would be entirely abolished for New York State residents (although until 1841 nonresidents could visit and bring their slaves with them to New York for up to nine months). In light of her excellent service, John Dumont promised to emancipate Isabella on July 4, 1826, a year before the date required by law. She worked dutifully under this impression, and early in 1826 she suffered a disfiguring hand injury while doing field work. Dumont used this injury as an excuse to breach his promise, arguing that as he had lost significant value in her due to her inability to perform hard labor, he was forced to keep her enslaved until 1827. Isabella was always a good servant, but the violation of honor that this breach represented was a turning point for her. Isabella determined that she would do no more as a slave than spin the wool for that season, and would be free as soon as the task was completed.

Remarkably, she followed through with her intention, and did so openly. Isabella left the Dumont residence with her youngest child, Sophia, and walked 5 miles to seek the aid of the Van Wageners (the name is sometimes given as Van Wagenen). Isaac and Maria Van Wagener were prominent members of the Dutch Reformed Church and opposed slavery. They provided Isabella and her daughter with shelter. When Dumont came to retrieve his property, the Van Wageners paid off the remainder of Isabella's service to him with $25.

Isabella worked for the Van Wageners for a time, but it was not long before she was tempted to return to slavery. Unlike many other slave narratives, Truth's *Narrative* dramatically renders the complex relationship between enslaved and enslavers, who are united by domesticity and rituals of cruelty. She wanted freedom, but she also was attached to her former life. In particular, she was tempted by a holiday called Pinkster (spelled Pingster in the *Narrative*), which means Pentecost in Dutch.

This holiday, celebrated on the day of Pentecost, the seventh Sunday after Easter, had become a sort of carnival for black New Yorkers. As a population that was largely dispersed, black New Yorkers had relatively minimal opportunity to exist in a culturally African or African-American community. Pinkster was a time when they could share traditions and subvert their subjugation through elaborate mimicry of the European ruling classes and general bacchanalia. The holiday involved a secular interpretation of the time of spiritual transcendence in the form of speaking in tongues and religious ecstasy represented by the day of Pentecost. They paraded, imbibed, and transcended conventions of subservience for one weekend a year. Isabella recalled the joy of the holiday and decided to return to her master out of her desire to participate. He arrived to pick her up just before the celebration but as she was about to get aboard his wagon and return to his home she experienced a divine intervention. In a flash she saw God and, later, incapable of remembering what had happened in the physical world, she found herself alone, standing still in her freedom. It was a true conversion, her first, marked by a vision, a break with the temporal world, and a transformed relationship to life.

Isabella's association of Pinkster with her rejection of slavery could be read as a disaffection for one of her few contacts with black culture, but in the context of her life as a political and religious figure, another interpretation is demanded. Isabella's association should be read as a religion-based rejection of Pinkster's excess; the holiday's drinking and wildness is exchanged for the deeply conservative religious life she had by then embraced. The *Narrative* also subtextually suggests that Isabella's association should be read as a rejection of the role Pinkster played in psychologically subjugating black people. Pinkster, we are led to think, was but a taste of freedom, perhaps an opiate of sorts, not freedom itself. For Isabella then, turning away from Pinkster was an embrace of her true freedom on multiple registers, legal, psychological, and spiritual.

Isabella's second conversion precipitated her name change to Sojourner. In 1829 Isabella moved with her son Peter to New York City, where she worked as a domestic servant. She began preaching and was known for inspiring religious conversions. During this time, as would become characteristic of her, she was influenced by one of the religious movements that had emerged as part of the Second Great Awakening, a liberalizing Protestant movement lasting from the 1790s to the 1840s. Spearheaded by Methodists and Baptists, this movement led to the transformation of Protestant denominations in the United States. Across the nation, itinerant ministers brought the Word to vast numbers of people, and converted them through electrifying revivals. The revivals were democratic. Preachers were not required to come from a certain class, nor to have vocational training. Hence, the revival space was in many ways socially subversive. The language of the revivals was often vernacular, and the leadership dependent upon charisma rather than pomp. The revivals displaced religious power from church hierarchies into humble, local hands. A proximate political liberty thus could begin to emerge through religious liberty.

Isabella began to participate in the community organized by followers of William Miller, a Second Adventist prophet committed to converting as many people as possible before the "end of time." Isabella was also motivated by what she considered to be the sin of grotesque poverty and economic cruelty suffered by so many New Yorkers. In the *Narrative* we read that she was called to the ministry in response to this reality, and was instructed by God to adopt the name that would carry her into the history books, Sojourner Truth. Sojourner indicated her intention to be itinerant, and to be "Truth," the pursuit and transmission of spiritual wisdom. As the *Narrative* recounts,

> She informed Mrs. Whiting, the woman of the house where she was stopping, that her name was no longer Isabella, but SOJOURNER; and that she was going east. And to her inquiry, 'What are you going east for?' her answer was, 'The Spirit calls me there, and I must go.' . . . Her mission was not merely to travel east, but to 'lecture,' as she designated it; 'testifying of the hope that was in her'—exhorting the people to embrace Jesus, and refrain from sin, the nature and origin of which she explained to them in accordance with her own . . . views (pp. 73–74).

She embarked on her life as Sojourner Truth on the Day of Pentecost (and Pinkster) June 1, 1843.

Once again her spiritual conversion, this time to a life of ministry, was tied to political commitments. Truth's Word was one of humanity and democracy. Her self-assertion as a preacher, given her race and gender, was a rejection of the hierarchies of society. Her transgressions of socially proscribed roles would only begin there, and her ability to engage in these transgressions came about because she took advantage of the movement known as the Second Great Awakening.

At the same time as revivals spread, so too did the existence of utopian communities (more than ninety appeared in the United States between 1800 and 1850). Over the course of her life, she would join a number of intentional communities that blended democratic ideologies with religious conviction.

The first such community she joined was the Kingdom of Matthias. In 1830 Robert Matthews, a fanatic carpenter of Scotch ancestry from Albany, New York, claimed to be the wandering biblical prophet Matthias. He enlisted several prominent New York businessmen to join his fervent faith and established, with their financial support, a "Kingdom" in Sing Sing (later Ossining), New York. Several of these members were people with whom Truth had associated, including Elijah Pierson, for whom she was a housekeeper. Initially Pierson believed himself to be the reincarnation of the biblical Elijah, but he would grow to believe that Robert Matthews, the "Prophet Matthias," was Christ in his second coming. Isabella, too, joined Matthias's Kingdom, which was established on a 29-acre estate in Westchester County. This would come to be remembered as a dark period in her life. While there was supposedly no hierarchy to the community, Matthias held absolute, cult-like power; he was patriarchal, hypersexual, and manipulative. The membership dutifully followed his word, until sexual scandal and murder charges tore the Kingdom apart. Elijah Pierson died suddenly, and Matthias was charged with poisoning him. Though Isabella and Matthias both escaped serious criminal charges, the degradation and failure of the Kingdom could have alienated Truth from her spiritual path. But it appears her faith just grew in the aftermath, and she went on to seek fellowship with others.

With few exceptions (the Zion African Church in New York City being the most notable) the spiritual communities Truth participated in were mainly white. While she undoubtedly faced racism in these contexts (it appears she did much of the domestic labor and suffered sexual abuse at the hands of a wealthy white woman at the Kingdom of Matthias) she continually asserted her authority to be a full member and spokesperson of the communities of the faithful no matter what their racial composition.

It was in the context of the racially progressive intentional community the Northampton Association, however, that she gave her first antislavery lecture in 1844. For the remainder of her life, her public work would be both religious and political, and she went on to become a star on the antislavery lecture circuit. She supported the Union troops with domestic labor during the Civil War, and she worked for the Freedman's Bureau subsequent to Union victory. The last major work of her life was petitioning to Congress to allocate lands in the West for the formerly enslaved squatters who had relocated to Washington, D.C., in search of a livelihood that would sustain them in freedom. In these years, the newspaper accounts, many of which are found in the "Book of Life," cite her powerful and unique oratory. Her language was called peculiar, and her appearance—she was almost six feet tall and had dark brown skin—Amazonian. She proved in word and deed to be an effective yet unusual advocate, a virtual Paul of her people.

The Litigant

Although popular discourses fail adequately to account for Truth as a minister, scholarly accounts almost without exception detail her spiritual life. What both sorts of writing address inadequately, by and large, is Truth as a significant figure in legal history. (Christina Accomando's article "Demanding a Voice Among the Pettifoggers: Sojourner Truth as Legal Actor" is a noteworthy exception; see "For Further Reading.") Truth was a litigant in several landmark lawsuits, and in them she powerfully asserted her citizenship, even before she had citizenship rights.

When she was emancipated, Truth's children were still enslaved, as a result of the vagaries of the gradual emancipation law. In 1826 her son Peter was sold by John Dumont to a doctor as an attendant to the doctor on his journey to England. The doctor found, however, that Peter, aged five or six, was too small for this responsibility. Rather than return him, the doctor sold him to his brother, Solomon Gedney, who sold Peter to a planter in Alabama named Fowler. Fowler happened to be married to Sally Dumont's second cousin, Eliza.

The sale of Peter was in violation of New York State law. As part of the gradual elimination of slavery, slave owners were prohibited from selling their slaves to any other state, to ensure that the enslaved would indeed gain their freedom at the designated date. However, efforts to circumvent this law were quite common. Truth was aware that the sale of her son was in violation of the law. Moreover, she had spent her childhood witnessing her parents mourning the dozen children who had been sold away from them. Their trauma became her own, both as she witnessed their grief and then grieved herself when she was sold away from her beloved Mau Mau Bett and Bomefree, unable even to nurse them in their old age. The utter powerlessness of the enslaved parent and abandoned child were perhaps the greatest wounds of slavery.

Against all odds, Truth insisted upon fighting for Peter. She first appealed to the Dumonts for his return. When ridiculed by her former mistress for demanding the return of a "little nigger," Truth responded with conviction, "I'll have my son." Contrary to the laws of slave society, which denied most rights to African Americans, slave or free, she claimed ownership of her child, an early black feminist gesture if there ever was one.

When Truth got nowhere with her former masters, she sought assistance from the Quakers and was advised to seek legal counsel. She borrowed money to obtain an attorney and paid him more than his stated fee, so that he might that much more vigorously be her advocate. She brought her case before the grand jury, and though Fowler and Gedney tried various means to prevent Peter's return, he was back in Truth's arms within a year. He returned to her, badly abused and traumatized to such an extent that at first he rejected his mother, but he was nonetheless alive and hers again. Truth would take Peter with her when she moved to New York City, and much of the *Narrative* recounts her great concern for his welfare, as he gets into trouble and fails to pursue a profession until becoming a member of a whaling crew as a young man. Gilbert's editorial comments in the *Narrative* call into question Truth's competence as a mother to her five children. However, the fair reading is that Truth was a deeply committed mother, much in love with her children, but confined by their enslavement, and sometimes torn between the mission of her life and the duties of motherhood.

The first man Sojourner Truth loved, we learn in the *Narrative*, was nearly beaten to death by his master for loving her, and he never returned to her after this violence. Her husband, with whom she raised five children, did not remain a partner past her emancipation. As a parent in many ways alone, she remarkably prevailed in her suit for the return of Peter. We can imagine that, given her extraordinary oratorical skills, she offered powerful testimony before the grand jury and perhaps aided the case prepared by her lawyers. The courage she exhibited in this episode was indicative of her sense of her rights as a mother and more generally as a human being. We must recall that this case was brought at a time when the majority of African Americans were seen as not only noncitizens, but chattel, property rather than property holders. Truth's case was brought twenty years before *Dred Scott vs. Sandford* was filed, and nonetheless she won.

Truth's articulation of her rights through motherhood makes it undeniable that she should be designated as one of the foremothers of black feminism. A recurrent theme in black feminist thought of the late twentieth century was a critique of the manner in which the control of black women's reproductivity, and the construction of black mothers as either unfit parents or the adoring mammies of white children under the oversight of white women, were signature features of black women's gendered and racial oppression. Contemporary scholars continue to recognize the reproductive realm as contested territory in black feminist struggles. Truth's fierce maternalism contravened both stereotype and the culture of American law.

Truth's second lawsuit concerned slander. In the midst of the downfall of the Kingdom of Matthias, Truth was accused of attempting to poison one of the wealthy couples who belonged to the cult, the Folgers. It seems likely that this accusation was an effort by the Folgers to deflect attention away from their participation in the disreputed organization by positing themselves as victims of an evil black woman. Truth was found not guilty in her criminal trial. But she was not satisfied with that. In 1835 she sued the Folgers for slander, and prevailed. It appears that she may have been the first black person to win a slander suit against a white person in the United States. She also made sure her name would be cleared in public accounts by giving full testimony to Gilbert Vale, the man who would write the most detailed account of the sensational cult.

This suit was also extraordinary. The overwhelming majority of African Americans in 1835 had a virtually nameless existence. By and large, they had neither last names nor recorded dates of birth. To the extent that they were named, it was as a record of them as property. Slander, in contrast, is a claim that one's name has been insulted, and moreover that the individual's property interest in her name has been damaged by a false accusation. Truth thus saw her name as something she owned and could protect against desecration by others, even those who were white and wealthy. Her investment in her reputation, at a time when black people were routinely subjected as an entire group to racist stereotypes that obviated any notion of a good name, is almost unbelievable.

Truth's lawsuits indicate that she was not just an extraordinary individual, but also an extraordinary representative of the myriad enslaved people, in particular the women. She took this representation seriously, despite the fact that with the exception of her years in New York City, she never lived fully immersed in a black community. At one point, the abolitionist Truth would personify the black southern wet nurse, claiming that while she had nursed many a white baby at her breasts, her own children went untended. This claim came about at an antislavery meeting in Indiana in 1858, during which several pro-slavery Democrats in the audience challenged her by shouting out that she was really a man masquerading as a woman. In response to their allegations, Truth bared her breasts, telling them that it was to their shame, not her own that she did so. Her opponents' claims were intended to delegitimize her message and humiliate her. But Truth, in the court of public opinion represented by that meeting tent, made the better argument. She gave them a powerful tongue-lashing and "told them that her breasts had suckled many a white babe to the exclusion of her own offspring; that some of those babies had grown to man's estate; that, although they had sucked her colored breasts, they were, in her estimation, far more manly than they (her persecutors) appeared to be; and she quietly asked them, as she disrobed her bosom, if they, too, wished to suck!" (p. 104).

While it is unlikely that she actually had been a wet nurse—it was a very uncommon role for northern slaves—she used the quotidian experience of southern black women to gain the upper hand in argumentation. The allegation that she was a man, which she discredited, was not unusual. Indeed, as a public speaker, Truth was venturing not only into white, but also male territory. It was not infrequent for white women speakers to be accused of being men as a sort of rhetorical punishment of their entrance into the authority of lecturer. Just as Truth took on the white and male space of the law in her suits for Peter and against slander, she took on the white male public forum to argue for her rights and those of her enslaved sisters.

Truth's last lawsuit came about after the Civil War, while she was working in Washington, D.C. In the aftermath of the Civil War, the states and the District of Columbia underwent a painful adjustment to the idea that blacks were citizens, although some below the Mason-Dixon line never fully accepted the notion until well into the twentieth century. Many southern states created black codes, which restricted the rights of black people, as an effort to reassert white supremacy. These statutes were clearly in violation of the Thirteenth Amendment's guarantee of freedom, and the Fourteenth Amendment's guarantees of due process and equal protection, as they included provisions such as disallowing blacks to vote or bear arms and mandated segregation of public facilities.

One of the routine manners of publicly demonstrating white supremacy was the segregation of streetcars. Indeed, this segregation in transportation, as we well know, would continue in parts of the nation well into the twentieth century; it was not until 1954, with the Supreme Court decision on *Brown vs. Board of Education of Topeka*, that the notion of "separate but equal" was legally dismantled and not until the Montgomery Bus Boycott of 1964 that it was culturally dismantled.

Sojourner Truth, along with other African American activists of the mid- to late-nineteenth century (such as Frederick Douglass, Harriet Tubman, Frances Ellen Watkins Harper, and Ida B. Wells), challenged early forms of segregation in transportation. Although in 1865 Washington, D.C., streetcars were declared desegregated by federal law, they seldom stopped for black passengers. Truth insisted upon her rights to ride both before and after legal desegregation. Once, when she tried to board a streetcar, the driver refused to stop, and she was dragged seven yards. She filed a formal complaint with the company and had the driver dismissed. In another attempt to ride, Truth was forced to ride with the horses instead of with the other passengers. A third driver attacked her for her insistence upon her legal right to ride. She complained and had this driver dismissed as well. She went further than that, however, and pressed criminal charges against the man. He was convicted of assault and battery.

Truth would influence the continued anti-segregationist interpretation of the Constitution in Washington, D.C. This, we must recall, was almost a century before Rosa Parks famously refused to give up her seat on a segregated bus in Montgomery, Alabama—a refusal that led to the Montgomery Bus Boycott—and marks Sojourner Truth as a foremother of the civil rights movement.

The treatment of black women on public streetcars was another indication of the particular oppression they faced. In contrast to white women, they were not seen as ladies in law or culture. In the case of Sallie Robinson, this insult would be dramatically demonstrated before the entire nation in an 1883 Supreme Court opinion. Robinson, traveling with her white-looking husband, was thrown off the ladies' car of a train in Tennessee because the conductors presumed that she must be a prostitute. The United States Supreme Court, which consolidated this case with others in the *Civil Rights Cases*, upheld the legitimacy of this presumption, and her expulsion. The contrasting image of the white woman as lady and the black one as whore revealed both how white women were confined by gender roles, and how black women were confined, insulted, and assaulted by them. The racialized sexism experienced by Truth was experienced by all the nation's black women. Truth's feminism, a sort that centrally located feminist arguments within black female consciousness, anticipated the efforts in the 1970s to expand the largely white feminist movement to include women of color. Truth was, along with women of the generation following hers, like Ida B. Wells, and Anna Julia Cooper, one of the first "womanists," to use a term coined by contemporary writer Alice Walker. Indeed, Alice Walker has described Sojourner as an inspiration for Walker's coinage of the term to describe black feminism.

Sojourner Truth, in arguing that she should be treated as a lady, joined the cause of the suffragists, and yet also reminded her audiences that white women had played a central role in her experience of oppression, and the experience of all black women. In her testimonies of her slave experience, she described the physical cruelty of white women who had power over her, how they defamed her, and how they had abused her, sexually and otherwise. In the *Narrative*, she describes how cruel Mrs. Dumont had been to her, and yet she is saddened by the fact that Fowler, who mercilessly beat her son, also murdered Sally Dumont's cousin Eliza in an episode of domestic violence. While Truth could understand the oppression faced by white women, even identify with it, as evinced by her work with women like Lucretia Mott and other suffragists, she also saw what black feminist theorist Patricia Hill Collins (in the essay "Black Feminist Thought in the Matrix of Domination" in her *Black Feminist Thought* [1990]) would describe as "the matrix of domination"—a matrix in which white women were under the thumbs of white men, while holding down black women.

Truth's multiple lawsuits demonstrated that she had an extraordinary sense of herself and the potential of her race, as did her petition to Congress for the repatriation of blacks to the western states. Between 1865 and 1868 she worked with the Freedman's Bureau, the national agency that was established to usher blacks from slavery to citizenship. Truth assisted the agency in finding refugees in Washington, D.C., jobs in other states. After the Bureau was dismantled, she recognized the continuing needs of freedmen and women, and, inspired by the model of the Indian Reservation system, she put together the following petition:

To the Senate and House of Representatives, in Congress assembled:—*Whereas*, From the faithful and earnest representations of Sojourner Truth (who has personally investigated the matter), we believe that the freed colored people in and about Washington, dependent upon government for support, would be greatly benefited and might become useful citizens by being placed in a position to support themselves: We, the undersigned, therefore earnestly request your honorable body to set apart for them a portion of the public land in the West, and erect buildings thereon for the aged and infirm, and otherwise legislate so as to secure the desired results (p. 145).

Truth circulated this petition among former abolitionist allies and even took it to Kansas, the state in which she hoped land would be secured for the blacks of Washington. This legislative effort was a fight Truth would not win, its goal far greater than any of the personal triumphs she earned. However, Truth was thrilled when the "Exodusters," who had attempted earlier settlements and were inspired anew by the testimonials and vision of black minister Benjamin "Pap" Singleton and motivated by the terrorism of white supremacists, migrated to Kansas in 1879, seeking freedom and land.

A number of Truth's contemporaries remarked that, in making the case for her Kansas plan, she spoke of the formerly enslaved as lazy, living off the state, and bereft of ambition. It seems likely that this, as is the case with many views attributed to her, entailed some fair degree of editorializing. It is hard to imagine that she had so pessimistic an opinion of her fellow blacks if she believed they would successfully make a way for themselves once given land and greater freedom in Kansas. In contrast to Truth's optimism, there were other members of the Freedman's Bureau who advocated the criminalization of any breach of labor contracts and pressured blacks to sign year-long labor contracts, because they believed blacks did not have the disposition to be good workers without compulsion. Truth clearly was not of that opinion.

In Truth's appeal to the legislative branch of the U.S. Government, she again blazed a trail for later civil rights activism that combined law and protest, such as that of Fannie Lou Hamer, who was a grassroots activist and delegate of the Mississippi Freedom Democratic Party, a protest party created in 1964 to challenge the all-white Mississippi Democratic Party, and the mass movement that led to the passage of the Voting Rights Act of 1965. For the overwhelming majority of African Americans it was not until 1954, when *Brown vs. Board of Education of Topeka* was decided, that law, litigation, or legislation even appeared to be a realm of appeal for denied rights. Sojourner Truth's lawsuits and petition did not change the nation, yet her legal actions embodied and prefigured the people's struggle to come.

The Icon

The iconographic role of Sojourner Truth has been treated with some ambivalence by historians, often because much of the iconography of her life depends upon myth rather than verifiable truth. In her biography of Sojourner Truth, Nell Irvin Painter describes the dilemma created by the emotional power of the rhetoric that has been attributed to Truth, and the reality that much of it was probably crafted by the imagination of others. Nowhere is this more dramatically illustrated than in the famous "Ar'n't (or Ain't) I a Woman?" speech, recorded by Frances Gage in 1863, soon after Harriet Beecher Stowe's acclaimed portrait had appeared. Gage corrects Stowe's assertion that Truth was dead and details a remembrance of a speech given by Truth in 1851. Gage's depiction contradicts that offered by newspaper accounts from 1851 of the same event. She describes the crowd as hostile and the newspaper as supportive of an antislavery crowd, and Gage attributes to Truth a rhetoric that bears little resemblance to how she was quoted at the time. However, Gage's account is one of high drama, and the words she placed in Sojourner Truth's mouth remain inspiring today:

"Dat man ober dar say dat women needs to be helped into carriages, and lifted ober ditches, and to have de best place every whar. Nobody eber help me into carriages, or ober mud puddles, or gives me any best place [and raising herself to her full height and her voice to a pitch like rolling thunder, she asked], and ar'n't I a woman? Look at me! Look at my arm! [and she bared her right arm to the shoulder, showing her tremendous muscular power.] I have plowed, and planted, and gathered into barns, and no man could head me—and ar'n't I a woman? I could work as much and eat as much as a man (when I could get it), and bear de lash as well—and ar'n't I a woman? I have borne thirteen chilern, and seen 'em mos' all sold off into slavery, and when I cried out with a mother's grief, none but Jesus heard—and ar'n't I a woman?" (p. 100).

Though the dialect and rhetorical flourishes were not likely, the spirit of the words are undeniably Truth. She did argue (in her actions) that, despite racist social conventions, she was a lady, and citizen, deserving of respect. Though she birthed only five children, the witness to her mother's desperate loss of a dozen came through in her testimony; though she lived in the North, the witness of the southern black female slave came through in her oratory. She argued for respect and for the respect of her class. And she inspired those outside her class: Despite her race and their racism, she was a useful symbol for the first wave of bourgeois white feminists like Stowe and Gage.

It was not only white women, however, who took poetic license with her story; Truth herself recognized the value of the "Sojourner Truth" iconography for the struggle for the rights of black people. She sometimes allowed false stories told about her to stand (though she did take exception to the misrepresentation of her dialect). It also appears that she represented her famous meeting with President Lincoln more favorably than factually. In her memoirs, abolitionist Lucy N. Colman recounts that Elizabeth Keckley (Mary Todd Lincoln's dressmaker and Truth's friend), reported to her that when Sojourner Truth met with Lincoln,

> Mr. Lincoln was not himself with this colored woman; he had no funny story for her, he called her aunty, as he would his washerwoman, and when she complimented him as the first Antislavery President, he said, "I'm not an Abolitionist; I wouldn't free the slaves if I could save the Union in any other way—I'm obliged to do it" (Lucy N. Colman, *Reminiscences*, Buffalo, NY: H. L. Green, 1891, p. 67).

Why then would Truth announce that he had treated her gently, favorably, recognizing her acclaim and humbly accepting her praise? It may be Truth understood that in her unique position as one of a few national black figures she spoke and stood for many more than just herself. As a preacher she allowed the word of God to come through her person, and as an abolitionist and activist she allowed the voices of black people to come through her person. Her cause needed Lincoln, a president, to be remembered as humane to an illiterate black woman, so that they might continue to hope and to hold dear the promises of Reconstruction—just as earlier her cause needed her to share the abuse of humanity wreaked by slavery in its worst iterations on thousands of black women. This was particularly significant because of the kind of representative Truth was. Although authors of other prominent slave narratives of Truth's time, such as Harriet Jacobs and Frederick Douglass, recount slavery that was geographically far closer to the majority experience of slavery, Truth was more like the majority of enslaved people on a personal level—a laborer, illiterate, female, and dark-skinned. She transcended the role white society accorded her—and represented the African-American cause—with neither the power of the pen nor the benefit of filial relationships to the whites around her.

Though Sojourner Truth may not have said, "Ar'n't I a Woman?" literally, she said it symbolically through her work, through her "shadows." For a woman who was not literate, a photograph could be a rare text under her own control. Her appearance in photographs is humble and proper. She wore modest, Quaker-style dress and spectacles. The clothes at once showed her humility, practicality, religiosity, and self-respect. At the time when Truth was having her portraits made and selling them to support herself, most photographs publicly circulating of black women were either those of mammies caring for white children as servants, or demeaning and embarrassing anthropological images that were also used for pornographic purposes, in which black women appeared vulnerable and exposed. In contrast, Truth, in her self-authored images, sat covered up in a distinctive sartorial statement, her knitting, both utilitarian and womanly, before her. Indeed, the frequency with which she had her shadow made suggests that not only was she arguing for the recognition of her womanhood, but also of her unrecognized beauty.

Moreover, the photographs stand as yet another example of how committed Truth was to ownership of herself, her image, and her reputation. In her preaching, her lawsuits, and her activism, she rejected the generalized image of blacks as beneath citizenship, and in the sale of her photographs she found a means of self-support in old age. Thus, she continued to defy her socially proscribed role by participating in a national economic marketplace during a time of poverty and the ugly backlash against Reconstruction in which many African Americans continued to struggle to exercise full contract and property rights. Through the sale of her image, Truth was able to spend her money on acquiring the often elusive accoutrements of citizenship. Truth was a property-holder, and the sale of the photographs helped pay for the second of two homes she would own, the one in Battle Creek, Michigan, in which she died. Property-owning for Truth, as for legions of the formerly enslaved, would be a powerful way of asserting freedom and citizenship and transcending the image of blacks as closer to chattel than citizens. This was why she wanted land for the black Washingtonians. For Truth, self-sufficiency was both the manifestation of religion, by way of her Protestant work ethic, and her emancipation as a black person. Truth, in selling her shadow, traded on her iconographic image, crafted by herself and by others, as a form of property, thereby both taking control of it and capitalizing on it for her own self-sufficiency.

Sojourner Truth died in Battle Creek in 1883. The final memorial chapter of the "Book of Life" comprises a series of remembrances of her life and legacy. Truth's contemporaries understood what an important figure she was, just as the contemporary world has. Sojourner Truth was not literate, yet she did all she could to leave a record of her life, and to our great fortune intellectuals and activists of the 1970s brought Truth back into the public eye. It should be seen as no coincidence that in the 1970s black feminist writers took on the charge of telling the stories of foremothers who were not able to tell their own stories. Sojourner Truth educates us all because she, innovatively and passionately, found a way to tell us her own story and those of her sisters. How thankful we are for her testimonial.

Imani Perry is an assistant professor of law at Rutgers Law School in Camden, New Jersey. She holds a Ph.D. from the Harvard Program in the History of American Civilization and a J.D. from Harvard Law School. Perry is the author of numerous scholarly articles on the intersection of law and literature in African-American cultural history, and the role of aesthetics in African-American political discourse. Her book *Prophets of the Hood: Politics and Poetics in Hip Hop* was published by Duke University Press in 2004.

NARRATIVE

OF

SOJOURNER TRUTH;

A Bondswoman of Olden Time,

Emancipated by the New York Legislature in the Early Part of
the Present Century;

WITH A HISTORY OF HER

LABORS AND CORRESPONDENCE

DRAWN FROM HER

"BOOK OF LIFE."

———→———

BATTLE CREEK, MICH.:
PUBLISHED FOR THE AUTHOR.
1878.

A PREFACE

WHICH WAS INTENDED FOR A POSTSCRIPT.

———————————

Sojourner Truth once remarked, in reply to an allusion to the late Horace Greeley, "You call him a self-made man; well, I am a self-made woman." The world is ever ready to sound the praises of the so-called self-made men; *i.e.*, those men who in the full possession of freedom, lacking nothing but wealth, achieve distinction and success.

It is now asked to accord a modicum of honor to a woman who labored forty long and weary years a slave; to whom the paths of literature and science were forever closed; one who bore the double burdens of poverty and the ban of caste, yet who, despite all these disabilities, has acquired fame, and gained hosts of friends among the noblest and best of the dominant race. The reasons for presenting the history of this remarkable woman to the public are twofold.

First, that the world, and more especially the young, may be benefited by the wisdom of one who escaped unscathed from the consuming fires of slavery, as did Shadrach, Meshach, and Abednego from the flames of the fiery furnace.

In the autumn of 1876, a report of her decease was widely circulated. How this occurred we know not. Possibly, because her twin sister, the Century, had just expired. No prayers addressed, or oblations poured out to the gods, could induce them to grant *it* an extra hour. But Sojourner grandly outrode the storm which wrecked the Century. Her mind is as clear and vigorous as in middle age. Her finely molded form is yet unbent, and its grand height and graceful, wavy movements remind the observer of her lofty cousins, the Palms, which keep guard over the sacred streams where her forefathers idled away their childhood days.

Doubtless, her blood is fed by those tropical fires which had slumberingly crept through many generations, but now awaken in her veins; akin to those rivers which mysteriously disappear in the bosom of the desert, and unexpectedly burst forth in springs of pure and living water. This heritage, and the law of the survival of the fittest, may explain the secret of her longevity.

The first 128 pages of this book are reprinted from stereotype plates made in 1850. Since then, momentous changes have taken place. Slavery has been swallowed up in a Red Sea of blood, and the slave has emerged from the conflict of races transformed from a chattel to a man. Holding the ballot, the black man enters the halls of legislation, and his rights are recognized there. "God was not dead," and in looking back to the Egypt of their captivity, Sojourner sees that her people have been guided through the dark wilderness of oppression by the "pillar of cloud and of fire."

Her race now stands on the Pisgah* of freedom, looking into the promised land, where the culture which has so long been denied them can, by their own efforts, be obtained. "The Lord executeth righteousness and judgment for all that are oppressed." "O give thanks unto the Lord; for he is good; for his mercy endureth forever." "Sing ye to the Lord, for he hath triumphed gloriously." "Who is like unto thee, O Lord? who is like thee, glorious in holiness, fearful in praises, doing wonders?"

Sojourner has stood before this nation many years, advocating the cause of human rights, and yet she presses on, feeling that her century of toil does not exonerate her from the service of her Divine Master, while his "Come labor in my vineyard," is responded to by so few.

Her sun of life is about to dip below the horizon; but flashes of wit and wisdom still emanate from her soul, like the rays of the natural sun as it bursts forth from a somber cloud, baptizing earth and sky with the radiance of its expiring glory.

Bishop Haven says, "There is no more deserving lady in the land than Sojourner Truth. As one of the famous women of these famous times, covering in her own experience the emancipation era, from the declaration of New York in 1817, to Abraham Lincoln's procla-

---

*Precipice; in the Bible (Deuteronomy 34:1), God shows Moses the promised land from Mount Pisgah.

mation, she deserves especial honor. The nation could rightfully grant her a pension for her services in the war, no less than for her labors since the war, for the amelioration of those yet half enslaved."

The second and most important reason for offering this book to the public is, that by its sale she may be kept from want in these her last days. Should it prove a success, the desired end will be accomplished.

The following letter appeared in the *Anti-Slavery Standard* after the first issue of the "Narrative and Book of Life" of Sojourner Truth. Wishing to give it to the public, we insert it in the preface:—

"Battle Creek, Mich., Apr. 14, 1863.

"OLIVER JOHNSON:—

"Dear Friend—Permit me, through the columns of *The Standard*, in behalf of Sojourner Truth, whom your readers so well remember, to acknowledge the receipt of the several donations from her many generous friends, all of which have been gratefully received by her. Printed words can never convey such deep and heartfelt gratitude as she feels. The donors needed but to have seen the expression of her dark, care-worn face and heard her words of genuine thankfulness, to have realized that indeed it is 'more blessed to give than to receive.'

"As we opened the letters, one by one, and read the words of sweet remembrance and kindness, she was quite overcome with joy, and more than once gave utterance to her feelings through her tears; praising the Lord who had so soon answered her prayer, which was, in language from the depths of her soul, as she sat weary and alone in her quiet little home: 'Lord, I'm too old to work—I'm too sick to hold meetings and speak to de people, and sell my books; Lord, you sent de ravens to feed 'Lijah in de wilderness; now send de good angels to feed me while I live on dy footstool.'

"No sooner had the appeal gone forth, than the answers came from the East and West, accompanied with material aid to supply her physical needs. Then again she exclaimed in words of deepest gratitude: 'Lord, I knew dy laws was sure, but I didn't t'ink dey would work so quick.' The words of friendship and sympathy that filled every letter were a source of great joy and consolation to her, and when the comforting message from Gerrit Smith came, saying,

'Sojourner, the God whom you so faithfully serve will abundantly bless you, he will suffer you to lack nothing either in body or soul,' she threw up her hands, and, in her deep-toned voice, said, 'De Lord bless de man! his heart is as big as de nation, and if he hadn't sent a penny, his words would feed my soul, and dat is what we all want.' Then she mentioned Samuel Hill, of Northampton, Mass., where she lived fifteen years, saying that his noble, generous heart had done a great deal for her. Ofttimes the ecstasy of her soul would gush forth in all its original vigor and freshness at the thought of her many friends and their quick responses. She once said to me, 'I tell you, chile, de Lord manages everything; you see when you wrote dat letter, you didn't think you was doing much, but I tell you, dear lamb, dat when a thing is done in de right spirit, God takes it up and spreads it all over de country.'

"She wishes the friends to know that the 'little curly-headed, jolly grandson,' whom Mrs. Stowe so graphically describes, is now grown to a tall, able-bodied lad, and *has just enlisted in the 54th Massachusetts Regiment;* gone forth with her prayers and blessings, she says, 'to redeem de white people from de curse dat God has sent upon them.' The glorious news of old Massachusetts leading in the van for the right of the colored man to fight, has just reached here, and she seems at times to be filled with all the fire and enthusiasm of her former years. She says if she were only ten years younger, she would be 'on hand as the Joan of Arc to lead de army of de Lord; for now is de day and now de hour for de colored man to save dis nation; for dere sin have been so great dat dey don't know God, nor God don't know dem.' I never heard her speak with greater force and power than she did the other day when some friends called to see her. She says this is all the way she has now to preach. She often speaks of T. W. Higginson and Frances D. Gage[1]—thinks 'dey are *appointed* of God to fill de position dey have taken.' As I closed the interview, Sojourner called down many blessings on all who have helped her to live and 'do good in de world.'

"I will give the names of the donors, so far as I know them, and if any have sent whose names do not appear, perhaps they will write, or they will yet come to hand.

"Yours truly,

"**Phebe H. M. Stickney.**"

At the time the foregoing letter was received, in 1863, Sojourner thought herself too old and infirm to either labor or lecture. But as the war of the Rebellion, which was then stirring the pulses of the nation so deeply, progressed, she experienced a new baptism, so to speak, of physical and mental vigor, which enabled her to take an active part in many of its stirring scenes. She received her commission from Abraham Lincoln, and labored in the hospitals and among the freedmen four years.

Since the war, her life has been one of activity. Now, in 1878, she oversees her own household matters, and often gives three public lectures in a week. Within the past year, she has held meetings in thirty-six towns in Michigan. Her health is good; her eyesight, for many years defective, has returned. Her gray locks are being succeeded by a luxuriant growth of black hair, without the use of any other renovator than that which kind Nature furnishes. She hopes that natural teeth will supersede the necessity of using false ones. May her ardent wish be realized! Her mental capacities are becoming intensified. A Chicago lady wrote to her, asking for a thought to inspire and cheer her on her life journey. Sojourner responded as follows:—

"God is from everlasting to everlasting." "There was no beginning till sin came." "All that had a beginning will have an end." "Truth burns up error." "God is the great house that will hold all his children." "We dwell in him as the fishes in the sea." Of the fashionable so-called *religious* world she says, "It is empty as the barren fig-tree, possessing nothing but leaves."

This is Sojourner Truth at a century old.

Would you like to meet her?

THE AUTHOR.

NARRATIVE OF
SOJOURNER TRUTH.

Her Birth and Parentage.

THE SUBJECT OF THIS BIOGRAPHY, SOJOURNER TRUTH, as she now calls herself—but whose name, originally, was Isabella—was born, as near as she can now calculate, between the years 1797 and 1800. She was the daughter of James and Betsey, slaves of one Colonel Ardinburgh, Hurley, Ulster County, New York.[2]

Colonel Ardinburgh belonged to that class of people called Low Dutch.

Of her first master, she can give no account, as she must have been a mere infant when he died; and she, with her parents and some ten or twelve other fellow human chattels, became the legal property of his son, Charles Ardinburgh. She distinctly remembers hearing her father and mother say, that their lot was a fortunate one, as Master Charles was the best of the family,—being, comparatively speaking, a kind master to his slaves.

James and Betsey having, by their faithfulness, docility, and respectful behavior, won his particular regard, received from him particular favors—among which was a lot of land, lying back on the slope of a mountain, where, by improving the pleasant evenings and Sundays, they managed to raise a little tobacco, corn, or flax; which they exchanged for extras, in the articles of food or clothing for themselves and children. She has no remembrance that Saturday afternoon was ever added to their own time, as it is by *some* masters in the Southern States.

Accommodations.

Among Isabella's earliest recollections was the removal of her master, Charles Ardinburgh, into his new house, which he had built for a hotel, soon after the decease of his father. A cellar, under this hotel, was assigned to his slaves, as their sleeping apartment,—all the slaves he possessed, of both sexes, sleeping (as is quite common in a state of slavery) in the same room. She carries in her mind, to this day, a vivid picture of this dismal chamber; its only lights consisting of a few panes of glass, through which she thinks the sun never shone, but with thrice reflected rays; and the space between the loose boards of the floor, and the uneven earth below, was often filled with mud and water, the uncomfortable splashings of which were as annoying as its noxious vapors must have been chilling and fatal to health. She shudders, even now, as she goes back in memory, and revisits this cellar, and sees its inmates, of both sexes and all ages, sleeping on those damp boards, like the horse, with a little straw and a blanket; and she wonders not at the rheumatisms, and fever-sores, and palsies, that distorted the limbs and racked the bodies of those fellow-slaves in after-life. Still, she does not attribute this cruelty—for cruelty it certainly is, to be so unmindful of the health and comfort of any being, leaving entirely out of sight his more important part, his everlasting interests,—so much to any innate or constitutional cruelty of the master, as to that gigantic inconsistency, that inherited habit among slaveholders, of expecting a willing and intelligent obedience from the slave, because he is a MAN—at the same time every thing belonging to the soul-harrowing system does its best to crush the last vestige of a man within him; and when it *is* crushed, and often before, he is denied the comforts of life, on the plea that he knows neither the want nor the use of them, and because he is considered to be little more or little *less* than a beast.

Her Brothers and Sisters.

Isabella's father was very tall and straight, when young, which gave him the name of 'Bomefree'—Low Dutch for tree—at least, this is SOJOURNER'S pronunciation of it—and by this name he usually went. The most familiar appellation of her mother was 'Mau-mau Bett.' She was the mother of some ten or twelve children; though Sojourner is far from knowing the exact number of her brothers and sisters; she being the youngest, save one, and all older than herself having been sold before her remembrance. She was privileged to behold six of them while she remained a slave.

Of the two that immediately preceded her in age, a boy of five years, and a girl of three, who were sold when she was an infant, she heard much; and she wishes that all who would fain believe that slave parents have not natural affection for their offspring could have listened as *she* did, while Bomefree and Mau-mau Bett,—their dark cellar lighted by a blazing pine-knot,—would sit for hours, recalling and recounting every endearing, as well as harrowing circumstance that taxed memory could supply, from the histories of those dear departed ones, of whom they had been robbed, and for whom their hearts still bled. Among the rest, they would relate how the little boy, on the last morning he was with them, arose with the birds, kindled a fire, calling for his Mau-mau to 'come, for all was now ready for her'—little dreaming of the dreadful separation which was so near at hand, but of which his parents had an uncertain, but all the more cruel foreboding. There was snow on the ground, at the time of which we are speaking; and a large old-fashioned sleigh was seen to drive up to the door of the late Col. Ardinburgh. This event was noticed with childish pleasure by the unsuspicious boy; but when he was taken and put into the sleigh, and saw his little sister actually shut and locked into the sleigh box, his eyes were at once opened to their intentions; and, like a frightened deer he sprang from the sleigh, and running into the house, concealed himself under a bed. But this availed him little. He was re-conveyed to the sleigh, and separated for ever from those whom God had constituted his natural guardians and protectors, and who should have found him, in return, a stay and a staff to them in their declining years. But I make no comments on facts like these, knowing that the heart of every slave parent will make its own comments, involuntarily and correctly, as soon as each heart shall make the case its own. Those who are not parents will draw their conclusions from the promptings of humanity and philanthropy:—these, enlightened by reason and revelation, are also unerring.

Her Religious Instruction.

Isabella and Peter, her youngest brother, remained, with their parents, the legal property of Charles Ardinburgh till his decease, which took place when Isabella was near nine years old.

After this event, she was often surprised to find her mother in tears; and when, in her simplicity, she inquired, 'Mau-mau, what makes you cry?' she would answer, 'Oh my child, I am thinking of your brothers and sisters that have been sold away from me.' And she would proceed to detail many circumstances respecting them. But Isabella long since concluded that it was the impending fate of her only remaining children, which her mother but too well understood, even then, that called up those memories from the past, and made them crucify her heart afresh.

In the evening, when her mother's work was done, she would sit down under the sparkling vault of heaven, and calling her children to her, would talk to them of the only Being that could effectually aid or protect them. Her teachings were delivered in Low Dutch, her only language, and, translated into English, ran nearly as follows:—

'My children, there is a God, who hears and sees you.' 'A *God*, mau-mau! Where does he live?' asked the children. 'He lives in the sky,' she replied; 'and when you are beaten, or cruelly treated, or fall into any trouble, you must ask help of him, and he will always hear and help you.' She taught them to kneel and say the Lord's prayer. She entreated them to refrain from lying and stealing, and to strive to obey their masters.

At times, a groan would escape her, and she would break out in the language of the Psalmist—'Oh Lord, how long?' 'Oh Lord, how long?' And in reply to Isabella's question—'What ails you, mau-mau?' her only answer was, 'Oh, a good deal ails me'—'Enough ails me.' Then again, she would point them to the stars, and say, in her peculiar language, 'Those are the same stars, and that is the same moon, that look down upon your brothers and sisters, and which they see as they look up to them, though they are ever so far away from us, and each other.'

Thus, in her humble way, did she endeavor to show them their Heavenly Father, as the only being who could protect them in their perilous condition; at the same time, she would strengthen and brighten the chain of family affection, which she trusted extended itself sufficiently to connect the widely scattered members of her precious flock. These instructions of the mother were treasured up and held sacred by Isabella, as our future narrative will show.

The Auction.

At length, the never-to be-forgotten day of the terrible auction arrived, when the 'slaves, horses, and other cattle' of Charles Ardinburgh, deceased, were to be put under the hammer, and again change masters. Not only Isabella and Peter, but their mother, was now destined to the auction block, and would have been struck off with the rest to the highest bidder, but for the following circumstance: A question arose among the heirs, 'Who shall be burdened with Bomefree, when we have sent away his faithful Mau-mau Bett?' He was becoming weak and infirm; his limbs were painfully rheumatic and distorted—more from exposure and hardship than from old age, though he was several years older than Mau-mau Bett: he was no longer considered of value, but must soon be a burden and care to some one. After some contention on the point at issue, none being willing to be burdened with him, it was finally agreed, as most expedient for the heirs, that the price of Mau-mau Bett should be sacrificed, and she receive her freedom, on condition that she take care of and support her faithful James,—faithful, not only to her as a husband, but proverbially faithful as a slave to those who would not willingly sacrifice a dollar for *his* comfort, now that he had commenced his descent into the dark vale of decrepitude and suffering. This important decision was received as joyful news indeed to our ancient couple, who were the objects of it, and who were trying to prepare their hearts for a severe struggle, and one altogether new to them, as they had never before been separated; for, though ignorant, helpless, crushed in spirit, and weighed down with hardship and cruel bereavement, they were still human, and their human hearts beat within them with as true an affection as ever caused a human heart to beat. And their anticipated separation now, in the decline of life, after the last child had been torn from them, must have been truly appalling. Another privilege was granted them—that of remaining occupants of the same dark, humid cellar I have before described: otherwise, they were to support themselves as they best could. And as her mother was still able to do considerable work, and her father a little, they got on for some time very comfortably. The strangers who rented the house were humane people, and very kind to them; they were not rich, and owned no slaves. How long this state of things continued, we are unable to say, as Isabella had not then sufficiently cultivated her organ of time to calculate years, or even weeks or hours. But she thinks her mother must have lived several years after the death of Master Charles. She remembers going to visit her parents some three or four times before the death of her mother, and a good deal of time seemed to her to intervene between each visit.

At length her mother's health began to decline—a fever-sore made its ravages on one of her limbs, and the palsy began to shake her frame; still, she and James tottered about, picking up a little here and there, which, added to the mites contributed by their kind neighbors, sufficed to sustain life, and drive famine from the door.

Death of Mau-Mau Bett.

One morning, in early autumn, (from the reason above mentioned, we cannot tell what year,) Mau-mau Bett told James she would make him a loaf of rye-bread, and get Mrs. Simmons, their kind neighbor, to bake it for them, as she would bake that forenoon. James told her he had engaged to rake after the cart for his neighbors that morning; but before he commenced, he would pole off some apples from a tree near, which they were allowed to gather; and if she could get some of them baked with the bread, it would give it a nice relish for their dinner. He beat off the apples, and soon after, saw Mau-mau Bett come out and gather them up.

At the blowing of the horn for dinner, he groped his way into his cellar, anticipating his humble, but warm and nourishing meal; when, lo! instead of being cheered by the sight and odor of fresh-baked bread and the savory apples, his cellar seemed more cheerless than usual, and at first neither sight nor sound met eye or ear. But, on groping his way through the room, his staff, which he used as a pioneer to go before, and warn him of danger, seemed to be impeded in its progress, and a low, gurgling, choking sound proceeded from the object before him, giving him the first intimation of the truth as it was, that Mau-mau Bett, his bosom companion, the only remaining member of his large family, had fallen in a fit of the palsy, and lay helpless and senseless on the earth! Who among us, located in pleasant homes, surrounded with every comfort, and so many kind and sympathizing friends, can picture to ourselves the dark and desolate state of poor old James—penniless, weak, lame, and nearly blind, as he was at the moment he found his companion was removed from him, and he was left alone in the world, with no one to aid, comfort, or console him? for she never revived again, and lived only a few hours after being discovered senseless by her poor bereaved James.

Last Days of Bomefree.

Isabella and Peter were permitted to see the remains of their mother laid in their last narrow dwelling, and to make their bereaved father a little visit, ere they returned to their servitude. And most piteous were the lamentations of the poor old man, when, at last, *they* also were obliged to bid him "Farewell!" Juan Fernandes, on his desolate island, was not so pitiable an object as this poor lame man. Blind and crippled, he was too superannuated to think for a moment of taking care of himself and he greatly feared no persons would interest themselves in his behalf. 'Oh,' he would exclaim, 'I had thought God would take me first,—Mau-mau was so much smarter than I, and could get about and take care of herself;—and I am *so old*, and *so helpless*. What *is* to become of me? I can't do any thing more—my children are all gone, and here I am left helpless and alone.' 'And then, as I was taking leave of him,' said his daughter, in relating it, 'he raised his voice, and cried aloud like a child—*Oh, how he* DID *cry!* I HEAR it *now*—and remember it as well as if it were but yesterday— *poor old man!!!* He thought *God* had done it all—and my heart bled within me at the sight of his misery. He begged me to get permission to come and see him sometimes, which I readily and heartily promised him.' But when all had left him, the Ardinburghs, having some feeling left for their faithful and favorite slave, 'took turns about' in keeping him—permitting him to stay a few weeks at one house, and then a while at another, and so around. If, when he made a removal, the place where he was going was not too far off, he took up his line of march, staff in hand, and asked for no assistance. If it was twelve or twenty miles, they gave him a ride. While he was living in this way, Isabella was twice permitted to visit him. Another time she walked twelve miles, and carried her infant in her arms to see him, but when she reached the place where she hoped to find him, he had just left for a place some twenty miles distant, and she never saw him more. The last time she *did* see him, she found him seated on a rock, by the road side, alone, and far from any house. He was then migrating from the house of one Ardinburgh to that of another, several miles distant. His hair was white like wool—he was almost blind—and his gait was more a creep than a walk—but the weather was warm and pleasant, and he did not dislike the journey. When Isabella addressed him, he recognized her voice, and was exceeding glad to see her. He was assisted to mount the wagon, was carried back to the famous cellar of which we have spoken, and there they held their last earthly conversation. He again, as usual, bewailed his loneliness,—spoke in tones of anguish of his many children, saying, 'They are all taken away from me! I have now not one to give me a cup of cold water—why should I live and not die?' Isabella, whose heart yearned over her father, and who would have made any sacrifice to have been able to be with, and take care of him, tried to comfort, by telling him that 'she had heard the white folks say, that all the slaves in the State would be freed in ten years, and that then she would come and take care of him.' 'I would take just as good care of you as Mau-mau would, if she was here'—continued Isabel. 'Oh, my child,' replied he, 'I cannot *live* that long.' 'Oh *do*, daddy, do live, and I will take such *good* care of you,' was her rejoinder. She now says, 'Why, I thought then, in my ignorance, that he *could* live, if he *would*. I just as much thought so, as I ever thought *any* thing in my life—and I *insisted* on his living: but he shook his head, and insisted he could not.'

But before Bomefree's good constitution would yield either to age, exposure, or a strong desire to die, the Ardinburghs again tired of him, and offered freedom to two old slaves—Cæsar, brother of Maumau Bett, and his wife Betsey—on condition that they should take care of James. (I was about to say, 'their brother-in-law'—but as slaves are neither *husbands* nor *wives* in law, the idea of being brothers-in-law is truly ludicrous.) And although they were too old and infirm to take care of themselves, (Cæsar having been afflicted for a long time with fever-sores, and his wife with the jaundice,) they eagerly accepted the boon of freedom, which had been the life-long desire of their souls—though at a time when emancipation was to them little more than destitution, and was a freedom more to be desired by the master than the slave. Sojourner declares of the slaves in their ignorance, that 'their thoughts are no longer than her finger.'

Death of Bomefree.

A rude cabin, in a lone wood, far from any neighbors, was granted to our freed friends, as the only assistance they were now to expect. Bomefree, from this time, found his poor needs hardly supplied, as his new providers were scarce able to administer to their *own* wants. However, the time drew near when things were to be decidedly worse rather than better; for they had not been together long, before Betty died, and shortly after, Cæsar followed her to 'that bourne from whence no traveller returns'—leaving poor James again desolate, and more helpless than ever before; as, this time, there was no kind family in the house, and the Ardinburghs no longer invited him to their homes. Yet, lone, blind and helpless as he was, James for a time lived on. One day, an aged colored woman, named Soan, called at his shanty, and James besought her, in the most moving manner, even with tears, to tarry awhile and wash and mend him up, so that he might once more be decent and comfortable; for he was suffering dreadfully with the filth and vermin that had collected upon him.

Soan was herself an emancipated slave, old and weak, with no one to care for her; and she lacked the courage to undertake a job of such seeming magnitude, fearing she might herself get sick, and perish there without assistance; and with great reluctance, and a heart swelling with pity, as she afterwards declared, she felt obliged to leave him in his wretchedness and filth. And shortly after her visit, this faithful slave, this deserted wreck of humanity, was found on his miserable pallet, frozen and stiff in death. The kind angel had come at last, and relieved him of the many miseries that his fellow-man had heaped upon him. Yes, he had died, chilled and starved, with none to speak a kindly word, or do a kindly deed for him, in that last dread hour of need!

The news of his death reached the ears of John Ardinburgh, a grandson of the old Colonel; and he declared that 'Bomefree, who had ever been a kind and faithful slave, should now have a *good* funeral.' And now, gentle reader, what think you constituted a good funeral? Answer—some black paint for the coffin, and—a jug of ardent spirits! What a compensation for a life of toil, of patient submission to repeated robberies of the most aggravated kind, and, also, far more than murderous neglect!! Mankind often vainly attempt to atone for unkindness or cruelty to the living, by honoring the same after death; but John Ardinburgh undoubtedly meant *his* pot of paint and jug of whisky should act as an opiate on his slaves, rather than on his own seared conscience.

Commencement of Isabella's Trials in Life.

Having seen the sad end of her parents, so far as it relates to *this* earthly life, we will return with Isabella to that memorable auction which threatened to separate her father and mother. A slave auction is a terrible affair to its victims, and its incidents and consequences are graven on their hearts as with a pen of burning steel.

At this memorable time, Isabella was struck off, for the sum of one hundred dollars, to one John Nealy, of Ulster County, New York; and she has an impression that in this sale she was connected with a lot of sheep. She was now nine years of age, and her trials in life may be dated from this period. She says, with emphasis, '*Now the war begun.*' She could only talk Dutch—and the Nealys could only talk English. Mr. Nealy could *understand* Dutch, but Isabel and her mistress could neither of them understand the language of the other—and this, of itself, was a formidable obstacle in the way of a *good* understanding between them, and for some time was a fruitful source of dissatisfaction to the mistress, and of punishment and suffering to Isabella. She says, 'If they sent me for a frying-pan, not knowing what they meant, perhaps I carried them the pot-hooks and trammels. Then, oh! how angry mistress would be with me!' Then she suffered '*terribly—terribly,*' with the cold. During the winter her feet were badly frozen, for want of proper covering. They gave her a plenty to eat, and also a plenty of whippings. One Sunday morning, in particular, she was told to go to the barn; on going there, she found her master with a bundle of rods, prepared in the embers, and bound together with cords. When he had tied her hands together before her, he gave her the most cruel whipping she was ever tortured with. He whipped her till the flesh was deeply lacerated, and the blood streamed from her wounds—and the scars remain to the present day, to testify to the fact. 'And now,' she says, 'when I hear 'em tell of whipping women on the bare flesh, it makes *my* flesh crawl, and my very hair rise on my head! Oh! my God!' she continues, 'what a way is this of treating human beings?' In these hours of her extremity, she did not forget the instructions of her mother, to go to God in all her trials, and every affliction; and she not only remembered, but obeyed: going to him, 'and telling him all—and asking Him if He thought it was right,' and begging him to protect and shield her from her persecutors.

She always asked with an unwavering faith that she should receive just what she plead for,—'And now,' she says, 'though it seems *curious*, I do not remember ever asking for any thing but what I got it. And I always received it as an answer to my prayers. When I got beaten, I never knew it long enough beforehand to pray; and I always thought if I only had *had* time to pray to God for help, I should have escaped the beating.' She had no idea God had any knowledge of her thoughts, save what she told him; or heard her prayers, unless they were spoken audibly. And consequently, she could not pray unless she had time and opportunity to go by herself, where she could talk to God without being overheard.

Trials Continued.

When she had been at Mr. Nealy's several months, she began to beg God most earnestly to send her father to her, and as soon as she commenced to pray, she began as confidently to look for his coming, and, ere it was long, to her great joy, he came. She had no opportunity to speak to him of the troubles that weighed so heavily on her spirit, while he remained; but when he left, she followed him to the gate, and unburdened her heart to him, inquiring if he could not do something to get her a new and better place. In this way the slaves often assist each other, by ascertaining who are kind to their slaves, comparatively; and then using their influence to get such an one to hire or buy their friends; and masters, often from policy, as well as from latent humanity, allow those they are about to sell or let, to choose their own places, if the persons they happen to select for masters are considered safe *pay*. He promised to do all he could, and they parted. But, every day, as long as the snow lasted, (for there was snow on the ground at the time,) she returned to the spot where they separated, and walking in the tracks her father had made in the snow, repeated her prayer that 'God would help her father get her a new and better place.'

A long time had not elapsed, when a fisherman by the name of Scriver appeared at Mr. Nealy's, and inquired of Isabel 'if she would like to go and live with him.' She eagerly answered 'Yes,' nothing doubting but he was sent in answer to her prayer; and she soon started off with him, walking while he rode; for he had bought her at the suggestion of her father, paying one hundred and five dollars for her. He also lived in Ulster County, but some five or six miles from Mr. Nealy's.

Scriver, besides being a fisherman, kept a tavern for the accommodation of people of his own class—for his was a rude, uneducated family, exceedingly profane in their language, but, on the whole, an honest, kind and well-disposed people.

They owned a large farm, but left it wholly unimproved; attending mainly to their vocations of fishing and inn-keeping. Isabella declares she can ill describe the life she led with them. It was a wild, out-of-door kind of lief.* She was expected to carry fish, to hoe corn, to bring roots and herbs from the wood for beers, go to the Strand for a gallon of molasses or liquor as the case might require, and 'browse around,' as she expresses it. It was a life that suited her well for the time—being as devoid of hardship or terror as it was of improvement; a need which had not yet become a want. Instead of improving at this place, morally, she retrograded, as their example taught her to curse; and it was here that she took her first oath. After

---

*Misspelling of "life."

living with them about a year and a half, she was sold to one John J. Dumont, for the sum of seventy pounds. This was in 1810. Mr. Dumont lived in the same county as her former masters, in the town of New Paltz, and she remained with him till a short time previous to her emancipation by the State, in 1828.*

Her Standing with Her New Master and Mistress.

Had Mrs. Dumont possessed that vein of kindness and considera-tion for the slaves, so perceptible in her husband's character, Isabella would have been as comfortable here, as one had *best* be, if one *must* be a slave. Mr. Dumont had been nursed in the very lap of slavery, and being naturally a man of kind feelings, treated his slaves with all the consideration he did his *other* animals, and *more*, perhaps. But Mrs. Dumont, who had been born and educated in a non-slaveholding family, and, like many others, used only to work-people, who, under the most stimulating of human motives, were willing to put forth their every energy, could not have patience with the creeping gait, the dull understanding, or see any cause for the listless manners and careless, slovenly habits of the poor down-trodden outcast—entirely forgetting that every high and efficient motive had been removed far from him; and that, had not his very intellect been crushed out of him, the slave would find little ground for aught but hopeless despondency. From this source arose a long series of trials in the life of our heroine, which we must pass over in silence; some from motives of delicacy,† and others, because the re-lation of them might inflict undeserved pain on some now living, whom Isabel remembers only with esteem and love; therefore, the reader will not be surprised if our narrative appear somewhat tame at this point, and may rest assured that it is not for want of facts, as the most thrilling incidents of this portion of her life are from vari-ous motives suppressed.

One comparatively trifling incident she wishes related, as it made

---

*In 1817 the New York State legislature passed a law requiring that enslaved per-sons born before 1799 be emancipated on July 4, 1827.

†Scholars generally agree that this passage indicates that Isabella's mistress, Sally Dumont, sexually abused her.

a deep impression on her mind at the time—showing, as *she* thinks, how God shields the innocent, and causes them to triumph over their enemies, and also how she stood between master and mistress. In her family, Mrs. Dumont employed two white girls, one of whom, named Kate, evinced a disposition to 'lord it over' Isabel, and, in her emphatic language, 'to *grind her down*.' Her master often shielded her from the attacks and accusations of others, praising her for her readiness and ability to work, and these praises seemed to foster a spirit of hostility to her, in the minds of Mrs. Dumont and her white servant, the latter of whom took every opportunity to cry up her faults, lessen her in the esteem of her master and increase against her the displeasure of her mistress, which was already more than sufficient for Isabel's comfort. Her master insisted that she could do as much work as half a dozen common people, and do it well, too; whilst her mistress insisted that the first was true, only because it ever came from her hand but half performed. A good deal of feeling arose from this difference of opinion, which was getting to rather an uncomfortable height, when, all at once, the potatoes that Isabel cooked for breakfast assumed a dingy, dirty look. Her mistress blamed her severely, asking her master to observe 'a fine specimen of Bell's work!'—adding, 'it is the way *all* her work is done.' Her master scolded also this time, and commanded her to be more careful in future. Kate joined with zest in the censures, and was very hard upon her. Isabella thought that she had done all she well could to have them nice; and became quite distressed at these appearances, and wondered what she should do to avoid them. In this dilemma, Gertrude Dumont, (Mr. D.'s eldest child, a good, kind-hearted girl of ten years, who pitied Isabel sincerely,) when she heard them all blame her so unsparingly, came forward, offering her sympathy and assistance; and when about to retire to bed, on the night of Isabella's humiliation, she advanced to Isabel, and told her, if she would wake her early next morning, she would get up and attend to her potatoes for her, while she (Isabella) went to milking, and they would see if they could not have them nice, and not have 'Poppee,' her word for father, and 'Matty,' her word for mother, and all of 'em, scolding so terribly.

Isabella gladly availed herself of this kindness, which touched her to the heart, amid so much of an opposite spirit. When Isabella had put the potatoes over to boil Getty told her she would herself tend the fire, while Isabel milked. She had not long been seated by the fire in performance of her promise, when Kate entered, and requested Gertrude to go out of the room and do something for her, which she refused, still keeping her place in the corner. While there, Kate came sweeping about the fire, caught up a chip, lifted some ashes with it, and dashed them into the kettle. Now the mystery was solved, the plot discovered! Kate was working a little too fast at making her mistress's words good, at showing that Mrs. Dumont and herself were on the right side of the dispute, and consequently at gaining power over Isabella. Yes, she was quite too fast, inasmuch as she had overlooked the little figure of justice, which sat in the corner, with scales nicely balanced, waiting to give all their dues.

But the time had come when she was to be overlooked no longer. It was Getty's turn to speak now. 'Oh. Poppee! oh, Poppee!' said she, 'Kate has been putting ashes in among the potatoes! I saw her do it! Look at those that fell on the outside of the kettle! You can now see what made the potatoes so dingy every morning, though Bell washed them clean!' And she repeated her story to every new comer, till the fraud was made as public as the censure of Isabella had been. Her mistress looked blank, and remained dumb—her master muttered something which sounded very like an oath—and poor Kate was so chop-fallen, she looked like a convicted criminal, who would gladly have hid herself (now that the baseness was out,) to conceal her mortified pride and deep chagrin.

It was a fine triumph for Isabella and her master, and she became more ambitious than ever to please him; and he stimulated her ambition by his commendation, and by boasting of her to his friends, telling them that '*that* wench' (pointing to Isabel) 'is better to me than a *man*—for she will do a good family's washing in the night, and be ready in the morning to go into the field, where she will do as much at raking and binding as my best hands.' Her ambition and desire to please were so great, that she often worked several nights in succession, sleeping only short snatches, as she sat in her chair; and some nights she would not allow herself to take any sleep, save what she could get resting herself against the wall, fearing that if she sat down, she would sleep too long. These extra exertions to please, and the praises consequent upon them, brought upon her head the envy of her fellow-slaves, and they taunted her with being the '*white folks' nigger.*' On the other hand, she received a larger share of the confidence of her master, and many small favors that were by them unattainable. I asked her if her master, Dumont, ever whipped her? She answered, 'Oh yes, he sometimes whipped me soundly, though never cruelly. And the most severe whipping he ever give me was because *I* was cruel to a cat.' At this time she looked upon her master as a *God;* and believed that he knew of and could see her at all times, even as God himself. And she used sometimes to confess her delinquencies, from the conviction that he already knew them, and that she should fare better if she confessed voluntarily: and if any one talked to her of the injustice of her being a slave, she answered them with contempt and immediately told her master. She then firmly believed that slavery was right and honorable. Yet she *now* sees very clearly the false position they were all in, both masters and slaves; and she looks back, with utter astonishment, at the absurdity of the claims so arrogantly set up by the masters, over beings designed by God to be as free as kings; and at the perfect stupidity of the slave, in admitting for one moment the validity of these claims.

In obedience to her mother's instructions, she had educated herself to such a sense of honesty, that, when she had become a mother, she would sometimes whip her child when it cried to her for bread, rather than give it a piece secretly, lest it should learn to take what was not its own! And the writer of this knows, from personal observation, that the slaveholders of the South feel it to be a *religious duty* to teach their slaves to be honest, and never to take what is not their own! Oh consistency, art thou not a jewel? Yet Isabella glories in the fact that she was faithful and true to her master; she says, 'It made me true to my God'—meaning, that it helped to form in her a character that loved truth, and hated a lie, and had saved her from the bitter pains and fears that are sure to follow in the wake of insincerity and hypocrisy.

As she advanced in years, an attachment sprung up between herself and a slave named Robert.* But his master, an Englishman by

---

*Truth biographer Nell Painter and others have considered that Robert might have been the father of her first two children, given the gap of several years between them and Truth's younger children.

the name of Catlin, anxious that no one's property but his own should be enhanced by the increase of his slaves, forbade Robert's visits to Isabella, and commanded him to take a wife among his fellow-servants. Notwithstanding this interdiction, Robert, following the bent of his inclinations, continued his visits to Isabel, though very stealthily, and, as he believed, without exciting the suspicion of his master; but one Saturday afternoon, hearing that Bell was ill, he took the liberty to go and see her. The first intimation *she* had of his visit was the appearance of her master, inquiring 'if she had seen Bob.' On her answering in the negative, he said to her, 'If you see him, tell him to take care of himself, for the Catlins are after him.' Almost at that instant, Bob made his appearance; and the first people he met were his old and his young masters. They were terribly enraged at finding him there, and the eldest began cursing, and calling upon his son to '*Knock down* the d——d black rascal;' at the same time, they both fell upon him like tigers, beating him with the heavy ends of their canes, bruising and mangling his head and face in the most awful manner, and causing the blood, which streamed from his wounds, to cover him like a slaughtered beast, constituting him a most shocking spectacle. Mr. Dumont interposed at this point, telling the ruffians they could no longer thus spill human blood on *his* premises—he would have 'no niggers killed there.' The Catlins then took a rope they had taken with them for the purpose, and tied Bob's hands behind him in such a manner, that Mr. Dumont insisted on loosening the cord, declaring that no brute should be tied in *that* manner, where *he* was. And as they led him away, like the greatest of criminals, the more humane Dumont followed them to their homes, as Robert's protector; and when he returned, he kindly went to Bell, as he called her, telling her he did not think they would strike him any more, as their wrath had greatly cooled before he left them. Isabella had witnessed this scene from her window, and was greatly shocked at the murderous treatment of poor Robert, whom she truly loved, and whose only crime, in the eye of his persecutors, was his affection for her. This beating, and we know not what after treatment, completely subdued the spirit of its victim, for Robert ventured no more to visit Isabella, but like an obedient and faithful chattel, took himself a wife from the house of his master. Robert did not live many years after his last visit to Isabel, but took his departure to that country, where 'they neither marry nor are given in marriage,' and where the oppressor cannot molest.

Isabella's Marriage.

Subsequently, Isabella was married to a fellow-slave, named Thomas, who had previously had two wives, one of whom, if not both, had been torn from him and sold far away. And it is more than probable, that he was not only allowed but encouraged to take another at each successive sale. I say it is probable, because the writer of this knows from personal observation, that such is the custom among slaveholders at the present day; and that in a twenty months' residence among them, we never knew any one to open the lip against the practice; and when we severely censured it, the slaveholder had nothing to say; and the slave pleaded that, under existing circumstances, he could do no better.

Such an abominable state of things is silently tolerated, to say the least, by slaveholders—deny it who may. And what is that religion that sanctions, even by its silence, all that is embraced in the '*Peculiar Institution?*' If there *can* be any thing more diametrically opposed to the religion of Jesus, than the working of this soul-killing system—which is as truly sanctioned by the religion of America as are her ministers and churches—we wish to be shown where it can be found.

We have said, Isabella was married to Thomas—she was, after the fashion of slavery, one of the slaves performing the ceremony for them; as no true minister of Christ *can* perform, as in the presence of God, what he knows to be a mere *farce*, a *mock* marriage, unrecognized by any civil law,[3] and liable to be annulled any moment, when the interest or caprice of the master should dictate.

With what feelings must slaveholders expect us to listen to their horror of amalgamation in prospect, while they are well aware that we know how calmly and quietly they contemplate the present state of licentiousness their own wicked laws have created, not only as it regards the slave, but as it regards the more privileged portion of the population of the South?

Slaveholders appear to me to take the same notice of the vices of the slave, as one does of the vicious disposition of his horse. They are often an inconvenience; further than that, they care not to trouble themselves about the matter.

Isabella as a Mother.

In process of time, Isabella found herself the mother of five children, and she rejoiced in being permitted to be the instrument of increasing the property of her oppressors! Think, dear reader, without a blush, if you can, for one moment, of a *mother* thus willingly, and with *pride*, laying her own children, the 'flesh of her flesh,' on the altar of slavery—a sacrifice to the bloody Moloch! But we must remember that beings capable of such sacrifices are not mothers; they are only 'things,' 'chattels,' 'property.'

But since that time, the subject of this narrative has made some advances from a state of chattelism towards that of a woman and a mother; and she now looks back upon her thoughts and feelings there, in her state of ignorance and degradation, as one does on the dark imagery of a fitful dream. One moment it seems but a frightful illusion; again it appears a terrible reality. I would to God it *were* but a dreamy myth, and not, as it now stands, a horrid reality to some three millions of chattelized human beings.

I have already alluded to her care not to teach her children to steal, by her example; and she says, with groanings that cannot be written, 'The Lord only knows how many times I let my children go hungry, rather than take secretly the bread I liked not to ask for.' All parents who annul their preceptive teachings by their daily practices would do well to profit by her example.

Another proof of her master's kindness of heart is found in the following fact. If her master came into the house and found her infant crying, (as she could not always attend to its wants and the commands of her mistress at the same time,) he would turn to his wife with a look of reproof, and ask her why she did not see the child taken care of; saying, most earnestly, 'I will not hear this crying; I can't bear it, and I will not hear any child cry so. Here, Bell, take care of this child, if no more work is done for a week.' And he would linger to see if his orders were obeyed, and not countermanded.

When Isabella went to the field to work, she used to put her infant in a basket, tying a rope to each handle, and suspending the basket to a branch of a tree, set another small child to swing it. It was thus secure from reptiles, and was easily administered to, and even lulled to sleep, by a child too young for other labors. I was quite struck with the ingenuity of such a baby-tender, as I have sometimes been with the swinging hammock the native mother prepares for her sick infant—apparently so much easier than aught we have in our more civilized homes; easier for the child, because it gets the motion without the least jar; and easier for the nurse, because the hammock is strung so high as to supersede the necessity of stooping.

Slaveholder's Promises.

After emancipation had been decreed by the State, some years before the time fixed for its consummation, Isabella's master told her if she would do well, and be faithful, he would give her 'free papers,' one year before she was legally free by statute. In the year 1826, she had a badly diseased hand, which greatly diminished her usefulness; but on the arrival of July 4, 1827, the time specified for her receiving her 'free papers,' she claimed the fulfilment of her master's promise; but he refused granting it, on account (as he alleged) of the loss he had sustained by her hand. She plead that she had worked all the time, and done many things she was not wholly able to do, although she knew she had been less useful than formerly; but her master remained inflexible. Her very faithfulness probably operated against her now, and he found it less easy than he thought to give up the profits of his faithful Bell, who had so long done him efficient service.

But Isabella inwardly determined that she would remain quietly with him only until she had spun his wool—about one hundred pounds—and then she would leave him, taking the rest of the time to herself. 'Ah!' she says, with emphasis that cannot be written, 'the slaveholders are TERRIBLE for promising to give you this or that, or such and such a privilege, if you will do thus and so; and when the time of fulfilment comes, and one claims the promise, they, forsooth, recollect nothing of the kind; and you are, like as not, taunted with being a LIAR; or, at best, the slave is accused of not having performed *his* part or condition of the contract.' 'Oh!' said she, 'I have felt as if I could not live through the *operation* sometimes. Just think of us! *so* eager for our pleasures, and just foolish enough to keep feeding and feeding ourselves up with the idea that we should get what had been thus fairly promised; and when we think it is almost in our hands, find ourselves flatly denied! Just think! how *could* we bear it? Why, there was Charles Brodhead promised his slave Ned, that when harvesting was over, he might go and see his wife, who lived some twenty or thirty miles off. So Ned worked early and late, and as soon as the harvest was all in, he claimed the promised boon. His master said, he had merely told him he 'would *see* if he could go, when the harvest was over; but now he saw that he *could not go*.' But Ned, who still claimed a positive promise, on which he had fully depended, went on cleaning his shoes. His master asked him if he intended going, and on his replying 'yes,' took up a sled-stick that lay near him, and gave him such a blow on the head as broke his skull, killing him dead on the spot. The poor colored people all felt struck down by the blow.' Ah! and well they might. Yet it was but one of a long series of bloody, and other most effectual blows, struck against their liberty and their lives.* But to return from our digression.

The subject of this narrative was to have been free July 4, 1827, but she continued with her master till the wool was spun, and the heaviest of the 'fall's work' closed up, when she concluded to take her freedom into her own hands, and seek her fortune in some other place.

Her Escape.

The question in her mind, and one not easily solved, now was, 'How can I get away?' So, as was her usual custom, she 'told God she was afraid to go in the night, and in the day every body would see her.' At length, the thought came to her that she could leave just before the day dawned, and get out of the neighborhood where she was known before the people were much astir. 'Yes,' said she, fervently, 'that's a good thought! Thank you, God, for *that* thought!' So, receiving it as coming direct from God, she acted upon it, and one fine morning, a little before day-break, she might have been seen step-

---

*Yet no official notice was taken of his more than brutal murder.

ping stealthily away from the rear of Master Dumont's house, her infant on one arm and her wardrobe on the other; the bulk and weight of which, probably, she never found so convenient as on the present occasion, a cotton handkerchief containing both her clothes and her provisions.

As she gained the summit of a high hill, a considerable distance from her master's, the sun offended her by coming forth in all his pristine splendor. She thought it never was so light before; indeed, she thought it much too light. She stopped to look about her, and ascertain if her pursuers were yet in sight. No one appeared, and, for the first time, the question came up for settlement, 'Where, and to whom, shall I go?' In all her thoughts of getting away, she had not once asked herself whither she should direct her steps. She sat down, fed her infant, and again turning her thoughts to God, her only help, she prayed him to direct her to some safe asylum. And soon it occurred to her, that there was a man living somewhere in the direction she had been pursuing, by the name of Levi Rowe, whom she had known, and who, she thought, would be likely to befriend her. She accordingly pursued her way to his house, where she found him ready to entertain and assist her, though he was then on his death-bed. He bade her partake of the hospitalities of his house, said he knew of two good places where she might get in, and requested his wife to show her where they were to be found. As soon as she came in sight of the first house, she recollected having seen it and its inhabitants before, and instantly exclaimed, 'That's the place for me; I shall stop there.' She went there, and found the good people of the house, Mr. and Mrs. Van Wagener,* absent, but was kindly received and hospitably entertained by their excellent mother, till the return of her children. When they arrived, she made her case known to them. They listened to her story, assuring her they never turned the needy away, and willingly gave her employment.

She had not been there long before her old master, Dumont, appeared, as she had anticipated; for when she took French leave of him, she resolved not to go too far from him, and not put him to as much trouble in looking her up—for the latter he was sure to do—

---

*Often spelled Van Wagenen.

as Tom and Jack had done when they ran away from him, a short time before. This was very considerate in her, to say the least, and a proof that 'like begets like.' He had often considered *her* feelings, though not always, and she was equally considerate.

When her master saw her, he said, 'Well, Bell, so you've run away from me.' 'No I did not *run* away; I walked away by day-light, and all because you had promised me a year of my time.' His reply was, 'You must go back with me.' Her decisive answer was, 'No, I *won't* go back with you.' He said, 'Well, I shall take the *child*.' *This* also was as stoutly negatived.

Mr. Isaac S. Van Wagener then interposed, saying, he had never been in the practice of buying and selling slaves; he did not believe in slavery; but, rather than have Isabella taken back by force, he would buy her services for the balance of the year—for which her master charged twenty dollars, and five in addition for the child. The sum was paid, and her master Dumont departed; but not till he had heard Mr. Van Wagener tell her not to call him master,— adding, 'there is but *one* master; and he who is *your* master is *my* master.' Isabella inquired what she *should* call him? He answered, 'Call me Isaac Van Wagener, and my wife is Maria Van Wagener.' Isabella could not understand this, and thought it a *mighty change*, as it most truly was from a master whose word was law, to simple Isaac S. Van Wagener, who was master to *no* one. With these noble people, who, though they could not be the masters of slaves, were undoubtedly a portion of God's nobility, she resided one year, and from them she derived the name of Van Wagener; he being her last master in the eye of the law, and a slave's surname is ever the same as his master; that is, if he is allowed to have any other name than Tom, Jack, or Guffin. Slaves have sometimes been severely punished for adding their master's name to their own.[4] But when they have no particular title to it, it is no particular offence.

Illegal Sale of Her Son.

A little previous to Isabel's leaving her old master, he had sold her child, a boy of five years, to a Dr. Gedney, who took him with him as far as New York City, on his way to England; but finding the boy too small for his service, he sent him back to his brother, Solomon

Gedney. This man disposed of him to his sister's husband, a wealthy planter, by the name of Fowler, who took him to his own home in Alabama.

This illegal and fraudulent transaction[5] had been perpetrated some months before Isabella knew of it, as she was now living at Mr. Van Wagener's. The law expressly prohibited the sale of any slave out of the State,—and all minors were to be free at twenty-one years of age; and Mr. Dumont had sold Peter with the express understanding, that he was soon to return to the State of New York, and be emancipated at the specified time.

When Isabel heard that her son had been sold South, she immediately started on foot and alone, to find the man who had thus dared, in the face of all law, human and divine, to sell her child out of the State; and if possible, to bring him to account for the deed.

Arriving at New Paltz, she went directly to her former mistress, Dumont, complaining bitterly of the removal of her son. Her mistress heard her through, and then replied—'*Ugh!* a *fine* fuss to make about a little *nigger!* Why, haven't you as many of 'em left as you can see to and take care of? A pity 'tis, the niggers are not all in Guinea!! Making such a halloo-balloo about the neighborhood; and all for a paltry nigger!!!' Isabella heard her through, and after a moment's hesitation, answered, in tones of deep determination—'*I'll have my child again.*' 'Have *your child* again!' repeated her mistress—her tones big with contempt, and scorning the absurd idea of her getting him. 'How can you get him? And what have you to support him with, if you could? Have you any money?' 'No,' answered Bell, 'I have no money, but God has enough, or what's better! And I'll have my child again.' These words were pronounced in the most slow, solemn and determined measure and manner. And in speaking of it, she says, 'Oh, my God! I know'd I'd have him agin. I was sure God would help me to get him. Why, I felt so *tall within*—I felt as if the *power of a nation* was with me!'

The impressions made by Isabella on her auditors, when moved by lofty or deep feeling, can never be transmitted to paper, (to use the words of another,) till by some Daguerrian art, we are enabled to transfer the look, the gesture, the tones of voice, in connection with the quaint, yet fit expressions used, and the spirit-stirring animation that, at such a time, pervades all she says.

After leaving her mistress, she called on Mrs. Gedney, mother of him who had sold her boy; who, after listening to her lamentations, her grief being mingled with indignation at the sale of her son, and her declaration that she would have him again—said, 'Dear me! What a disturbance to make about your child! What, is *your* child better than *my* child? My child is gone out there, and yours is gone to live with her, to have enough of everything, and to be treated like a gentleman!' And here she laughed at Isabel's absurd fears, as she would represent them to be. 'Yes,' said Isabel, '*your* child has gone there, but she is *married*, and my boy has gone as a *slave*, and he is too little to go so far from his mother. Oh, I must have my child.' And here the continued laugh of Mrs. G. seemed to Isabel, in this time of anguish and distress, almost demoniacal. And well it was for Mrs. Gedney, that, at that time, she could not even dream of the awful fate awaiting her own beloved daughter, at the hands of him whom she had chosen as worthy the wealth of her love and confidence, and in whose society her young heart had calculated on a happiness, purer and more elevated than was ever conferred by a kingly crown. But, alas! she was doomed to disappointment, as we shall relate by and by. At this point, Isabella earnestly begged of God that he would show to those about her that He was her helper; and she adds, in narrating, 'And He *did;* or, if He did not show them, he did me.'

It Is Often Darkest Just Before Dawn.

This homely proverb was illustrated in the case of our sufferer; for, at the period at which we have arrived in our narrative, to her the darkness seemed palpable, and the waters of affliction covered her soul; yet light was about to break in upon her.

Soon after the scenes related in our last chapter, which had harrowed up her very soul to agony, she met a man, (we would like to tell you *who*, dear reader, but it would be doing him no kindness, even at the present day, to do so,) who evidently sympathized with her, and counselled her to go to the Quakers, telling her they were already feeling very indignant at the fraudulent sale of her son, and assuring her that they would readily assist her, and direct her what to do. He pointed out to her two houses, where lived some of those

people, who formerly, more than any other sect, perhaps, lived out
the principles of the gospel of Christ. She wended her way to their
dwellings, was listened to, unknown as she personally was to them,
with patience, and soon gained their sympathies and active co-
operation.

They gave her lodgings for the night; and it is very amusing to
hear her tell of the 'nice, high, clean, white, *beautiful* bed' assigned
her to sleep in, which contrasted so strangely with her former pal-
lets, that she sat down and contemplated it, perfectly absorbed in
wonder that *such* a bed should have been appropriated to one like
herself. For some time she thought that she would lie down beneath
it, on her usual bedstead, the floor. 'I did, indeed,' says she, laughing
heartily at her former self. However, she finally concluded to make
use of the bed, for fear that not to do so might injure the feelings of
her good hostess. In the morning, the Quaker saw that she was
taken and set down near Kingston, with directions to go to the
Court House, and enter complaint to the Grand Jury.*

By a little inquiry, she found which was the building she sought,
went into the door, and taking the first man she saw of imposing appearance for the *grand* jury, she commenced her complaint. But he
very civilly informed her there was no Grand Jury there; she must
go up stairs. When she had with some difficulty ascended the flight
through the crowd that filled them, she again turned to the '*grandest*' looking man she could select, telling him she had come to enter
a complaint to the Grand Jury. For his own amusement, he inquired
what her complaint was; but, when he saw it was a serious matter,
he said to her, 'This is no place to enter a complaint—go in there,'
pointing in a particular direction.

She then went in, where she found the Grand Jurors indeed sitting, and again commenced to relate her injuries. After holding
some conversation among themselves, one of them rose, and bidding her follow him, led the way to a side office, where he heard her
story, and asked her 'if she could *swear* that the child she spoke of
was her son?' 'Yes,' she answered, 'I *swear* it's my son.' 'Stop, stop!'
said the lawyer, 'you must swear by this book '—giving her a book,

---

*In Truth's day, grand juries often performed civil oversight functions that in the
contemporary era are controlled by administrative agencies and local government.

which she thinks must have been the Bible. She took it, and putting it to her lips, began again to swear it was her child. The clerks, unable to preserve their gravity any longer, burst into an uproarious laugh; and one of them inquired of lawyer Chip of what use it could be to make *her* swear. 'It will answer the law,' replied the officer. He then made her comprehend just what he wished her to do, and she took a lawful oath, as far as the outward ceremony could make it one. All can judge how far she understood its spirit and meaning.

He now gave her a writ,* directing her to take it to the constable of New Paltz, and have him serve it on Solomon Gedney. She obeyed, walking, or rather *trotting*, in her haste, some eight or nine miles.

But while the constable, through mistake, served the writ on a brother of the real culprit, Solomon Gedney slipped into a boat, and was nearly across the North River, on whose banks they were standing, before the dull Dutch constable was aware of his mistake. Solomon Gedney, meanwhile, consulted a lawyer, who advised him to go to Alabama and bring back the boy, otherwise it might cost him fourteen years' imprisonment, and a thousand dollars in cash.† By this time, it is hoped he began to feel that selling slaves unlawfully was not so good a business as he had wished to find it. He secreted himself till due preparations could be made, and soon set sail for Alabama. Steamboats and railroads had not then annihilated distance to the extent they now have, and although he left in the fall of the year, spring came ere he returned, bringing the boy with him—but holding on to him as his property. It had ever been Isabella's prayer, not only that her son might be returned, but that he should be delivered from bondage, and into her own hands, lest he should be punished out of mere spite to her, who was so greatly annoying and irritating to her oppressors; and if her suit was gained, her very triumph would add vastly to their irritation.

She again sought advice of Esquire Chip, whose counsel was, that the aforesaid constable serve the before-mentioned writ upon

---

*Official court document that commands the person to whom it is addressed to do something specific; that person is typically a defendant who must answer to this notice of legal action.

†Penalty for the sale of a slave out of state.

the right person. This being done, soon brought Solomon Gedney up to Kingston, where he gave bonds for his appearance at court, in the sum of $600.

Esquire Chip next informed his client, that her case must now lie over till the next session of the court, some months in the future. 'The law must take its course,' said he.

'What! wait another court! wait *months?*' said the persevering mother. 'Why, long before that time, he can go clear off; and take my child with him—no one knows where. I *cannot* wait; I *must* have him *now*, whilst he is to be had.' 'Well,' said the lawyer, very coolly, 'if he puts the boy out of the way, he must pay the $600—one half of which will be yours;' supposing, perhaps, that $300 would pay for a 'heap of children,' in the eye of a slave who never, in all her life, called a dollar her own. But in this instance, he was mistaken in his reckoning. She assured him, that she had not been seeking money, neither would money satisfy her; it was her son, and her son alone she wanted, and her son she must have. Neither could she wait court, not she. The lawyer used his every argument to convince her, that she ought to be very thankful for what they had done for her; that it was a great deal, and it was but reasonable that she should now wait patiently the time of the court.

Yet she never felt, for a moment, like being influenced by these suggestions. She felt confident she was to receive a full and literal answer to her prayer, the burden of which had been—'O Lord, give my son into my hands, and that speedily! Let not the spoilers have him any longer.' Notwithstanding, she very distinctly saw that those who had thus far helped her on so kindly were *wearied* of her, and she feared God was wearied also. She had a short time previous learned that Jesus was a Saviour, and an intercessor; and she thought that if Jesus could but be induced to plead for her in the present trial, God would listen to *him*, though he were wearied of *her* importunities. To him, of course, she applied. As she was walking about, scarcely knowing whither she went, asking within herself, 'Who will show me any good, and lend a helping hand in this matter,' she was accosted by a perfect stranger, and one whose name she has never learned, in the following terms: 'Halloo, there; how do you get along with your boy? do they give him up to you?' She told him all, adding that now every body was tired, and she had none to help

her. He said, 'Look here! I'll tell you what you'd better do. Do you
see that stone house yonder?' pointing in a particular direction.
'Well, lawyer Demain lives there, and do you go to him, and lay your
case before him; I think he'll help you. *Stick to him.* Don't give him
peace till he does. I feel sure if you press him, he'll do it for you.' She
needed no further urging, but trotted off at her peculiar gait in the
direction of his house, as fast as possible,—and she was not encumbered with stockings, shoes, or any other heavy article of dress.
When she had told him her story, in her impassioned manner, he
looked at her a few moments, as if to ascertain if he were contemplating a new variety of the genus homo, and then told her, if she
would give him five dollars, he would get her son for her, in twenty-
four hours. 'Why,' she replied, '*I* have no *money*, and never had a
dollar in my life!' Said he, 'If you will go to those Quakers in Poppletown, who carried you to court, they will help you to five dollars
in cash, I have no doubt; and you shall have your son in twenty-four
hours, from the time you bring me that sum.' She performed the
journey to Poppletown, a distance of some ten miles, very expedi-
tiously; collected considerable more than the sum specified by the
barrister; then, shutting the money tightly in her hand, she trotted
back, and paid the lawyer a larger fee than he had demanded. When
inquired of by people what she had done with the overplus, she answered, 'Oh, I got it for lawyer Demain, and I gave it to him.' They
assured her she was a *fool* to do so; that she should have kept all over
five dollars, and purchased herself shoes with it. 'Oh, I do not want
money or clothes now, I only want my son; and if five dollars will
get him, more will *surely* get him.' And if the lawyer had returned it
to her, she avers she would not have accepted it. She was perfectly
willing he should have every coin she could raise, if he would but restore her lost son to her. Moreover, the five dollars he required were
for the remuneration of him who should go after her son and his
master, and not for his own services.

The lawyer now renewed his promise, that she should have her
son in twenty-four hours. But Isabella, having no idea of this space
of time, went several times in a day, to ascertain if her son had come.
Once, when the servant opened the door and saw her, she said, in a
tone expressive of much surprise, 'Why, this woman's come again!'
She then wondered if she went too often. When the lawyer ap-

peared, he told her the twenty-four hours would not expire till the next morning; if she would call then, she would see her son. The next morning saw Isabel at the lawyer's door, while he was yet in his bed. He now assured her it was morning till noon; and that before noon her son would be there, for he had sent the famous 'Matty Styles' after him, who would not fail to have the boy and his master on hand in due season, either dead or alive; of that he was sure. Telling her she need not come again; he would himself inform her of their arrival.

After dinner, he appeared at Mr. Rutzer's, (a place the lawyer had procured for her, while she awaited the arrival of her boy,) assuring her, her son had come; but that he stoutly denied having any mother, or any relatives in that place; and said, 'she must go over and identify him.' She went to the office, but at sight of her the boy cried aloud, and regarded her as some terrible being, who was about to take him away from a kind and loving friend. He knelt, even, and begged them, with tears, not to take him away from his dear master, who had brought him from the dreadful South, and been so kind to him.

When he was questioned relative to the bad scar on his forehead, he said, 'Fowler's horse hove him.' And of the one on his cheek, 'That was done by running against the carriage.' In answering these questions he looked imploringly at his master, as much as to say, 'If they are falsehoods, you bade me say them; may they be satisfactory to you, at least.'

The justice, noting his appearance, bade him forget his master and attend only to him. But the boy persisted in denying his mother, and clinging to his master, saying his mother did not live in such a place as that. However, they allowed the mother to identify her son; and Esquire Demain pleaded that he claimed the boy for her, on the ground that he had been sold out of the State, contrary to the laws in such cases made and provided—spoke of the penalties annexed to said crime, and of the sum of money the delinquent was to pay, in case any one chose to prosecute him for the offence he had committed. Isabella, who was sitting in a corner, scarcely daring to breathe, thought within herself; 'If I can but get the boy, the $200 may remain for whoever else chooses to prosecute—*I* have done enough to make myself enemies already'—and she trembled at the thought of the formidable enemies she had probably arrayed against herself—helpless and despised as she was. When the pleading was at an end, Isabella understood the Judge to declare, as the sentence of the Court, that the 'boy be delivered into the hands of the mother—having no other master, no other controller, no other conductor, but his mother.' This sentence was obeyed; he was delivered into her hands, the boy meanwhile begging, most piteously, *not* to be taken from his dear master, saying she was not his mother, and that his mother did not live in such a place as that. And it was some time before lawyer Demain, the clerks, and Isabella, could collectively succeed in calming the child's fears, and in convincing him that Isabella was not some terrible monster, as he had for the last months, probably, been trained to believe; and who, in taking him away from his master, was taking him from all good, and consigning him to all evil.

When at last kind words and *bon bons* had quieted his fears, and he could listen to their explanations, he said to Isabella—'Well, you *do* look like my mother *used* to;' and she was soon able to make him comprehend some of the obligations he was under, and the relation he stood in, both to herself and his master. She commenced as soon as practicable to examine the boy, and found, to her utter astonishment, that from the crown of his head to the sole of his foot, the callosities and indurations on his entire body were most frightful to behold. His back she described as being like her fingers, as she laid them side by side.

'Heavens! what is all *this?*' said Isabel. He answered, 'It is where Fowler whipped, kicked, and beat me.' She exclaimed, 'Oh, Lord Jesus, look! see my poor child! Oh Lord, "render unto them double" for all this! Oh my God! Pete, how *did* you bear it?'

'Oh, this is nothing, mammy—if you should see Phillis, I guess you'd *scare!* She had a little baby, and Fowler cut her till the milk as well as blood ran down *her* body. You would *scare* to see Phillis, mammy.'

When Isabella inquired, 'What did Miss Eliza* say, Pete, when you were treated so badly?' he replied, 'Oh, mammy, she said she wished I was with Bell. Sometimes I crawled under the stoop,

---

*Meaning Mrs. Eliza Fowler.

mammy, the blood running all about me, and my back would stick to the boards; and sometimes Miss Eliza would come and grease my sores, when all were abed and asleep.'

Death of Mrs. Eliza Fowler.

As soon as possible she procured a place for Peter, as tender of locks, at a place called Wahkendall, near Greenkills. After he was thus disposed of, she visited her sister Sophia, who resided at Newburg, and spent the winter in several different families where she was acquainted. She remained some time in the family of a Mr. Latin, who was a visiting relative of Solomon Gedney; and the latter, when he found Isabel with his cousin, used all his influence to persuade him she was a great mischief-maker and a very troublesome person,— that she had put him to some hundreds of dollars expense, by fabricating lies about him, and especially his sister and her family, concerning her boy, when the latter was living so like a gentleman with them; and, for his part, he would not advise his friends to harbor or encourage her. However, his cousins, the Latins, could not see with the eyes of *his* feelings, and consequently his words fell powerless on them, and they retained her in their service as long as they had aught for her to do.

She then went to visit her former master, Dumont. She had scarcely arrived there, when Mr. Fred. Waring entered, and seeing Isabel, pleasantly accosted her, and asked her 'what she was driving at now-a-days.' On her answering 'nothing particular,' he requested her to go over to his place, and assist his folks, as some of them were sick, and they needed an extra hand. She very gladly assented. When Mr. W. retired, her master wanted to know why she wished to help people, that called her the 'worst of devils,' as Mr. Waring had done in the court-house—for he was the uncle of Solomon Gedney, and attended the trial we have described—and declared 'that she was a *fool* to; *he* wouldn't do it.' 'Oh,' she told him, 'she would not mind that, but was very glad to have people forget their anger towards her.' She went over, but too happy to feel that their resentment was passed, and, commenced her work with a light heart and a strong will. She had not worked long in this frame of mind, before a young daughter of Mr. Waring rushed into the room, exclaiming, with uplifted hands—'Heavens and earth, Isabella! Fowler's murdered Cousin Eliza!' 'Ho,' said Isabel, '*that's* nothing—he liked to have killed *my* child; nothing saved him but God.' Meaning, that she was not at all surprised at it, for a man whose heart was sufficiently hardened to treat a mere child as hers had been treated, was, in her opinion, more fiend than human, and prepared for the commission of any crime that his passions might prompt him to. The child further informed her, that a letter had arrived by mail bringing the news.

Immediately after this announcement, Solomon Gedney and his mother came in, going direct to Mrs. Waring's room, where she soon heard tones as of some one reading. She thought something said to her inwardly, 'Go up stairs and hear.' At first she hesitated, but it seemed to press her the more—'Go up and hear!' She went up, unusual as it is for slaves to leave their work and enter unbidden their mistress's room, for the sole purpose of seeing or hearing what may be seen or heard there. But on this occasion, Isabella says, she walked in at the door, shut it, placed her back against it, and listened. She saw them and heard them read—'He knocked her down with his fist, jumped on her with his knees, broke her collar bone, and tore out her wind-pipe! He then attempted his escape, but was pursued and arrested, and put in an iron bank for safe-keeping!' And the friends were requested to go down and take away the poor innocent children who had thus been made in one short day more than orphans.

If this narrative should ever meet the eye of those innocent sufferers for another's guilt, let them not be too deeply affected by the relation; but, placing their confidence in Him who sees the end from the beginning, and controls the results, rest secure in the faith, that, although they may physically suffer for the sins of others, if they remain but true to themselves, their highest and more enduring interests can never suffer from such a cause. This relation should be suppressed for their sakes, were it not even now so often denied, that slavery is fast undermining all true regard for human life. We know this one instance is not a demonstration to the contrary; but, adding this to the lists of tragedies that weekly come up to us through the Southern mails, may we not admit them as proofs irrefragable? The newspapers confirm this account of the terrible affair.

When Isabella had heard the letter, all being too much absorbed in their own feelings to take note of her, she returned to her work, her heart swelling with conflicting emotions. She was awed at the dreadful deed; she mourned the fate of the loved Eliza, who had in such an undeserved and barbarous manner been put away from her labors and watchings as a tender mother; and, 'last though not least,' in the development of her character and spirit, her heart bled for the afflicted relatives; even those of them who 'laughed at her calamity, and mocked when her fear came.' Her thoughts dwelt long and intently on the subject, and the wonderful chain of events that had conspired to bring her that day to that house, to listen to that piece of intelligence—to that house, where she never was before or afterwards in her life, and invited there by people who had so lately been hotly incensed against her. It all seemed very remarkable to her, and she viewed it as flowing from a special providence of God. She thought she saw clearly, that their unnatural bereavement was a blow dealt in retributive justice: but she found it not in her heart to exult or rejoice over them. She felt as if God had more than answered her petition, when she ejaculated, in her anguish of mind, 'Oh, Lord, render unto them double!' She said, 'I dared not find fault with God, exactly; but the language of my heart was, 'Oh, my God! that's too much—I did not mean quite so much, God!' It was a terrible blow to the friends of the deceased; and her selfish mother (who, said Isabella, made such a 'to-do about *her* boy, not from affection, 'but to have her own will and way') went deranged, and walking to and fro in her delirium, called aloud for her poor murdered daughter—'*Eliza! Eliza!*'

The derangement of Mrs. G. was a matter of hearsay, as Isabella saw her not after the trial; but she has no reason to doubt the truth of what she heard. Isabel could never learn the subsequent fate of Fowler, but heard in the spring of '49 that his children had been seen in Kingston—one of whom was spoken of as a fine, interesting girl, albeit a halo of sadness fell like a veil about her.

Isabella's Religious Experience.

We will now turn from the outward and temporal to the inward and spiritual life of our subject. It is ever both interesting and instructive to trace the exercises of a human mind, through the trials and mysteries of life; and especially a naturally powerful mind, left as hers was almost entirely to its own workings, and the chance influences it met on its way; and especially to note its reception of that divine 'light, that lighteth every man that cometh into the world.'

We see, as knowledge dawns upon it, truth and error strangely commingled; here, a bright spot illuminated by truth—and there, one darkened and distorted by error; and the state of such a soul may be compared to a landscape at early dawn, where the sun is seen superbly gilding some objects, and causing others to send forth their lengthened, distorted, and sometimes hideous shadows.

Her mother, as we have already said, talked to her of God. From these conversations, her incipient mind drew the conclusion, that God was 'a great man;' greatly superior to other men in power; and being located 'high in the sky,' could see all that transpired on the earth. She believed he not only saw, but noted down all her actions in a great book, even as her master kept a record of whatever he wished not to forget. But she had no idea that God knew a thought of hers till she had uttered it aloud.

As we have before mentioned, she had ever been mindful of her mother's injunctions, spreading out in detail all her troubles before God, imploring and firmly trusting him to send her deliverance from them. Whilst yet a child, she listened to a story of a wounded soldier, left alone in the trail of a flying army, helpless and starving, who hardened the very ground about him with kneeling in his supplications to God for relief, until it arrived. From this narrative, she was deeply impressed with the idea, that if *she* also were to present her petitions under the open canopy of heaven, speaking very loud, she should the more readily be heard; consequently, she sought a fitting spot for this, her rural sanctuary. The place she selected, in which to offer up her daily orisons,* was a small island in a small stream, covered with large willow shrubbery, beneath which the sheep had made their pleasant winding paths; and sheltering themselves from the scorching rays of a noon-tide sun, luxuriated in the cool shadows of the graceful willows, as they listened to the tiny falls of the silver waters. It was a lonely spot, and chosen by her for its

---

*Prayers or supplications.

beauty, its retirement, and because she thought that there, in the noise of those waters, she could speak louder to God, without being overheard by any who might pass that way. When she had made choice of her sanctum, at a point of the island where the stream met, after having been separated, she improved it by pulling away the branches of the shrubs from the centre, and weaving them together for a wall on the outside, forming a circular arched alcove, made entirely of the graceful willow. To this place she resorted daily, and in pressing times much more frequently.

At this time, her prayers, or, more appropriately, 'talks with God,' were perfectly original and unique, and would be well worth preserving, were it possible to give the tones and manner with the words; but no adequate idea of them can be written while the tones and manner remain inexpressible.

She would sometimes repeat, 'Our Father in heaven,' in her Low Dutch, as taught her by her mother, after that, all was from the suggestions of her own rude mind. She related to God, in minute detail, all her troubles and sufferings, inquiring, as she proceeded, 'Do you think that's right, God?' and closed by begging to be delivered from the evil, whatever it might be.

She talked to God as familiarly as if he had been a creature like herself; and a thousand times more so, than if she had been in the presence of some earthly potentate. She demanded, with little expenditure of reverence or fear, a supply of all her more pressing wants, and at times her demands approached very near to commands. She felt as if God was under obligation to her, much more than she was to him. He seemed to her benighted vision in some manner bound to do her bidding.

Her heart recoils now, with very dread, when she recalls these shocking, almost blasphemous conversations with the great Jehovah. And well for herself did she deem it, that, unlike earthly potentates, his infinite character combined the tender father with the omniscient and omnipotent Creator of the universe.

She at first commenced promising God, that if he would help her out of all her difficulties, she would pay him by being very good; and this goodness she intended as a remuneration to God. She could think of no benefit that was to accrue to herself or her fellow-creatures, from her leading a life of purity and generous self-sacrifice for the good of others; as far, as any but God was concerned, she saw nothing in it but heart-trying penance, sustained by the sternest exertion; and this she soon found much more easily promised than performed.

Days wore away—new trials came—God's aid was invoked, and the same promises repeated; and every successive night found her part of the contract unfulfilled. She now began to excuse herself; by telling God she could not be good in her present circumstances; but if he would give her a new place, and a good master and mistress, she could and would be good; and she expressly stipulated, that she would be good *one* day to show God how good she would be *all* of the time, when he should surround her with the right influences, and she should be delivered from the temptations that then so sorely beset her. But, alas! when night came, and she became conscious that she had yielded to all her temptations, and entirely failed of keeping her word with God, having prayed and promised one hour, and fallen into the sins of anger and profanity the next, the mortifying reflection weighed on her mind, and blunted her enjoyment. Still, she did not lay it deeply to heart, but continued to repeat her demands for aid, and her promises of pay, with full purpose of heart, at each particular time, that *that* day she would not fail to keep her plighted word.

Thus perished the inward spark, like a flame just igniting, when one waits to see whether it will burn on or die out, till the long desired change came, and she found herself in a new place, with a good mistress, and one who never instigated an otherwise kind master to be unkind to her; in short, a place where she had literally nothing to complain of, and where, for a time, she was more happy than she could well express. 'Oh, every thing there was *so* pleasant, and kind, and good, and all so comfortable; enough of every thing; indeed, it was beautiful!' she exclaimed.

Here, at Mr. Van Wagener's,—as the reader will readily perceive she must have been,—she was so happy and satisfied, that God was entirely forgotten. Why should her thoughts turn to Him, who was only known to her as a help in trouble? She had no trouble now; her every prayer had been answered in every minute particular. She had been delivered from her persecutors and temptations, her youngest child had been given her, and the others she knew she had no means of sustaining if she had them with her, and was content to leave them behind. Their father, who was much older than Isabel, and who preferred serving his time out in slavery, to the trouble and dangers of the course she pursued, remained with and could keep an eye on them—though it is comparatively little that they can do for each other while they remain in slavery; and this little the slave, like persons in every other situation of life, is not always disposed to perform. There *are* slaves, who, copying the selfishness of their superiors in power, in their conduct towards their fellows who may be thrown upon their mercy, by infirmity or illness, allow them to suffer for want of that kindness and care which it is fully in their power to render them.

The slaves in this country have ever been allowed to celebrate the principal, if not some of the lesser festivals observed by the Catholics and Church of England; many of them not being required to do the least service for several days, and at Christmas they have almost universally an entire week to themselves, except, perhaps, the attending to a few duties, which are absolutely required for the comfort of the families they belong to. If much service is desired, they are hired to do it, and paid for it as if they were free. The more sober portion of them spend these holidays in earning a little money. Most of them visit and attend parties and balls, and not a few of them spend it in the lowest dissipation. This respite from toil is granted them by all religionists, of whatever persuasion, and probably originated from the fact that many of the first slaveholders were members of the Church of England.

Frederick Douglass,[6] who has devoted his great heart and noble talents entirely to the furtherance of the cause of his down-trodden race, has said—'From what I know of the effect of their holidays upon the slave, I believe them to be among the most effective means, in the hands of the slaveholder, in keeping down the spirit of insurrection. Were the slaveholders at once to abandon this practice, I have not the slightest doubt it would lead to an immediate insurrection among the slaves. These holidays serve as conductors, or safety-valves, to carry off the rebellious spirit of enslaved humanity. But for these, the slave would be forced up to the wildest desperation; and woe betide the slaveholder, the day he ventures to remove or hinder the operation of those conductors! I warn him that, in such an event, a spirit will go forth in their midst, more to be dreaded than the most appalling earthquake.'

When Isabella had been at Mr. Van Wagener's a few months, she saw in prospect one of the festivals approaching. She knows it by none but the Dutch name, Pingster,* as she calls it—but I think it must have been Whitsuntide, in English. She says she 'looked back into Egypt,' and everything looked 'so pleasant there,' as she saw retrospectively all her former companions enjoying their freedom for at least a little space, as well as their wonted convivialities, and in her heart she longed to be with them. With this picture before her mind's eye, she contrasted the quiet, peaceful life she was living with the excellent people of Wahkendall, and it seemed so dull and void of incident, that the very contrast served but to heighten her desire to return, that, at least, she might enjoy with them, once more, the coming festivities. These feelings had occupied a secret corner of her breast for some time, when, one morning, she told Mrs. Van Wagener that her old master Dumont would come that day, and that she should go home with him on his return. They expressed some surprise, and asked her where she obtained her information. She replied, that no one had told her, but she felt that he would come.

It seemed to have been one of those 'events that cast their shadows before;' for, before night, Mr. Dumont made his appearance. She informed him of her intention to accompany him home. He answered, with a smile, 'I shall not take you back again; you ran away from me.' Thinking his manner contradicted his words, she did not feel repulsed, but made herself and child ready; and when her former master had seated himself in the open dearborn, she walked towards it, intending to place herself and child in the rear, and go with him. But, ere she reached the vehicle, she says that God revealed himself to her, with all the suddenness of a flash of lightning, showing her, 'in the twinkling of an eye, that he was *all over*'—that he pervaded the universe—'and that there was no place where God was not.' She became instantly conscious of her great sin in forgetting

---

*Often spelled Pinkster, this Dutch celebration of Pentecost, the seventh Sunday after Easter, had developed by the late eighteenth century into a carnival for African-American New Yorkers.

her almighty Friend and 'ever-present help in time of trouble.' All
her unfulfilled promises arose before her, like a vexed sea whose
waves run mountains high; and her soul, which seemed but one
mass of lies, shrunk back aghast from the 'awful look' of Him whom
she had formerly talked as if he had been a being like herself; and
she would now fain have hid herself in the bowels of the earth, to
have escaped his dread presence. But she plainly saw there was no
place, not even in hell, where he was not: and where could she flee?
Another such 'a look,' as she expressed it, and she felt that she must
be extinguished forever, even as one, with the breath of his mouth,
'blows out a lamp,' so that no spark remains.

A dire dread of annihilation now seized her, and she waited to see
if, by 'another look,' she was to be stricken from existence,—swallowed up, even as the fire licketh up the oil with which it comes in
contact.

When at last the second look came not, and her attention was
once more called to outward things, she observed her master had
left, and exclaiming aloud, 'Oh, God, I did not know you were so
big,' walked into the house, and made an effort to resume her work.
But the workings of the inward man were too absorbing to admit of
much attention to her avocations. She desired to talk to God, but
her vileness utterly forbade it, and she was not able to prefer a petition. 'What!' said she, 'shall I lie again to God? I have told him
nothing but lies; and shall I speak again, and tell another lie to
God?' She could not; and now she began to wish for some one to
speak to God for her. Then a space seemed opening between her
and God, and she felt that if some one, who was worthy in the sight
of heaven, would but plead *for* her in their own name, and not let
God know it came from *her*, who was so unworthy, God might grant
it. At length a friend appeared to stand between herself and an insulted Deity; and she felt as sensibly refreshed as when, on a hot day,
an umbrella had been interposed between her scorching head and a
burning sun. But who was this friend? became the next inquiry. Was
it Deencia, who had so often befriended her? She looked at her with
her new power of sight—and, lo! she, too, seemed all 'bruises and
putrifying sores,' like herself. No, it was some one very different
from Deencia.

'Who *are* you?' she exclaimed, as the vision brightened into a form distinct, beaming with the beauty of holiness, and radiant with love. She then said, audibly addressing the mysterious visitant—'I *know* you, and I *don't* know you. Meaning, 'You seem perfectly familiar; I feel that you not only love me, but that you always have loved me—yet I know you not—I cannot call you by name.' When she said, 'I know you,' the subject of the vision remained distinct and quiet. When she said, 'I don't know you,' it moved restlessly about, like agitated waters. So while she repeated, without intermission, 'I know you, I know you,' that the vision might remain—'Who are you?' was the cry of her heart, and her whole soul was in one deep prayer that this heavenly personage might be revealed to her, and remain with her. At length, after bending both soul and body with the intensity of this desire, till breath and strength seemed failing, and she could maintain her position no longer, an answer came to her, saying distinctly, 'It is Jesus.' 'Yes,' she responded, 'it is *Jesus.*'

Previous to these exercises of mind, she heard Jesus mentioned in reading or speaking, but had received from what she heard no impression that he was any other than an eminent man, like a Washington or a Lafayette. Now he appeared to her delighted mental vision as so mild, so good, and so every way lovely, and he loved her so much! And, how strange that he had always loved her, and she had never known it! And how great a blessing he conferred, in that he should stand between her and God! And God was no longer a terror and a dread to her.

She stopped not to argue the point, even in her own mind, whether he had reconciled her to God, or God to herself, (though she thinks the former now,) being but too happy that God was no longer to her as a consuming fire, and Jesus was 'altogether lovely.' Her heart was now full of joy and gladness, as it had been of terror, and at one time of despair. In the light of her great happiness, the world was clad in new beauty, the very air sparkled as with diamonds, and was redolent of heaven. She contemplated the unapproachable barriers that existed between herself and the great of this world, as the world calls greatness, and made surprising comparisons between them, and the union existing between herself and Jesus,—Jesus, the transcendently lovely as well as great and powerful; for so he appeared to her, though he seemed but human; and she watched for his bodily appearance, feeling that she should know him, if she saw him; and when he came, she should go and dwell with him, as with a dear friend.

It was not given her to see that he loved any other; and she thought if others came to know and love him, as she did, she should be thrust aside and forgotten, being herself but a poor ignorant slave, with little to recommend her to his notice. And when she heard him spoken of, she said mentally—'What! others know Jesus! I thought no one knew Jesus but me!' and she felt a sort of jealousy, lest she should be robbed of her newly found treasure.

She conceived, one day, as she listened to reading, that she heard an intimation that Jesus was married, and hastily inquired if Jesus had a wife. 'What!' said the reader, '*God* have a wife?' 'Is Jesus *God?*' inquired Isabella. 'Yes, to be sure he is,' was the answer returned. From this time, her conceptions of Jesus became more elevated and spiritual; and she sometimes spoke of him as God, in accordance with the teaching she had received.

But when she was simply told, that the Christian world was much divided on the subject of Christ's nature—some believing him to be coequal with the Father—to be God in and of himself, 'very God, of very God;'—some, that he is the 'well-beloved,' 'only be-gotten Son of God;'—and others, that he is, or was, rather, but a mere man—she said, 'Of that I only know as I saw. I did not see him to be God; else, how could he stand between me and God? I saw him as a friend, standing between me and God, through whom, love flowed as from a fountain.' Now, so far from expressing her views of Christ's character and office in accordance with any system of theology extant, she says she believes Jesus is the same spirit that was in our first parents, Adam and Eve, in the beginning, when they came from the hand of their Creator. When they sinned through disobedience, this pure spirit forsook them, and fled to heaven; that there it remained, until it returned again in the person of Jesus; and that, previous to a personal union with him, man is but a brute, possessing only the spirit of an animal.

She avers that, in her darkest hours, she had no fear of any worse hell than the one she then carried in her bosom; though it had ever been pictured to her in its deepest colors, and threatened her as a reward for all her misdemeanors. Her vileness and God's holiness and all-pervading presence, which filled immensity, and threatened her with instant annihilation, composed the burden of her vision of terror. Her faith in prayer is equal to her faith in the love of Jesus. Her language is, 'Let others say what they will of the efficacy of prayer, *I* believe in it, and *I* shall pray. Thank God! Yes, *I shall always pray,*' she exclaims, putting her hands together with the greatest enthusiasm.

For some time subsequent to the happy change we have spoken of, Isabella's prayers partook largely of their former character; and while, in deep affliction, she labored for the recovery of her son, she prayed with constancy and fervor; and the following may be taken as a specimen:—'Oh, God, you know how much I am distressed, for I have told you again and again. Now, God, help me get my son. If you were in trouble, as I am, and I could help you, as you can me, think I wouldn't do it? Yes, God, you *know* I would do it.' 'Oh, God, you know I have no money, but you can make the people do for me, and you must make the people do for me. I will never give you peace till you do, God.' 'Oh, God, make the people hear me—don't let them turn me off, without hearing and helping me.' And she has not a particle of doubt, that God heard her, and especially disposed the hearts of thoughtless clerks, eminent lawyers, and grave judges and others—between whom and herself there seemed to her almost an infinite remove—to listen to her suit with patient and respectful attention, backing it with needed aid. The sense of her nothingness, in the eyes of those with whom she contended for her rights, sometimes fell on her like a heavy weight, which nothing but her unwavering confidence in an arm which she believed to be stronger than all others combined could have raised from her sinking spirit. 'Oh! how little I did feel,' she repeated, with a powerful emphasis. 'Neither would you wonder, if you could have seen me, in my ignorance and destitution, trotting about the streets, meanly clad, bareheaded, and bare-footed! Oh, God only could have made such people hear me; and he did it in answer to my prayers.' And this perfect trust, based on the rock of Deity, was a soul-protecting fortress, which, raising her above the battlements of fear, and shielding her from the machinations of the enemy, impelled her onward in the struggle, till the foe was vanquished, and the victory gained.

We have now seen Isabella, her youngest daughter, and her only son, in possession of, at least, their nominal freedom. It has been said that the freedom of the most free of the colored people of this country is but nominal; but stinted and limited as it is, at best, it is an *immense* remove from chattel slavery. This fact is disputed, I know; but I have no confidence in the honesty of such questionings. If they are made in sincerity, I honor not the judgment that thus decides.

Her husband, quite advanced in age, and infirm of health, was emancipated, with the balance of the adult slaves of the State, according to law, the following summer, July 4, 1828.

For a few years after this event, he was able to earn a scanty living, and when he failed to do that, he was dependent on the 'world's cold charity,' and died in a poor-house. Isabella had herself and two children to provide for; her wages were trifling, for at that time the wages of females were at a small advance from nothing; and she doubtless had to learn the first elements of economy—for what slaves, that were never allowed to make any stipulations or calculations for themselves, ever possessed an adequate idea of the true value of time, or, in fact, of any material thing in the universe? To such, 'prudent using' is meanness—and 'saving' is a word to be sneered at. Of course, it was not in her power to make to herself a home, around whose sacred hearthstone she could collect her family, as they gradually emerged from their prison-house of bondage; a home, where she could cultivate their affection, administer to their wants, and instil into the opening minds of her children those principles of virtue, and that love of purity, truth and benevolence, which must ever form the foundation of a life of usefulness and happiness. No—all this was far beyond her power or means, in more senses than one; and it should be taken into the account, whenever a comparison is instituted between the progress made by her children in virtue and goodness, and the progress of those who have been nurtured in the genial warmth of a sunny home, where good influences cluster, and bad ones are carefully excluded—where 'line upon line, and precept upon precept,' are daily brought to their quotidian tasks—and where, in short, every appliance is brought in requisition, that self-denying parents can bring to bear on one of the dearest objects of a parent's life, the promotion of the welfare of their children. But God forbid that this suggestion should be wrested from its original intent, and made to shield any one from merited rebuke! Isabella's children are now of an age to know good from evil, and may easily inform themselves on any point where they may yet be in doubt; and if they now suffer themselves to be drawn by temptation into the paths of the destroyer, or forget what is due to the mother who has done and suffered so much for them, and who, now that she is descending into the vale of years, and feels her health and strength declining, will turn her expecting eyes to them for aid and comfort, just as instinctively as the child turns its confiding eye to its fond parent, when it seeks for succor or for sympathy—(for it is now their turn to do the work, and bear the burdens of life, as all must bear them in turn, as the wheel of life rolls on)—if, I say, they forget this, their duty and their happiness, and pursue an opposite course of sin and folly, they must lose the respect of the wise and good, and find, when too late, that 'the way of the transgressor is hard.'

New Trials.

The reader will pardon this passing homily, while we return to our narrative.

We were saying that the day-dreams of Isabella and her husband—the plan they drew of what they would do, and the comforts they thought to have, when they should obtain their freedom, and a little home of their own—had all turned to 'thin air,' by the postponement of their freedom to so late a day. These delusive hopes were never to be realized, and a new set of trials was gradually to open before her. These were the heart-wasting trials of watching over her children, scattered, and imminently exposed to the temptations of the adversary, with few, if any, fixed principles to sustain them.

'Oh,' she says, 'how little did I know myself of the best way to instruct and counsel them! Yet I did the best I then knew, when with them. I took them to the religious meetings; I talked to, and prayed for and with them; when they did wrong, I scolded at and whipped them.'

Isabella and her son had been free about a year, when they went to reside in the city of New York; a place which she would doubtless have avoided, could she have seen what was there in store for her; for this view into the future would have taught her what she only learned by bitter experience, that the baneful influences going up from such a city were not the best helps to education, commenced as the education of *her* children had been.

Her son Peter was, at the time of which we are speaking, just at that age when no lad should be subjected to the temptations of such a place, unprotected as he was, save by the feeble arm of a mother, herself a servant there. He was growing up to be a tall, well-formed, active lad, of quick perceptions, mild and cheerful in his disposition, with much that was open, generous and winning about him, but with little power to withstand temptation, and a ready ingenuity to provide himself with ways and means to carry out his plans, and conceal from his mother and her friends, all such as he knew would not meet their approbation. As will be readily believed, he was soon drawn into a circle of associates who did not improve either his habits or his morals.

Two years passed before Isabella knew what character Peter was establishing for himself among his low and worthless comrades— passing under the assumed name of Peter Williams;[7] and she began to feel a parent's pride in the promising appearance of her only son. But, alas! this pride and pleasure were shortly dissipated, as distressing facts relative to him came one by one to her astonished ear. A friend of Isabella's, a lady, who was much pleased with the good humor, ingenuity, and open confessions of Peter, when driven into a corner, and who, she said, 'was so smart, he ought to have an education, if any one ought,'—paid ten dollars, as tuition fee, for him to attend a navigation school. But Peter, little inclined to spend his leisure hours in study, when he might be enjoying himself in the dance, or otherwise, with his boon companions, went regularly and made some plausible excuses to the teacher, who received them as genuine, along with the ten dollars of Mrs. ——, and while his mother and her friend believed him improving at school, he was, to their latent sorrow, improving in a very different place or places, and on entirely opposite principles. They also procured him an excellent place as a coachman. But, wanting money, he sold his livery, and other things belonging to his master; who, having conceived a kind regard for him, considered his youth, and prevented the law from falling, with all its rigor, upon his head. Still he continued to abuse his privileges, and to involve himself in repeated difficulties, from which his mother as often extricated him. At each time, she talked much, and reasoned and remonstrated with him; and he would, with such perfect frankness, lay open his whole soul to her, telling her he had never intended doing harm,—how he had been led along, little by little, till, before he was aware, he found himself in trouble—how he had *tried* to be good—and how, when he would have been so, 'evil was present with him,'—indeed he knew not *how* it was.

His mother, beginning to feel that the city was no place for him, urged his going to sea, and would have shipped him on board a man-of-war; but Peter was not disposed to consent to that proposition, while the city and its pleasures were accessible to him. Isabella now became a prey to distressing fears, dreading lest the next day or hour come fraught with the report of some dreadful crime, committed or abetted by her son. She thanks the Lord for sparing her that giant sorrow, as all his wrong doings never ranked higher, in the eye of the law, than misdemeanors. But as she could see no improvement in Peter, as a last resort, she resolved to leave him, for a time, unassisted, to bear the penalty of his conduct, and see what effect that would have on him. In the trial hour, she remained firm in her resolution. Peter again fell into the hands of the police, and sent for his mother, as usual; but she went not to his relief. In his extremity, he sent for Peter Williams, a respectable colored barber, whose name he had been wearing, and who sometimes helped young culprits out of their troubles, and sent them from city dangers, by shipping them on board of whaling vessels.

The curiosity of this man was awakened by the culprit's bearing his own name. He went to the Tombs and inquired into his case, but could not believe what Peter told him respecting his mother and family. Yet he redeemed him, and Peter promised to leave New York in a vessel that was to sail in the course of a week. He went to see his mother, and informed her of what had happened to him. She listened incredulously, as to an idle tale. He asked her to go with him and see for herself. She went, giving no credence to his story till she found herself in the presence of Mr. Williams, and heard him saying to her, 'I am very glad I have assisted your son; he stood in great need of sympathy and assistance; but I could not think he had such a mother here, although he assured me he had.'

Isabella's great trouble now was, a fear lest her son should deceive his benefactor, and be missing when the vessel sailed; but he begged her earnestly to trust him, for he said he had resolved to do better, and meant to abide by the resolve. Isabella's heart gave her no peace till the time of sailing, when Peter sent Mr. Williams and another messenger whom she knew, to tell her he had sailed. But for a month afterwards, she looked to see him emerging from some by-place in the city, and appearing before her; so afraid was she that he was still unfaithful, and doing wrong. But he did not appear, and at length she believed him really gone. He left in the summer of 1839, and his friends heard nothing further from him till his mother received the following letter, dated 'October 17, 1840':—

'My Dear and Beloved Mother:

'I take this opportunity to write to you and inform you that I am well, and in hopes for to find you the same. I am got on board the same unlucky ship Done, of Nantucket. I am sorry for to say, that I have been punished once severely, by shoving my head in the fire for other folks. We have had bad luck, but in hopes to have better. We have about 230 on board, but in hopes, if don't have good luck, that my parents will receive me with thanks. I would like to know how my sisters are. Does my cousins live in New York yet? Have you got my letter? If not, inquire to Mr. Pierce Whiting's. I wish you would write me an answer as soon as possible. I am your only son, that is so far from your home, in the wide, briny ocean. I have seen more of the world than ever I expected, and if I ever should return home safe, I will tell you all my troubles and hardships. Mother, I hope you do not forget me, your dear and only son. I should like to know how Sophia, and Betsey, and Hannah, come on. I hope you all will forgive me for all that I have done.

'Your son,

'Peter Van Wagener.'

Another letter reads as follows, dated 'March 22, 1841':—

'My Dear Mother:

'I take this opportunity to write to you, and inform you that I have been well and in good health. I have wrote you a letter before, but have received no answer from you, and was very anxious to see you. I hope to see you in a short time. I have had very hard luck, but are in hopes to have better in time to come. I should like if my sisters are well, and all the people round the neighborhood. I expect to be home in twenty-two months or thereabouts. I have seen Samuel Laterett. Beware! There has happened very bad news to tell you, that Peter Jackson is dead. He died within two days' sail of Otaheite, one of the Society Islands. The Peter Jackson that used to live at Laterett's; he died on board the ship Done, of Nantucket, Captain Miller, in the latitude 15 53, and longitude 148 30 W. I have no more to say at present, but write as soon as possible.

'Your only son,

'PETER VAN WAGENER.'

Another, containing the last intelligence she has had from her son, reads as follows, and was dated 'Sept. 19, 1841':—

'DEAR MOTHER:

'I take this opportunity to write to you and inform you that I am well and in good health, and in hopes to find you in the same. This is the fifth letter that I have wrote to you, and have received no answer, and it makes me very uneasy. So pray write as quick as you can, and tell me how all the people is about the neighborhood. We are out from home twenty-three months, and in hopes to be home in fifteen months. I have not much to say; but tell me if you have been up home since I left or not. I want to know what sort of a time is at home. We had very bad luck when we first came out, but since we have had very good; so I am in hopes to do well yet; but if I don't do well, you need not expect me home these five years. So write as quick as you can, won't you? So now I am going to put an end to my writing, at present. Notice—when this you see, remember me, and place me in your mind.

> Get me to my home, that's in the far distant west,
> To the scenes of my childhood, that I like the best;
> There the tall cedars grow, and the bright waters flow,
> Where my parents will greet me, white man, let me go!

Let me go to the spot where the cateract plays,
Where oft I have sported in my boyish days;
And there is my poor mother, whose heart ever flows,
At the sight of her poor child, to her let me go, let me go!

'Your only son,
'PETER VAN WAGENER.'

Since the date of the last letter, Isabella has heard no tidings from
her long-absent son, though ardently does her mother's heart long
for such tidings, as her thoughts follow him around the world, in his
perilous vocation, saying within herself—'He is good now, I have no
doubt; I feel sure that he has persevered, and kept the resolve he
made before he left home;—he seemed so different before he went,
so determined to do better.' His letters are inserted here for preservation, in case they prove the last she ever hears from him in this
world.

Finding a Brother and Sister.

When Isabella had obtained the freedom of her son, she remained in
Kingston, where she had been drawn by the judicial process, about a
year, during which time she became a member of the Methodist
Church there: and when she went to New York, she took a letter
missive from that church to the Methodist Church in John street.
Afterwards, she withdrew her connection with that church and
joined Zion's Church, in Church street, composed entirely of colored
people. With the latter church she remained until she went to reside
with Mr. Pierson, after which, she was gradually drawn into the
'kingdom' set up by the prophet Matthias,[8] in the name of God the
Father; for he said the spirit of God the Father dwelt in him.

While Isabella was in New York, her sister Sophia came from
Newburg to reside in the former place. Isabel had been favored with
occasional interviews with this sister, although at one time she lost
sight of her for the space of seventeen years—almost the entire period of her being at Mr. Dumont's—and when she appeared before
her again, handsomely dressed, she did not recognize her, till in-

formed who she was. Sophia informed her that her brother Michael—a brother she had never seen—was in the city; and when she introduced him to Isabella, *he* informed her that their sister Nancy had been living in the city, and had deceased a few months before. He described her features, her dress, her manner, and said she had for some time been a member in Zion's Church, naming the class she belonged to. Isabella almost instantly recognized her as a sister in the church, with whom she had knelt at the altar, and with whom she had exchanged the speaking pressure of the hand, in recognition of their spiritual sisterhood; little thinking, at the time, that they were also children of the same earthly parents—even Bomefree and Mau-mau Bett. As inquiries and answers rapidly passed, and the conviction deepened that this was their sister, the very sister they had heard so much of, but had never seen, (for she was the self-same sister that had been locked in the great old fashioned sleigh-box, when she was taken away, never to behold her mother's face again this side the spirit-land, and Michael, the narrator, was the brother who had shared her fate,) Isabella thought, 'D——n! here she was; we met; and was I not, at the time, struck with the peculiar feeling of her hand—the bony hardness so just like mine? and yet I could not know she was my sister; and now I see she looked *so* like my mother!" And Isabella wept, and not alone; Sophia wept, and the strong man, Michael, mingled his tears with theirs. 'Oh Lord,' inquired Isabella, 'what is this slavery, that it can do such dreadful things? what evil can it not do?' Well may she ask; for surely the evils it can and does do daily and hourly, can never be summed up, till we can see them as they are recorded by him who writes no errors, and reckons without mistake. This account, which now varies so widely in the estimate of different minds, will be viewed alike by all.

Think you, dear reader, when that day comes, the most 'rabid abolitionist' will say—'Behold, I saw all this while on the earth?' Will he not rather say, 'Oh, who has conceived the breadth and depth of this moral malaria, this putrescent plague-spot?' Perhaps the pioneers in the slave's cause will be as much surprised as any to find that with all *their* looking, there remained so much unseen.

Gleanings.

There are some hard things that crossed Isabella's life while in slavery, that she has no desire to publish, for various reasons. First, because the parties from whose hands she suffered them have rendered up their account to a higher tribunal, and their innocent friends alone are living, to have their feelings injured by the recital; secondly, because they are not all for the public ear, from their very nature; thirdly, and not least, because, she says, were she to tell all that happened to her as a slave—all that she knows is 'God's truth'—it would seem to others, especially the uninitiated, so unaccountable, so unreasonable, and what is usually called so unnatural, (though it may be questioned whether people do not always act naturally,) they would not easily believe it. 'Why, no!' she says, 'they'd call me a liar! they would, indeed! and I do not wish to say anything to destroy my own character for veracity, though what I say is strictly true.' Some things have been omitted through forgetfulness, which not having been mentioned in their places, can only be briefly spoken of here;—such as, that her father Bomefree had had two wives before he took Mau-mau Bett; one of whom, if not both, were torn from him by the iron hand of the ruthless trafficker in human flesh;—that her husband, Thomas, after one of *his* wives had been sold away from him, ran away to New York City, where he remained a year or two, before he was discovered and taken back to the prison-house of slavery;—that her master Dumont, when he promised Isabella one year of her time, before the State should make her free, made the same promise to her husband, and in addition to freedom, they were promised a log cabin for a home of their own; all of which, with the one-thousand-and-one day-dreams resulting therefrom, went into the repository of unfulfilled promises and unrealized hopes;—that she had often heard her father repeat a thrilling story of a little slave-child, which, because it annoyed the family with its cries, was caught up by a white man, who dashed its brains out against the wall. An Indian (for Indians were plenty in that region then) passed along as the bereaved mother washed the bloody corpse of her murdered child, and learning the cause of its death, said, with characteristic vehemence, 'If I had been here, I would have put my tomahawk in his head!' meaning the murderer's.

Of the cruelty of one Hasbrouck.—He had a sick slave-woman, who was lingering with a slow consumption, whom he made to spin, regardless of her weakness and suffering; and this woman had a child, that was unable to walk or talk, at the age of five years, neither could it cry like other children, but made a constant, piteous, moaning sound. This exhibition of helplessness and imbecility, instead of exciting the master's pity, stung his cupidity, and so enraged him, that he would kick the poor thing about like a foot-ball.

Isabella's informant had seen this brute of a man, when the child was curled up under a chair, innocently amusing itself with a few sticks, drag it thence, that he might have the pleasure of tormenting it. She had seen him, with one blow of his foot, send it rolling quite across the room, and down the steps at the door. Oh, how she wished it might instantly die! 'But,' she said, 'it seemed as tough as a moccasin.' Though it *did* die at last, and made glad the heart of its friends; and its persecutor, no doubt, rejoiced with them, but from very different motives. But the day of his retribution was not far off—for he sickened, and his reason fled. It was fearful to hear his old slave soon tell how, in the day of his calamity, she treated *him*.

She was very strong, and was therefore selected to support her master, as he sat up in bed, by putting her arms around, while she stood behind him. It was then that she did her best to wreak her vengeance on him. She would clutch his feeble frame in her iron grasp, as in a vice; and, when her mistress did not see, would give him a squeeze, a shake, and lifting him up, set him down again, as *hard as possible*. If his breathing betrayed too tight a grasp, and her mistress said, 'Be careful, don't hurt him, Soan!' her ever-ready answer was, 'Oh no, Missus, no,' in her most pleasant tone—and then, as soon as Missus's eyes and ears were engaged away, another grasp—another shake—another bounce. She was afraid the disease alone would let him recover,—an event she dreaded more than to do wrong herself. Isabella asked her, if she were not afraid his spirit would haunt her. 'Oh, no,' says Soan; 'he was *so* wicked, the devil will never let him out of hell long enough for that.'

Many slaveholders boast of the love of their slaves. How would it freeze the blood of some of them to know what kind of love rankles in the bosoms of slaves for them! Witness the attempt to poison Mrs. Calhoun, and hundreds of similar cases. Most '*surprising*' to every body, because committed by slaves supposed to be so *grateful* for their chains.

These reflections bring to mind a discussion on this point, between the writer and a slaveholding friend in Kentucky, on Christmas morning, 1846. We had asserted, that until mankind were far in advance of what they now are, irresponsible power over our fellow-beings would be, as it is, abused. Our friend declared it *his* conviction, that the cruelties of slavery existed chiefly in imagination, and that no person in D—— County, where we then were, but would be above ill-treating a helpless slave. We answered, that if his belief was well-founded, the people in Kentucky were greatly in advance of the people of New England—for we would not dare say as much as that of any school-district there, letting alone counties. No, we would not answer for our own conduct even on so delicate a point.

The next evening, he very magnanimously overthrew his own position and established ours, by informing us that, on the morning previous, and as near as we could learn, at the very hour in which we were earnestly discussing the probabilities of the case, a young woman of fine appearance, and high standing in society, the pride of her husband, and the mother of an infant daughter, only a few miles from us, ay, in D—— County, too, was actually beating in the skull of a slave-woman called Tabby; and not content with that, had her tied up and whipped, after her skull was broken, and she died hanging to the bedstead, to which she had been fastened. When informed that Tabby was dead, she answered, 'I am *glad of it*, for she has worried my life out of me.' But Tabby's highest good was probably not the end proposed by Mrs. M——, for no one supposed she meant to kill her. Tabby was considered quite lacking in good sense, and no doubt belonged to that class at the South, that are silly enough to 'die of moderate correction.'

A mob collected around the house for an hour or two, in that manner expressing a momentary indignation. But was she treated as a murderess? Not at all! She was allowed to take boat (for her residence was near the beautiful Ohio) that evening, to spend a few months with her absent friends, after which she returned and remained with her husband, no one to 'molest or make her afraid.'

Had she been left to the punishment of an outraged conscience from right motives, I would have 'rejoiced with exceeding joy.' But to see the life of one woman, and she a murderess, put in the balance against the lives of three millions of innocent slaves, and to contrast her punishment with what I felt would be the punishment of one who was merely suspected of being an equal friend of all mankind, regardless of color or condition, caused my blood to stir within me, and my heart to sicken at the thought. The husband of Mrs. M—— was absent from home, at the time alluded to; and when he arrived, some weeks afterwards, bringing beautiful presents to his cherished companion, he beheld his once happy home deserted, Tabby murdered and buried in the garden, and the wife of his bosom, and the mother of his child, the doer of the dreadful deed, a *murderess!*

When Isabella went to New York City, she went in company with a Miss Grear, who introduced her to the family of Mr. James Latourette, a wealthy merchant, and a Methodist in religion; but who, the latter part of his life, felt that he had outgrown ordinances, and advocated free meetings, holding them at his own dwelling-house for several years previous to his death. She worked for them, and they generously gave her a home while she labored for others, and in their kindness made her as one of their own.

At that time, the 'moral reform' movement* was awakening the attention of the benevolent in that city. Many women, among whom were Mrs. Latourette and Miss Grear, became deeply interested in making an attempt to reform their fallen sisters, even the most degraded of them; and in this enterprise of labor and danger, they enlisted Isabella and others, who for a time put forth their most zealous efforts, and performed the work of missionaries with much apparent success. Isabella accompanied those ladies to the most wretched abodes of vice and misery and sometimes she went where they dared not follow. They even succeeded in establishing prayer-meetings in several places, where such a thing might least have been expected.

But these meetings soon became the most noisy, shouting, ranting, and boisterous of gatherings; where they became delirious with

---

*Campaign in New England and New York to rescue women leading "indecent" lives as prostitutes or hustlers.

excitement, and then exhausted from over-action. Such meetings Isabel had not much sympathy with, at best. But one evening she attended one of them, where the members of it, in a fit of ecstasy, jumped upon her cloak in such a manner as to drag her to the floor—and then, thinking she had fallen in a spiritual trance, they increased their glorifications on her account,—jumping, shouting, stamping, and clapping of hands; rejoicing so much over her spirit, and so entirely overlooking her body, that she suffered much, both from fear and bruises; and ever after refused to attend any more such meetings, doubting much whether God had any thing to do with such worship.

The Matthias Delusion.

We now come to an eventful period in the life of Isabella, as identified with one of the most extraordinary religious delusions of modern times; but the limits prescribed for the present work forbid a minute narration of all the occurrences that transpired in relation to it.

After she had joined the African Church in Church street, and during her membership there, she frequently attended Mr. Latourette's meetings, at one of which, Mr. Smith invited her to go to a prayer-meeting, or to instruct the girls at the Magdalene Asylum, Bowery Hill, then under the protection of Mr. Pierson, and some other persons, chiefly respectable females. To reach the Asylum, Isabella called on Katy, Mr. Pierson's colored servant, of whom she had some knowledge. Mr. Pierson saw her there, conversed with her, asked her if she had been baptized, and was answered, characteristically, 'by the Holy Ghost.' After this, Isabella saw Katy several times, and occasionally Mr. Pierson, who engaged her to keep his house while Katy went to Virginia to see her children. This engagement was considered an answer to prayer by Mr. Pierson, who had both fasted and prayed on the subject, while Katy and Isabella appeared to see in it the hand of God.

Mr. Pierson was characterized by a strong devotional spirit, which finally became highly fanatical. He assumed the title of Prophet, asserting that God had called him in an omnibus, in these words:—'Thou art Elijah, the Tishbite. Gather unto me all the

members of Israel at the foot of Mount Carmel'; which he understood as meaning the gathering of his friends at Bowery Hill. Not
long afterward, he became acquainted with the notorious Matthias,
whose career was as extraordinary as it was brief. Robert Matthews,
or Matthias, (as he was usually called,) was of Scotch extraction, but
a native of Washington county, New York, and at that time about
forty-seven years of age. He was religiously brought up, among the
Anti-Burghers, a sect of Presbyterians; the clergyman, the Rev. Mr.
Bevridge, visiting the family after the manner of the church, and
being pleased with Robert, put his hand on his head, when a boy,
and pronounced a blessing, and this blessing, with his natural qualities, determined his character; for he ever after thought he should
be a distinguished man. Matthias was brought up a farmer till nearly
eighteen years of age, but acquired indirectly the art of a carpenter,
without any regular apprenticeship, and showed considerable me-
chanical skill. He obtained property from his uncle, Robert Thompson, and then he went into business as a store-keeper, was
considered respectable, and became a member of the Scotch Presbyterian church. He married in 1813, and continued in business in
Cambridge. In 1816, he ruined himself by a building speculation,
and the derangement of the currency which denied bank facilities,
and soon after he came to New York with his family, and worked at
his trade. He afterwards removed to Albany, and became a hearer at
the Dutch Reformed Church, then under Dr. Ludlow's charge. He
was frequently much excited on religious subjects.

In 1829, he was well known, if not for street preaching, for loud
discussions and pavement exhortations, but he did not make set sermons. In the beginning of 1830, he was only considered zealous; but
in the same year he prophesied the destruction of the Albanians and
their capital, and while preparing to shave, with the Bible before
him, he suddenly put down the soap and exclaimed, 'I have found it!
I have found a text which proves that no man who shaves his beard
can be a true Christian;' and shortly afterwards, without shaving, he
went to the Mission House to deliver an address which he had
promised, and in this address he proclaimed his new character, pronounced vengeance on the land, and that the law of God was the
only rule of government, and that he was commanded to take possession of the world in the name of the King of kings. His harangue

was cut short by the trustees putting out the lights. About this time, Matthias laid by his implements of industry, and in June, he advised his wife to fly with him from the destruction which awaited them in the city; and on her refusal, partly on account of Matthias calling himself a Jew, whom she was unwilling to retain as a husband, he left her, taking some of the children to his sister in Argyle, forty miles from Albany. At Argyle he entered the church and interrupted the minister, declaring the congregation in darkness, and warning them to repentance. He was, of course, taken out of the church, and as he was advertised in the Albany papers, he was sent back to his family. His beard had now obtained a respectable length, and thus he attracted attention, and easily obtained an audience in the streets. For this he was sometimes arrested, once by mistake for Adam Paine, who collected the crowd, and then left Matthias with it on the approach of the officers. He repeatedly urged his wife to accompany him on a mission to convert the world, declaring that food could be obtained from the roots of the forest, if not administered otherwise. At this time he assumed the name of Matthias, called himself a Jew, and set out on a mission, taking a western course, and visiting a brother at Rochester, a skilful mechanic, since dead. Leaving his brother, he proceeded on his mission over the Northern States, occasionally returning to Albany.

After visiting Washington, and passing through Pennsylvania, he came to New York. His appearance at that time was mean, but grotesque, and his sentiments were but little known.

On May the 5th, 1832, he first called on Mr. Pierson, in Fourth street, in his absence. Isabella was alone in the house, in which she had lived since the previous autumn. On opening the door, she, for the first time, beheld Matthias, and her early impression of seeing Jesus in the flesh rushed into her mind. She heard his inquiry and invited him into the parlor; and being naturally curious, and much excited, and possessing a good deal of tact, she drew him into conversation, stated her own opinions, and heard his replies and explanations. Her faith was at first staggered by his declaring himself a Jew; but on this point she was relieved by his saying, 'Do you not remember how Jesus prayed?' and repeated part of the Lord's prayer, in proof that the Father's kingdom was to come, and not the Son's. She then understood him to be a converted Jew, and in the conclusion she says she '*felt* as if God had sent him to set up the kingdom.' Thus Matthias at once secured the good will of Isabella, and we may suppose obtained from her some information in relation to Mr. Pierson, especially that Mrs. Pierson declared there was no true church, and approved of Mr. Pierson's preaching. Matthias left the house, promising to return on Saturday evening. Mr. P. at this time had not seen Matthias.

Isabella, desirous of hearing the expected conversation between Matthias and Mr. Pierson on Saturday, hurried her work, got it finished, and was permitted to be present. Indeed, the sameness of belief made her familiar with her employer, while her attention to her work, and characteristic faithfulness, increased his confidence. This intimacy, the result of holding the same faith, and the principle afterwards adopted of having but one table, and all things in common, made her at once the domestic and the equal, and the depositary of very curious, if not valuable information. To this object, even her color assisted. Persons who have travelled in the South know the manner in which the colored people, and especially slaves, are treated; they are scarcely regarded as being present. This trait in our American character has been frequently noticed by foreign travellers. One English lady remarks that she discovered, in course of conversation with a Southern married gentleman, that a colored girl slept in his bedroom, in which also was his wife; and when he saw that it occasioned some surprise, he remarked, 'What would he do if he wanted a glass of water in the night?' Other travellers have remarked that the presence of colored people never seemed to interrupt conversation of any kind for one moment. Isabella, then, was present at the first interview between Matthias and Pierson. At this interview, Mr. Pierson asked Matthias if he had a family, to which he replied in the affirmative; he asked him about his beard, and he gave a scriptural reason, asserting also that the Jews did not shave, and that Adam had a beard. Mr. Pierson detailed to Matthias his experience, and Matthias gave his, and they mutually discovered that they held the same sentiments, both admitting the direct influence of the Spirit, and the transmission of spirits from one body to another. Matthias admitted the call of Mr. Pierson, in the omnibus in Wall street, which, on this occasion, he gave in these words:— 'Thou art Elijah the Tishbite, and thou shalt go before me in the

spirit and power of Elias, to prepare my way before me.' And Mr.
Pierson admitted Matthias' call, who *completed* his declaration on
the 20th of June, in Argyle, which, by a curious coincidence, was the
very day on which Pierson had received his call in the omnibus.
Such singular coincidences have a powerful effect on excited minds.
From that discovery, Pierson and Matthias rejoiced in each other,
and became kindred spirits—Matthias, however, claiming to be the
Father, or to possess the spirit of the Father—he was God upon
earth, because the spirit of God dwelt in him; while Pierson then
understood that his mission was like that of John the Baptist, which
the name Elias meant. This conference ended with an invitation to
supper, and Matthias and Pierson washing each other's feet. Mr.
Pierson preached on the following Sunday, but after which, he declined in favor of Matthias, and some of the party believed that the
'kingdom had then come.'

As a specimen of Matthias' preaching and sentiments, the following is said to be reliable:

'The spirit that built the Tower of Babel is now in the world—it
is the spirit of the devil. The spirit of man never goes upon the
clouds; all who think so are Babylonians. The only heaven is on the
earth. All who are ignorant of truth are Ninevites. The Jews did not
crucify Christ—it was the Gentiles. Every Jew has his guardian
angel attending him in this world. God don't speak through preachers; he speaks through me, his prophet.

' "John the Baptist," (addressing Mr. Pierson,) "read the tenth
chapter of Revelations." After the reading of the chapter, the
prophet resumed speaking, as follows:—

'Ours is the mustard-seed kingdom which is to spread all over the
earth. Our creed is truth, and no man can find truth unless he obeys
John the Baptist, and comes clean into the church.

'All *real* men will be saved; all *mock* men will be damned. When
a person has the Holy Ghost, then he is a man, and not till then.
They who teach women are of the wicked. The communion is all
nonsense; so is prayer. Eating a nip of bread and drinking a little
wine won't do any good. All who admit members into their church,
and suffer them to hold their lands and houses, their sentence is,
"Depart, ye wicked, I know you not." All females who lecture their
husbands, their sentence is the same. The sons of truth are to enjoy

all the good things of this world, and must use their means to bring it about. Every thing that has the smell of woman will be destroyed. Woman is the capsheaf of the abomination of desolation—full of all deviltry. In a short time, the world will take fire and dissolve; it is combustible already. All women, not obedient, had better become so as soon as possible, and let the wicked spirit depart, and become temples of truth. Praying is all mocking. When you see any one wring the neck of a fowl, instead of cutting off its head, he has not got the Holy Ghost. (Cutting gives the least pain.)

'All who eat swine's flesh are of the devil; and just as certain as he eats it, he will tell a lie in less than half an hour. If you eat a piece of pork, it will go crooked through you, and the Holy Ghost will not stay in you but one or the other must leave the house pretty soon. The pork will be as crooked in you as rams' horns, and as great a nuisance as the hogs in the street.

'The cholera is not the right word; it is choler, which means God's wrath. Abraham, Isaac, and Jacob are now in this world; they did not go up in the clouds, as some believe—why should they go there? They don't want to go there to box the compass from one place to another. The Christians now-a-days are for setting up the *Son's* kingdom. It is not his; it is the *Father's* kingdom. It puts me in mind of the man in the country, who took his son in business, and had his sign made, "Hitchcock & Son;" but the son wanted it "Hitchcock & Father"—and that is the way with your Christians. They talk of the Son's kingdom first, and not the Father's kingdom.'

Matthias and his disciples at this time did not believe in a resurrection of the body, but that the spirits of the former saints would enter the bodies of the present generation, and thus begin heaven upon earth, of which he and Mr. Pierson were the first fruits.

Matthias made the residence of Mr. Pierson his own; but the latter, being apprehensive of popular violence in his house, if Matthias remained there, proposed a monthly allowance to him, and advised him to occupy another dwelling. Matthias accordingly took a house in Clarkson street, and then sent for his family at Albany, but they declined coming to the city. However, his brother George complied with a similar offer, bringing his family with him, where they found very comfortable quarters. Isabella was employed to do the housework. In May, 1833, Matthias left his house, and placed the furniture, part of which was Isabella's, elsewhere, living himself at the hotel corner of Marketfield and West streets. Isabella found employment at Mr. Whiting's, Canal street, and did the washing for Matthias by Mrs. Whiting's permission.

Of the subsequent removal of Matthias to the farm and residence of Mr. B. Folger, at Sing Sing,* where he was joined by Mr. Pierson, and others laboring under a similar religious delusion—the sudden, melancholy and somewhat suspicious death of Mr. Pierson, and the arrest of Matthias on the charge of his murder, ending in a verdict of not guilty—the criminal connection that subsisted between Matthias, Mrs. Folger, and other members of the 'Kingdom,' as 'match-spirits'—the final disperson of this deluded company, and the voluntary exilement of Matthias in the far West, after his release—&c. &c., we do not deem it useful or necessary to give any particulars. Those who are curious to know what there transpired are referred to a work published in New York in 1835, entitled 'Fanaticism; its Sources and Influence; illustrated by the simple Narrative of Isabella, in the case of Matthias, Mr. and Mrs. B. Folger, Mr. Pierson, Mr. Mills, Catharine, Isabella, &c. &c. By G. Vale, 84 Roosevelt street.' Suffice it to say, that while Isabella was a member of the household at Sing Sing, doing much laborious service in the spirit of religious disinterestedness, and gradually getting her vision purged and her mind cured of its illusions, she happily escaped the contamination that surrounded her,—assiduously endeavoring to discharge all her duties in a becoming manner.[9]

Fasting.

When Isabella resided with Mr. Pierson, he was in the habit of fasting every Friday; not eating or drinking anything from Thursday evening to six o' clock on Friday evening.

Then, again, he would fast two nights and three days, neither eating nor drinking; refusing himself even a cup of cold water till the third day at night, when he took supper again, as usual.

Isabella asked him why he fasted. He answered, that fasting gave

---

*Ossining, New York.

him great light in the things of God; which answer gave birth to the following train of thought in the mind of his auditor:—'Well, if fasting will give light inwardly and spiritually, I need it as much as any body,—and I'll fast too. If Mr. Pierson needs to fast two nights and three days, then I, who need light more than he does, ought to fast more, and I will fast three nights and three days.'

This resolution she carried out to the letter, putting not so much as a drop of water in her mouth for three whole days and nights. The fourth morning, as she arose to her feet, not having power to stand, she fell to the floor; but recovering herself sufficiently, she made her way to the pantry, and feeling herself quite voracious, and fearing that she might now offend God by her voracity, compelled herself to breakfast on dry bread and water—eating a large six-penny loaf before she felt at all stayed or satisfied. She says she did get light, but it was all in her body and none in her mind—and this lightness of body lasted a long time. Oh! she was so light, and felt so well, she could 'skim around like a gull.'

The Cause of Her Leaving the City.

The first years spent by Isabella in the city, she accumulated more than enough to supply all her wants, and she placed all the overplus in the Savings' Bank. Afterwards, while living with Mr. Pierson, he prevailed on her to take it thence, and invest it in a common fund which he was about establishing, as a fund to be drawn from by all the faithful; the faithful, of course, were the handful that should subscribe to his peculiar creed. This fund, commenced by Mr. Pierson, afterwards became part and parcel of the kingdom of which Matthias assumed to be head; and at the breaking up of the kingdom, her little property was merged in the general ruin—or went to enrich those who profited by the loss of others, if any such there were. Mr. Pierson and others had so assured her, that the fund would supply all her wants, at all times, and in all emergencies, and to the end of life, that she became perfectly careless on the subject—asking for no interest when she drew her money from the bank, and taking no account of the sum she placed in the fund. She recovered a few articles of furniture from the wreck of the kingdom, and received a small sum of money from Mr. B. Folger, as the price of Mrs.

Folger's attempt to convict her of murder. With this to start upon, she commenced anew her labors, in the hope of yet being able to accumulate a sufficiency to make a little home for herself, in her advancing age. With this stimulus before her, she toiled hard, working early and late, doing a great deal for a little money, and turning her hand to almost any thing that promised good pay. Still, she did not prosper; and somehow, could not contrive to lay by a single dollar for a 'rainy day.'

When this had been the state of her affairs some time, she suddenly paused, and taking a retrospective view of what had passed, inquired within herself, why it was that, for all her unwearied labors, she had nothing to show; why it was that others, with much less care and labor, could hoard up treasures for themselves and children? She became more and more convinced, as she reasoned, that every thing she had undertaken in the city of New York had finally proved a failure; and where her hopes had been raised the highest, there she felt the failure had been the greatest, and the disappointment most severe.

After turning it in her mind for some time, she came to the conclusion, that she had been taking part in a great drama, which was, in itself, but one great system of robbery and wrong. 'Yes,' she said, 'the rich rob the poor, and the poor rob one another.' True, she had not received labor from others, and stinted their pay, as she felt had been practised against her; but she had taken their work from them, which was their only means to get money, and was the same to them in the end. For instance—a gentleman where she lived would give her a half dollar to hire a poor man to clear the new-fallen snow from the steps and side-walks. She would arise early, and perform the labor herself, putting the money into her own pocket. A poor man would come along, saying she ought to have let him have the job; he was poor, and needed the pay for his family. She would harden her heart against him, and answer—'I am poor too, and I need it for mine. But, in her retrospection, she thought of all the misery she might have been adding to, in her selfish grasping, and it troubled her conscience sorely; and this insensibility to the claims of human brotherhood, and the wants of the destitute and wretched poor, she now saw, as she never had done before, to be unfeeling, selfish and wicked. These reflections and convictions gave rise to a sudden revulsion of feeling in the heart of Isabella, and she began to look upon money and property with great indifference, if not contempt—being at that time unable, probably, to discern any difference between a miserly grasping at and hoarding of money and means, and a true use of the good things of this life for one's own comfort, and the relief of such as she might be enabled to befriend and assist. One thing she was sure of—that the precepts, 'Do unto others as ye would that others should do unto you,' 'Love your neighbor as yourself,' and so forth, were maxims that had been but little thought of by herself, or practised by those about her.

Her next decision was, that she must leave the city; it was no place for her; yea, she felt called in spirit to leave it, and to travel east and lecture. She had never been further east than the city, neither had she any friends there of whom she had particular reason to expect any thing; yet to her it was plain that her mission lay in the east, and that she would find friends there. She determined on leaving; but these determinations and convictions she kept close locked in her own breast, knowing that if her children and friends were aware of it, they would make such an ado about it as would render it very unpleasant, if not distressing to all parties. Having made what preparations for leaving she deemed necessary,—which was, to put up a few articles of clothing in a pillow-case, all else being deemed an unnecessary incumbrance,—about an hour before she left, she informed Mrs. Whiting, the woman of the house where she was stopping, that her name was no longer Isabella, but SOJOURNER; and that she was going east. And to her inquiry, 'What are you going east for?' her answer was, 'The Spirit calls me there, and I must go.'

She left the city on the morning of the 1st of June, 1843, crossing over to Brooklyn, L. I.; and taking the rising sun for her only compass and guide, she 'remembered Lot's wife,' and hoping to avoid her fate, she resolved not to look back till she felt sure the wicked city from which she was fleeing was left too far behind to be visible in the distance; and when she first ventured to look back, she could just discern the blue cloud of smoke that hung over it, and she thanked the Lord that she was thus far removed from what seemed to *her* a second Sodom.

She was now fairly started on her pilgrimage; her bundle in one hand, and a little basket of provisions in the other, and two York shillings in her purse—her heart strong in the faith that her true work lay before her, and that the Lord was her director; and she doubted not he would provide for and protect her, and that it would be very censurable in her to burden herself with any thing more than a moderate supply for her then present needs. Her mission was not merely to travel east, but to 'lecture,' as she designated it; 'testifying of the hope that was in her'—exhorting the people to embrace Jesus, and refrain from sin, the nature and origin of which she explained to them in accordance with her own most curious and original views. Through her life, and all its chequered changes, she has ever clung fast to her first permanent impressions on religious subjects.

Wherever night overtook her, there she sought for lodgings—free, if she might—if not, she paid; at a tavern, if she chanced to be at one—if not, at a private dwelling; with the rich, if they would receive her—if not, with the poor.

But she soon discovered that the largest houses were nearly always full; if not quite full, company was soon expected; and that it was much easier to find an unoccupied corner in a small house than in a large one; and if a person possessed but a miserable roof over his head, you might be sure of a welcome to part of it.

But this, she had penetration enough to see, was quite as much the effect of a want of sympathy as of benevolence; and this was also very apparent in her religious conversations with people who were strangers to her. She said, 'she never could find out that the rich had any religion. If *I* had been rich and accomplished, I could; for the rich could always find religion in the rich, and *I* could find it among the poor.'

At first, she attended such meetings as she heard of, in the vicinity of her travels, and spoke to the people as she found them assembled. Afterwards, she advertised meetings of her own, and held forth to large audiences, having, as she said, 'a good time.'

When she became weary of travelling, and wished a place to stop a while and rest herself, she said some opening for her was always near at hand; and the first time she needed rest, a man accosted her as she was walking, inquiring if she was looking for work. She told him that was not the object of her travels, but that she would willingly work a few days, if any one wanted. He requested her to go to his family, who were sadly in want of assistance, which he had been thus far unable to supply. She went to the house where she was directed, and was received by his family, one of whom was ill, as a 'Godsend;' and when she felt constrained to resume her journey, they were very sorry, and would fain have detained her longer; but as she urged the necessity of leaving, they offered her what seemed in her eyes a great deal of money as a remuneration for her labor, and an expression of their gratitude for her opportune assistance; but she would only receive a very little of it; enough, as she says, to enable her to pay tribute to Cæsar, if it was demanded of her; and two or three York shillings at a time were all she allowed herself to take; and then, with purse replenished, and strength renewed, she would once more set out to perform her mission.

The Consequences of Refusing a Traveller a Night's Lodging.

As she drew near the centre of the Island, she commenced, one evening at nightfall, to solicit the favor of a night's lodging. She had repeated her request a great many, it seemed to her some twenty times, and as many times she received a negative answer. She walked on, the stars and the tiny horns of the new moon shed but a dim light on her lonely way, when she was familiarly accosted by two Indians, who took her for an acquaintance. She told them they were mistaken in the person; she was a stranger there, and asked them the direction to a tavern. They informed her it was yet a long way—some two miles or so; and inquired if she were alone. Not wishing for their protection, or knowing what might be the character of their kindness, she answered, 'No, not exactly,' and passed on. At the end of a weary way, she came to the tavern,—or, rather, to a large building, which was occupied as court-house, tavern, and jail,—and on asking for a night's lodging, was informed she could stay, if she would consent to be locked in. This to her mind was an insuperable objection. To have a key turned on her was a thing not to be thought of, at least not to be endured, and she again took up her line of march, preferring to walk beneath the open sky, to being locked up by a stranger in such a place. She had not walked far, before she heard the voice of a woman under an open shed; she ventured to accost her, and inquired if she knew where she could get in for the night. The woman answered, that she did not, unless she went home with them; and turning to her 'good man,' asked him if the stranger could not share their home for the night, to which he cheerfully assented. Sojourner thought it evident he had been taking a drop too much, but as he was civil and good-natured, and she did not feel inclined to spend the night alone in the open air, she felt driven to the necessity of accepting their hospitality, whatever it might prove to be. The woman soon informed her that there was a ball in the place, at which they would like to drop in a while, before they went to their home.

Balls being no part of Sojourner's mission, she was not desirous of attending; but her hostess could be satisfied with nothing short of a taste of it, and she was forced to go with her, or relinquish their company at once, in which move there might be more exposure than in accompanying her. She went, and soon found herself surrounded by an assemblage of people, collected from the very dregs of society, too ignorant and degraded to understand, much less entertain, a high or bright idea,—in a dirty hovel, destitute of every comfort, and where the fumes of whisky were abundant and powerful.

Sojourner's guide there was too much charmed with the combined entertainments of the place to be able to tear herself away, till she found her faculties for enjoyment failing her, from a too free use of liquor; and she betook herself to bed till she could recover them. Sojourner, seated in a corner, had time for many reflections, and refrained from lecturing them in obedience to the recommendation, 'Cast not your pearls,' &c. When the night was far spent, the husband of the sleeping woman aroused the sleeper, and reminded her that she was not very polite to the woman she had invited to sleep at her house, and of the propriety of returning home. They once more emerged into the pure air, which to our friend Sojourner, after so long breathing the noisome air of the ball-room, was most refreshing and grateful. Just as day dawned, they reached the place they called their home. Sojourner now saw that she had lost nothing in the shape of rest by remaining so long at the ball, as their miserable cabin afforded but one bunk or pallet for sleeping; and had there been many such, she would have preferred sitting up all night to occupying one like it. They very politely offered her the bed, if she would use it; but civilly declining, she waited for morning with an eagerness of desire she never felt before on the subject, and was never more happy than when the eye of day shed its golden light once more over the earth. She was once more free, and while daylight should last, independent, and needed no invitation to pursue her journey. Let these facts teach us, that every pedestrian in the world is not a vagabond, and that it is a dangerous thing to compel any one to receive that hospitality from the vicious and abandoned which they should have received from us,—as thousands can testify, who have thus been caught in the snares of the wicked.

The fourth of July, Isabella arrived at Huntingdon; from thence she went to Cold Springs, where she found the people making preparations for a mass temperance-meeting.* With her usual alacrity, she entered into their labors, getting up dishes *a la New York*, greatly to the satisfaction of those she assisted. After remaining at Cold Springs some three weeks, she returned to Huntingdon, where she took boat for Connecticut. Landing at Bridgeport, she again resumed her travels towards the north-east, lecturing some, and working some, to get wherewith to pay tribute to Cæsar, as she called it; and in this manner she presently came to the city of New Haven, where she found many meetings, which she attended—at some of which, she was allowed to express her views freely, and without reservation. She also called meetings expressly to give herself an opportunity to be heard; and found in the city many true friends of Jesus, as she judged, with whom she held communion of spirit, having no preference for one sect more than another, but being well satisfied with all who gave her evidence of having known or loved the Saviour.

After thus delivering her testimony in this pleasant city, feeling she had not as yet found an abiding place, she went from thence to Bristol, at the request of a zealous sister, who desired her to go to the latter place, and hold a religious conversation with some friends of hers there. She went as requested, found the people kindly and religiously disposed, and through them she became acquainted with several very interesting persons.

A spiritually-minded brother in Bristol, becoming interested in

---

*Gathering of supporters of the temperance movement, which blamed the use of alcohol and spirits for moral failure and other social ills. Women were central among the leadership of the movement.

her new views and original opinions, requested as a favor that she would go to Hartford, to see and converse with friends of his there. Standing ready to perform any service in the Lord, she went to Hartford as desired, bearing in her hand the following note from this brother:—

'SISTER,—

'I send you this living messenger, as I believe her to be one that God loves. Ethiopia is stretching forth her hands unto God. You can see by this sister, that God does by his Spirit alone teach his own children things to come. Please receive her, and she will tell you some new things. Let her tell her story without interrupting her, and give close attention, and you will see she has got the lever of truth, that God helps her to pry where but few can. She cannot read or write, but the law is in her heart.

'Send her to brother ——, brother ——, and where she can do the most good.

'FROM YOUR BROTHER, H. L. B.'

Some of Her Views and Reasonings.

As soon as Isabella saw God as an all-powerful, all-pervading spirit, she became desirous of hearing all that had been written of him, and listened to the account of the creation of the world and its first inhabitants, as contained in the first chapters of Genesis, with peculiar interest. For some time she received it all literally, though it appeared strange to her that 'God worked by the day, got tired, and stopped to rest,' &c. But after a little time, she began to reason upon it, thus—'Why, if God works by the day, and one day's work tires him, and he is obliged to rest, either from weariness or on account of darkness, or if he waited for the "cool of the day to walk in the garden," because he was inconvenienced by the heat of the sun, why then it seems that God cannot do as much as *I* can; for *I* can bear the sun at noon, and work several days and nights in succession without being much tired. Or, if he rested nights because of the darkness, it is very queer that he should make the night so dark that he could not see himself. If *I* had been God, I would have made night light enough for my own convenience, surely.' But the moment she placed this idea of God by the side of the impression she had once so suddenly received of his inconceivable greatness and entire spirituality, that moment she exclaimed mentally, 'No, God does not stop to rest, for he is a spirit, and cannot tire; he cannot want light, for he hath all light in himself. And if "God is all in all," and "worketh all in all," as I have heard them read, then it is impossible he should rest at all; for if he did, every other thing would stop and rest too; the waters would not flow, and the fishes could not swim; and all motion must cease. God could have no pauses in his work, and he needed no Sabbaths of rest. Man might need them, and he should take them when he needed them, whenever he required rest. As it regarded the worship God, he was to be worshipped at all times and in all places; and one portion of time never seemed to her more holy than another.'

These views, which were the result of the workings of her own mind, assisted solely by the light of her own experience and very limited knowledge, were, for a long time after their adoption, closely locked in her own breast, fearing lest their avowal might bring upon her the imputation of 'infidelity,'—the usual charge preferred by all religionists, against those who entertain religious views and feelings differing materially from their own. If, from their own sad experience, they are withheld from shouting the cry of 'infidel,' they fail not to see and to feel, ay, and to say, that the dissenters are not of the right spirit, and that their spiritual eyes have never been unsealed.

While travelling in Connecticut, she met a minister, with whom she held a long discussion on these points, as well as on various other topics, such as the origin of all things, especially the origin of evil, at the same time bearing her testimony strongly against a paid ministry. He belonged to that class, and, as a matter of course, as strongly advocated his own side of the question.

I had forgotten to mention, in its proper place, a very important fact, that when she was examining the Scriptures, she wished to hear them without comment; but if she employed adult persons to read them to her, and she asked them to read a passage over again, they invariably commenced to explain, by giving her their version of it; and in this way, they tried her feelings exceedingly. In consequence of this, she ceased to ask adult persons to read the Bible to her, and substituted children in their stead. Children, as soon as they could read distinctly, would re-read the same sentence to her, as often as she wished, and without comment; and in that way she was enabled to see what her own mind could make out of the record, and that, she said, was what she wanted, and not what others thought it to mean. She wished to compare the teachings of the Bible with the witness within her; and she came to the conclusion, that the spirit of truth spoke in those records; but that the recorders of those truths had intermingled with them ideas and suppositions of their own. This is one among the many proofs of her energy and independence of character.

When it became known to her children, that Sojourner had left New York, they were filled with wonder and alarm. Where could she have gone, and why had she left? were questions no one could answer satisfactorily. Now, their imaginations painted her as a wandering maniac—and again they feared she had been left to commit suicide; and many were the tears they shed at the loss of her.

But when she reached Berlin, Conn., she wrote to them by amanuensis, informing them of her whereabouts, and waiting an answer to her letter; thus quieting their fears, and gladdening their hearts once more with assurances of her continued life and her love.

*The Second Advent Doctrines.**

In Hartford and vicinity, she met with several persons who believed in the 'Second Advent' doctrines; or, the immediate personal appearance of Jesus Christ. At first she thought she had never heard of 'Second Advent.' But when it was explained to her, she recollected having once attended Mr. Miller's meeting in New York, where she saw a great many enigmatical pictures hanging on the wall, which she could not understand, and which, being out of the reach of her understanding, failed to interest her. In this section of country, she attended two camp-meetings of the believers in these doctrines—the 'second advent' excitement being then at its greatest

---

*Body of ideas that entailed a belief that the Second Coming of Christ was near, and that God would soon judge the world.

height. The last meeting was at Windsor Lock. The people, as a matter of course, eagerly inquired of her concerning her belief, as it regarded their most important tenet. She told them it had not been revealed to her; perhaps, if she could read, she might see it differently. Sometimes, to their eager inquiry, 'Oh, don't you believe the Lord is coming?' she answered, 'I believe the Lord is as near as he can be, and not be it.' With these evasive and non-exciting answers, she kept their minds calm as it respected her unbelief, till she could have an opportunity to hear their views fairly stated, in order to judge more understandingly of this matter, and see if, in her estimation, there was any good ground for expecting an event which was, in the minds of so many, as it were, shaking the very foundations of the universe. She was invited to join them in their religious exercises, and accepted the invitation—praying, and talking in her own peculiar style, and attracting many about her by her singing.

When she had convinced the people that she was a lover of God and his cause, and had gained a good standing with them, so that she could get a hearing among them, she had become quite sure in her own mind that they were laboring under a delusion, and she commenced to use her influence to calm the fears of the people, and pour oil upon the troubled waters. In one part of the grounds, she found a knot of people greatly excited: she mounted a stump and called out, 'Hear! hear!' When the people had gathered around her, as they were in a state to listen to any thing new, she addressed them as 'children,' and asked them why they made such a 'To-do;—are you not commanded to "watch and pray?" You are neither watching nor praying.' And she bade them, with the tones of a kind mother, retire to their tents, and there watch and pray, without noise or tumult, for the Lord would not come to such a scene of confusion; 'the Lord came still and quiet.' She assured them, 'the Lord might come, move all through the camp, and go away again, and they never know it,' in the state they then were.

They seemed glad to seize upon any reason for being less agitated and distressed, and many of them suppressed their noisy terror, and retired to their tents to 'watch and pray;' begging others to do the same, and listen to the advice of the good sister. She felt she had done some good, and then went to listen further to the preachers. They appeared to her to be doing their utmost to agitate and excite the people, who were already too much excited; and when she had listened till her feelings would let her listen silently no longer, she arose and addressed the preachers. The following are specimens of her speech:—

'Here you are talking about being "changed in the twinkling of an eye." If the Lord should come, he'd change you to *nothing!* for there is nothing to you.

'You seem to be expecting to go to some parlor *away up* somewhere, and when the wicked have been burnt, you are coming back to walk in triumph over their ashes—this is to be your New Jerusalem!! Now *I* can't see any thing so very *nice* in that, coming back to such a *muss* as that will be, a world covered with the ashes of the wicked! Besides, if the Lord comes and burns—as you say he will—I am not going away; *I* am going to stay here and *stand the fire*, like Shadrach, Meshach, and Abednego! And Jesus will walk with me through the fire, and keep me from harm. Nothing belonging to God can burn, any more than God himself; such shall have no need to go away to escape the fire! No, *I* shall remain. Do you tell me that God's children *can't stand fire?*' And her manner and tone spoke louder than words, saying, 'It is *absurd* to think so!'

The ministers were taken quite aback at so unexpected an opposer, and one of them, in the kindest possible manner, commenced a discussion with her, by asking her questions, and quoting scripture to her; concluding finally, that although she had learned nothing of the great doctrine which was so exclusively occupying their minds at the time, she had learned much that man had never taught her.

At this meeting, she received the address of different persons, residing in various places, with an invitation to visit them. She promised to go soon to Cabotville, and started, shaping her course for that place. She arrived at Springfield one evening at six o'clock, and immediately began to search for a lodging for the night. She walked from six till past nine, and was then on the road from Springfield to Cabotville,* before she found any one sufficiently hospitable to give her a night's shelter under their roof. Then a man gave her twenty-five cents, and bade her go to a tavern and stay all night. She did so, returning in the morning to thank him, assuring him she had put

---

*Chicopee, Massachusetts.

his money to its legitimate use. She found a number of the friends she had seen at Windsor when she reached the manufacturing town of Cabotville, (which has lately taken the name of Chicopee,) and with them she spent a pleasant week or more; after which, she left them to visit the Shaker village in Enfield. She now began to think of finding a resting place, at least, for a season; for she had performed quite a long journey, considering she had walked most of the way; and she had a mind to look in upon the Shakers, and see how things were there, and whether there was any opening there for her. But on her way back to Springfield, she called at a house and asked for a piece of bread; her request was granted, and she was kindly invited to tarry all night, as it was getting late, and she would not be able to stay at every house in that vicinity, which invitation she cheerfully accepted. When the man of the house came in, he recollected having seen her at the camp-meeting, and repeated some conversations, by which she recognized him again. He soon proposed having a meeting that evening, went out and notified his friends and neighbors, who came together, and she once more held forth to them in her peculiar style. Through the agency of this meeting, she became acquainted with several people residing in Springfield, to whose houses she was cordially invited, and with whom she spent some pleasant time.

One of these friends, writing of her arrival there, speaks as follows. After saying that she and her people belonged to that class of persons who believed in the second advent doctrines; and that this class, believing also in freedom of speech and action, often found at their meetings many singular people, who did not agree with them in their principal doctrine; and that, being thus prepared to hear new and strange things, 'They listened eagerly to Sojourner, and drank in all she said;'—and also, that she 'soon became a favorite among them; that when she arose to speak in their assemblies, her commanding figure and dignified manner hushed every trifler into silence, and her singular and sometimes uncouth modes of expression never provoked a laugh, but often were the whole audience melted into tears by her touching stories.' She also adds, 'Many were the lessons of wisdom and faith I have delighted to learn from her.'. . . . "She continued a great favorite in our meetings, both on account of her remarkable gift in prayer, and still more remarkable

talent for singing, . . . and the aptness and point of her remarks, frequently illustrated by figures the most original and expressive.

'As we were walking the other day, she said she had often thought
what a beautiful world this would be, when we should see every
thing right side up. Now, we see every thing topsy-turvy, and all is
confusion.' For a person who knows nothing of this fact in the science of optics, this seemed quite a remarkable idea.

'We also loved her for her sincere and ardent piety, her unwavering faith in God, and her contempt of what the world calls fashion,
and what we call folly.

'She was in search of a quiet place, where a way-worn traveller
might rest. She had heard of Fruitlands, and was inclined to go
there; but the friends she found here thought it best for her to visit
Northampton. She passed her time, while with us, working wherever her work was needed, and talking where work was not needed.

'She would not receive money for her work, saying she worked
for the Lord; and if her wants were supplied, she received it as from
the Lord.

'She remained with us till far into winter, when we introduced
her at the Northampton Association.'. . . . 'She wrote to me from
thence, that she had found the quiet resting place she had so long
desired. And she has remained there ever since.'

Another Camp-Meeting.

When Sojourner had been at Northampton a few months, she attended another camp-meeting, at which she performed a very
important part.

A party of wild young men, with no motive but that of entertaining themselves by annoying and injuring the feelings of others,
had assembled at the meeting, hooting and yelling, and in various
ways interrupting the services, and causing much disturbance.
Those who had the charge of the meeting, having tried their persuasive powers in vain, grew impatient and tried threatening.

The young men, considering themselves insulted, collected their
friends, to the number of a hundred or more, dispersed themselves
through the grounds, making the most frightful noises, and threatening to fire the tents. It was said the authorities of the meeting sat

in grave consultation, decided to have the ring-leaders arrested, and sent for the constable, to the great displeasure of some of the company, who were opposed to such an appeal to force and arms. Be that as it may, Sojourner, seeing great consternation depicted in every countenance, caught the contagion, and, ere she was aware, found herself quaking with fear.

Under the impulse of this sudden emotion, she fled to the most retired corner of a tent, and secreted herself behind a trunk, saying to herself, 'I am the only colored person here, and on me, probably, their wicked mischief will fall first, and perhaps fatally.' But feeling how great was her insecurity even there, as the very tent began to shake from its foundations, she began to soliloquize as follows:—

'Shall I run away and hide from the Devil? Me, a servant of the living God? Have I not faith enough to go out and quell that mob, when I know it is written—"One shall chase a thousand, and two put ten thousand to flight"? I know there are not a thousand here; and I know I am a servant of the living God. I'll go to the rescue, and the Lord shall go with and protect me.

'Oh,' said she, 'I felt as if I had *three hearts!* and that they were so large, my body could hardly hold them!'

She now came forth from her hiding-place, and invited several to go with her and see what they could do to still the raging of the moral elements. They declined, and considered her wild to think of it.

The meeting was in the open fields—the full moon shed its saddened light over all—and the woman who was that evening to address them was trembling on the preachers' stand. The noise and confusion were now terrific. Sojourner left the tent alone and unaided, and walking some thirty rods to the top of a small rise of ground, commenced to sing, in her most fervid manner, with all the strength of her most powerful voice, the hymn on the resurrection of Christ—

'It was early in the morning—it was early in the morning,
    Just at the break of day—
When he rose—when he rose—when he rose,
    And went to heaven on a cloud.'

All who have ever heard her sing this hymn will probably remember it as long as they remember her. The hymn, the tune, the style, are each too closely associated with to be easily separated from herself, and when sung in one of her most animated moods, in the open air, with the utmost strength of her most powerful voice, must have been truly thrilling.

As she commenced to sing, the young men made a rush towards her, and she was immediately encircled by a dense body of the rioters, many of them armed with sticks or clubs as their weapons of defence, if not of attack. As the circle narrowed around her, she ceased singing, and after a short pause, inquired, in a gentle but firm tone, 'Why do you come about me with clubs and sticks? I am not doing harm to any one.' 'We ar'n't a going to hurt you, old woman; we came to hear you sing,' cried many voices, simultaneously. 'Sing to us, old woman,' cries one. 'Talk to us, old woman,' says another. 'Pray, old woman,' says a third. 'Tell us your experience,' says a fourth. 'You stand and smoke so near me, I cannot sing or talk,' she answered.

'Stand back,' said several authoritative voices, with not the most gentle or courteous accompaniments, raising their rude weapons in the air. The crowd suddenly gave back, the circle became larger, as many voices again called for singing, talking, or praying, backed by assurances that no one should be allowed to hurt her—the speakers declaring with an oath, that they would '*knock down*' any person who should offer her the least indignity.

She looked about her, and with her usual discrimination, said inwardly—'Here must be many young men in all this assemblage, bearing within them hearts susceptible of good impressions. I will speak to them.' She did speak; they silently heard, and civilly asked her many questions. It seemed to her to be given her at the time to answer them with truth and wisdom beyond herself. Her speech had operated on the roused passions of the mob like oil on agitated waters; they were, as a whole, entirely subdued, and only clamored when she ceased to speak or sing. Those who stood in the background, after the circle was enlarged, cried out, 'Sing aloud, old woman, we can't hear.' Those who held the sceptre of power among them requested that she should make a pulpit of a neighboring wagon. She said, 'If I do, they'll overthrow it.' 'No, they sha'n't—he who dares hurt you, we'll knock him down instantly, d—n him,' cried the chiefs. 'No we won't, no we won't, nobody shall hurt you,' answered the many voices of the mob. They kindly assisted her to mount the wagon, from which she spoke and sung to them about an hour. Of all she said to them on the occasion, she remembers only the following:—

'Well, there are two congregations on this ground. It is written that there shall be a separation, and the sheep shall be separated from the goats. The other preachers have the sheep, *I* have the goats. And I have a few sheep among my goats, but they are *very* ragged.' This exordium produced great laughter. When she became wearied with talking, she began to cast about her to contrive some way to induce them to disperse. While she paused, they loudly clamored for 'more,' 'more,'—'sing,' 'sing more.' She motioned them to be quiet, and called out to them: 'Children, I have talked and sung to you, as you asked me; and now I have a request to make of you: will you grant it?' 'Yes, yes, yes,' resounded from every quarter. 'Well, it is this,' she answered: 'if I will sing one more hymn for you, will you then go away, and leave us this night in peace?' 'Yes, yes,' came faintly, feebly from a few. 'I repeat it,' says Sojourner, 'and I want an answer from you all, as of one accord. If I will sing you one more, you will go away, and leave us this night in peace?' 'Yes, yes, yes,' shouted many voices, with hearty emphasis. 'I repeat my request once more,' said she, 'and I want you *all* to answer.' And she reiterated the words again. This time a long, loud 'Yes—yes—yes,' came up, as from the multitudinous mouth of the entire mob. 'AMEN! it is SEALED, repeated Sojourner, in the deepest and most solemn tones of her powerful and sonorous voice. Its effect ran through the multitude, like an electric shock; and the most of them considered themselves bound by their promise, as they might have failed to do under less imposing circumstances. Some of them began instantly to leave; others said, 'Are we not to have one more hymn?' 'Yes,' answered their entertainer, and she commenced to sing:

> 'I bless the Lord I've got my seal—to-day and to-day—
> To slay Goliath in the field—to-day and to-day;
> The good old way is a righteous way,
> I mean to take the kingdom in the good old way.'

While singing, she heard some enforcing obedience to their promise, while a few seemed refusing to abide by it. But before she had
quite concluded, she saw them turn from her, and in the course of a
few minutes, they were running as fast as they well could in a solid
body; and she says she can compare them to nothing but a swarm of
bees, so dense was their phalanx, so straight their course, so hurried
their march. As they passed with a rush very near the stand of the
other preachers, the hearts of the people were smitten with fear,
thinking that their entertainer had failed to enchain them longer
with her spell, and that they were coming upon them with redou-
bled and remorseless fury. But they found they were mistaken, and
that their fears were groundless; for, before they could well recover
from their surprise, every rioter was gone, and not one was left on
the grounds, or seen there again during the meeting. Sojourner was
informed that as her audience reached the main road, some distance
from the tents, a few of the rebellious spirits refused to go on, and
proposed returning; but their leaders said, 'No—we have promised
to leave—all promised, and we must go, all go, and you shall none
of you return again.'

She did not fall in love at first sight with the Northampton Association, for she arrived there at a time when appearances did not
correspond with the ideas of associationists, as they had been spread
out in their writings; for their phalanx was a factory, and they were
wanting in means to carry out their ideas of beauty and elegance, as
they would have done in different circumstances. But she thought
she would make an effort to tarry* with them one night, though that
seemed to her no desirable affair. But as soon as she saw that accomplished, literary and refined persons were living in that plain
and simple manner, and submitting to the labors and privations† incident to such an infant institution, she said, 'Well, if these can live
here, *I* can.' Afterwards, she gradually became pleased with, and attached to, the place and the people, as well she might; for it must
have been no small thing to have found a home in a 'Community
composed of some of the choicest spirits of the age,' where all was
characterized by an equality of feeling, a liberty of thought and

---

*Stay.
†Deprivations.

speech, and a largeness of soul, she could not have before met with, to the same extent, in any of her wanderings.

Our first knowledge of her was derived from a friend who had resided for a time in the 'Community,' and who, after describing her, and singing one of her hymns, wished that we might see her. But we little thought, at that time, that we should ever pen these 'simple annals' of this child of nature.

When we first saw her, she was working with a hearty good will; saying she would not be induced to take regular wages, believing, as once before, that now Providence had provided her with a never-failing fount, from which her every want might be perpetually supplied through her mortal life. In this, she had calculated too fast. For the Associationists found, that, taking every thing into consideration, they would find it most expedient to act individually; and again, the subject of this sketch found her dreams unreal, and herself flung back upon her own resources for the supply of her needs. This she might have found more inconvenient at her time of life—for labor, exposure and hardship had made sad inroads upon her iron constitution, by inducing chronic disease and premature old age—had she not remained under the shadow of one,* who never wearies in doing good, giving to the needy, and supplying the wants of the destitute. She has now set her heart upon having a little home of her own, even at this late hour of life, where she may feel a greater freedom than she can in the house of another, and where she can repose a little, after her day of action has passed by. And for such a 'home' she is now dependent on the charities of the benevolent, and to them we appeal with confidence.

Through all the scenes of her eventful life may be traced the energy of a naturally powerful mind—the fearlessness and child-like simplicity of one untrammelled by education or conventional customs—purity of character—an unflinching adherence to principle—and a native enthusiasm, which, under different circumstances, might easily have produced another Joan of Arc.

With all her fervor, and enthusiasm, and speculation, her religion is not tinctured in the least with gloom. No doubt, no hesitation, no despondency, spreads a cloud over her soul; but all is bright, clear,

---

*George W. Benson.

positive, and at times ecstatic. Her trust is in God, and from him she looks for good, and not evil. She feels that 'perfect love casteth out fear.'

Having more than once found herself awaking from a mortifying delusion,—as in the case of the Sing-Sing kingdom,—and resolving not to be thus deluded again, she has set suspicion to guard the door of her heart, and allows it perhaps to be aroused by too slight causes, on certain subjects—her vivid imagination assisting to magnify the phantoms of her fears into gigantic proportions, much beyond their real size; instead of resolutely adhering to the rule we all like best, when it is to be applied to ourselves—that of placing every thing we see to the account of the best possible motive, until time and circumstance prove that we were wrong. Where no good motive can be assigned, it may become our duty to suspend our judgment till evidence can be had.

In the application of this rule, it is an undoubted duty to exercise a commendable prudence, by refusing to repose any important trust to the keeping of persons who may be strangers to us, and whose trustworthiness we have never seen tried. But no possible good, but incalculable evil may and does arise from the too common practice of placing all conduct, the source of which we do not fully understand, to the worst of intentions. How often is the gentle, timid soul discouraged, and driven perhaps to despondency, by finding its 'good evil spoken of;' and a well-meant but mistaken action loaded with an evil design!

If the world would but sedulously set about reforming itself on this one point, who can calculate the change it would produce—the evil it would annihilate, and the happiness it would confer! None but an all-seeing eye could at once embrace so vast a result. A result, how desirable! and one that can be brought about only by the most simple process—that of every individual seeing to it that he commit not this sin himself. For why should we allow in ourselves, the very fault we most dislike, when committed against us? Shall we not at least aim at consistency?

Had she possessed less generous self-sacrifice, more knowledge of the world and of business matters in general, and had she failed to take it for granted that others were like herself, and would, when her turn came to need, do as she had done, and find it 'more blessed to give than to receive,' she might have laid by something for the future. For few, perhaps, have ever possessed the power and inclination, in the same degree, at one and the same time, to labor as she has done, both day and night, for so long a period of time. And had these energies been well-directed, and the proceeds well husbanded, since she has been her own mistress, they would have given her an independence during her natural life. But her constitutional biases, and her early training, or rather want of training, prevented this result; and it is too late now to remedy the great mistake. Shall she then be left to want? Who will not answer, 'No!'

Last Interview with Her Master.

In the spring of 1849, Sojourner made a visit to her eldest daughter, Diana, who has ever suffered from ill health, and remained with Mr. Dumont, Isabella's humane master. She found him still living, though advanced in age, and reduced in property, (as he had been for a number of years,) but greatly enlightened on the subject of slavery. He said he could then see, that 'slavery was the wickedest thing in the world, the greatest curse the earth had ever felt—that it was then very clear to his mind that it was so, though, while he was a slaveholder himself, he did not see it so, and thought it was as right as holding any other property.' Sojourner remarked to him, that it might be the same with those who are now slaveholders. 'O, no,' replied he, with warmth, 'it cannot be. For, now, the sin of slavery is so clearly written out, and so much talked against,—(why, the whole world cries out against it!)—that if any one says he don't know, and has not heard, he must, I think, be a liar. In my slaveholding days, there were few that spoke against it, and these few made little impression on any one. Had it been as it is now, think you I could have held slaves? No! I should not have dared to do it, but should have emancipated every one of them. Now, it is very different; all may hear if they will.'

Yes, reader, if any one feels that the tocsin of alarm, or the antislavery trump, must sound a louder note before they can hear it, one would think they must be very hard of hearing—yea, that they belong to that class, of whom it may be truly said, 'they have stopped their ears that they may not hear.'

She received a letter from her daughter Diana, dated Hyde Park, December 19, 1849, which informed her that Mr. Dumont had 'gone West' with some of his sons—that he had taken along with him, probably through mistake, the few articles of furniture she had left with him. 'Never mind,' says Sojourner, 'what we give to the poor, we lend to the Lord.' She thanked the Lord with fervor, that she had lived to hear her master say such blessed things! She recalled the lectures he used to give his slaves, on speaking the truth and being honest, and laughing, she says he taught us not to lie and steal, when *he* was stealing all the time himself and did not know it! Oh! how sweet to my mind was this confession! And what a confession for a master to make to a slave! A slaveholding master turned to a brother! Poor old man, may the Lord bless him, and all slaveholders partake of his spirit!

THE VALIANT SOLDIERS.

TUNE.—"John Brown."

The following song, written for the first Michigan Regiment of colored soldiers, was composed by SOJOURNER TRUTH during the war, and was sung by her in Detroit and Washington.

We are the valiant soldiers who've 'listed for the war;
We are fighting for the Union, we are fighting for the law;
We can shoot a rebel farther than a white man ever saw,
            As we go marching on.

   Chorus.—
            Glory, glory, hallelujah! Glory, glory, hallelujah!
            Glory, glory, hallelujah, as we go marching on.

Look there above the center, where the flag is waving bright;
We are going out of slavery, we are bound for freedom's light;
We mean to show Jeff Davis how the Africans can fight,
            As we go marching on.—CHO.

We are done with hoeing cotton, we are done with hoeing corn;
We are colored Yankee soldiers as sure as you are born.
When massa hears us shouting, he will think 'tis Gabriel's horn,
            As we go marching on.—CHO.

They will have to pay us wages, the wages of their sin;
They will have to bow their foreheads to their colored kith and kin;
They will have to give us house-room, or the roof will tumble in,
              As we go marching on.—CHO.

We hear the proclamation, massa, hush it as you will;
The birds will sing it to us, hopping on the cotton hill;
The possum up the gum tree couldn't keep it still,
              As he went climbing on.—CHO.

Father Abraham has spoken, and the message has been sent;
The prison doors have opened, and out the prisoners went
To join the sable army of African descent,
              As we go marching on.—CHO.

"BOOK OF LIFE."

SOJOURNER TRUTH.

A Picture taken in the days of her Physical Strength.

PART SECOND.

"Book of Life."

THE PRECEDING NARRATIVE HAS given us a partial history of Sojourner Truth. This biography was published not many years after
her freedom had been secured to her. Having but recently emerged
from the gloomy night of slavery, ignorant and untaught in all that
gives value to human existence, she was still suffering from the burden of acquired and transmitted habits incidental to her past condition of servitude. Yet she was one whose life forces and moral
perceptions were so powerful and clear cut that she not only came
out from this moral gutter herself, but largely assisted in elevating
others of her race from a similar state of degradation. It was the "oil
of divine origin" which quickened her soul and fed the vital spark,
that her own indomitable courage fanned to an undying flame. She
was one of the first to enlist in the war against slavery, and fought
the battles for freedom by the side of its noble leaders.

A true sentinel, she slumbered not at her post. To hasten the enfranchisement of her own people was the great work to which she
consecrated her life; yet, ever responsive to the calls of humanity, she
cheerfully lent her aid to the advancement of other reforms, especially woman's rights and temperance.

During the last twenty-five years, she has traveled thousands of
miles, lectured in many States of the Union, spoken in Congress,
and has received tokens of friendship such as few can produce. The
following article was published in a Washington Sunday paper during the administration of President Lincoln:—

"It was our good fortune to be in the marble room of the senate chamber, a few days ago, when that old land-mark of the past—the representative of the forever-gone age—Sojourner Truth, made her appearance. It was an hour not soon to be forgotten; for it is not often, even in this magnanimous age of progress, that we see reverend senators—even him that holds the second chair in the gift of the Republic—vacate their seats in the hall of State, to extend the hand of welcome, the meed of praise, and substantial blessings, to a poor negro woman, whose poor old form, bending under the burden of nearly four-score and ten years, tells but too plainly that her marvelously strange life is drawing to a close. But it was as refreshing as it was strange to see her who had served in the shackles of slavery in the great State of New York for nearly a quarter of a century before a majority of these senators were born now holding a levee with them in the marble room, where less than a decade ago she would have been spurned from its outer corridor by the lowest menial, much less could she have taken the hand of a senator. Truly, the spirit of progress is abroad in the land, and the leaven of love is working in the hearts of the people, pointing with unerring certainty to the not far distant future, when the ties of affection shall cement all nations, kindreds and tongues into one common brotherhood."

She carries with her a book that she calls the Book of Life, which contains the autographs of many distinguished personages—the good and great of the land. No better idea can be given of the estimation in which she is held than by transcribing these testimonials and giving them to the public. It will be difficult to arrange these accounts in the chronological order of events, but no effort has been spared to furnish correct dates.

In the year 1851 she left her home in Northampton, Mass., for a lecturing tour in Western New York, accompanied by the Hon. George Thompson of England,[1] and other distinguished abolitionists. To advocate the cause of the enslaved at this period was both unpopular and unsafe. Their meetings were frequently disturbed or broken up by the pro-slavery mob, and their lives imperiled. At such times, Sojourner fearlessly maintained her ground, and by her dignified manner and opportune remarks would disperse the rabble and restore order.

She spent several months in Western New York, making

Rochester her head-quarters. Leaving this State, she traveled west-ward, and the next glimpse we get of her is in a Woman's Rights Convention at Akron, Ohio. Mrs. Frances D. Gage, who presided at that meeting, relates the following:—

"The cause was unpopular then. The leaders of the movement trembled on seeing a tall, gaunt black woman, in a gray dress and white turban, surmounted by an uncouth sun-bonnet, march delib-erately into the church, walk with the air of a queen up the aisle, and take her seat upon the pulpit steps. A buzz of disapprobation was heard all over the house, and such words as these fell upon listening ears:—

" 'An abolition affair!' 'Woman's rights and niggers!' 'We told you so!' 'Go it, old darkey!'[2]

"I chanced upon that occasion to wear my first laurels in public life as president of the meeting. At my request, order was restored and the business of the hour went on. The morning session was held; the evening exercises came and went. Old Sojourner, quiet and reticent as the 'Libyan Statue,' sat crouched against the wall on the corner of the pulpit stairs, her sun-bonnet shading her eyes, her el-bows on her knees, and her chin resting upon her broad, hard palm. At intermission she was busy, selling 'The Life of Sojourner Truth,' a narrative of her own strange and adventurous life. Again and again timorous and trembling ones came to me and said with earnestness, 'Don't let her speak, Mrs. Gage, it will ruin us. Every newspaper in the land will have our cause mixed with abolition and niggers, and we shall be utterly denounced.' My only answer was, 'We shall see when the time comes.'

"The second day the work waxed warm. Methodist, Baptist, Episcopal, Presbyterian, and Universalist ministers came in to hear and discuss the resolutions presented. One claimed superior rights and privileges for man on the ground of superior intellect; another, because of the manhood of Christ. 'If God had desired the equality of woman, he would have given some token of his will through the birth, life, and death of the Saviour.' Another gave us a theological view of the sin of our first mother. There were few women in those days that dared to 'speak in meeting,' and the august teachers of the people were seeming to get the better of us, while the boys in the galleries and the sneerers among the pews were hugely enjoying

the discomfiture, as they supposed, of the 'strong minded.' Some
of the tender-skinned friends were on the point of losing dignity,
and the atmosphere of the convention betokened a storm.

"Slowly from her seat in the corner rose Sojourner Truth, who,
till now, had scarcely lifted her head. 'Don't let her speak!' gasped
half a dozen in my ear. She moved slowly and solemnly to the front,
laid her old bonnet at her feet, and turned her great, speaking eyes
to me. There was a hissing sound of disapprobation above and
below. I rose and announced 'Sojourner Truth,' and begged the audience to keep silence for a few moments. The tumult subsided at
once, and every eye was fixed on this almost Amazon form, which
stood nearly six feet high, head erect, and eye piercing the upper air,
like one in a dream. At her first word, there was a profound hush.
She spoke in deep tones, which, though not loud, reached every ear
in the house, and away through the throng at the doors and windows:—

"'Well, chilern, what dar is so much racket dar must be something out o' kilter.[3] I tink dat 'twixt de niggers of de Souf and de
women at de Norf all a talkin' 'bout rights, de white men will be in
a fix pretty soon. But what's all dis here talkin' 'bout? Dat man ober
dar say dat women needs to be helped into carriages, and lifted ober
ditches, and to have de best place every whar. Nobody eber help me
into carriages, or ober mud puddles, or gives me any best place [and
raising herself to her full height and her voice to a pitch like rolling
thunder, she asked], and ar'n't I a woman? Look at me! Look at my
arm! [And she bared her right arm to the shoulder, showing her
tremendous muscular power.] I have plowed, and planted, and gathered into barns, and no man could head me—and ar'n't I a woman?
I could work as much and eat as much as a man (when I could get
it), and bear de lash as well—and ar'n't I a woman? I have borne
thirteen chilern and seen 'em mos' all sold off into slavery, and when
I cried out with a mother's grief, none but Jesus heard—and ar'n't I
a woman? Den dey talks 'bout dis ting in de head—what dis dey call
it?' 'Intellect,' whispered some one near. 'Dat's it honey. What's dat
got to do with women's rights or niggers' rights? If my cup won't
hold but a pint and yourn holds a quart, wouldn't ye be mean not to
let me have my little half-measure full?' And she pointed her signif-

icant finger and sent a keen glance at the minister who had made the argument. The cheering was long and loud.

" 'Den dat little man in black dar, he say women can't have as much rights as man, cause Christ want a woman. What did your Christ come from?' Rolling thunder could not have stilled that crowd as did those deep, wonderful tones, as she stood there with outstretched arms and eye of fire. Raising her voice still louder, she repeated, 'Whar did your Christ come from? From God and a woman. Man had nothing to do with him.' Oh! what a rebuke she gave the little man.

" 'Turning again to another objector, she took up the defense of mother Eve. I cannot follow her through it all. It was pointed, and witty, and solemn, eliciting at almost every sentence deafening applause; and she ended by asserting that 'if de fust woman God ever made was strong enough to turn the world upside down, all 'lone, dese togedder [and she glanced her eye over us], ought to be able to turn it back and get it right side up again, and now dey is asking to do it, de men better let 'em.' Long-continued cheering. 'Bleeged to ye for hearin' on me, and now ole Sojourner ha'n't got nothing more to say.'

"Amid roars of applause, she turned to her corner, leaving more than one of us with streaming eyes and hearts beating with gratitude. She had taken us up in her strong arms and carried us safely over the slough of difficulty, turning the whole tide in our favor. I have never in my life seen anything like the magical influence that subdued the mobbish spirit of the day and turned the jibes and sneers of an excited crowd into notes of respect and admiration. Hundreds rushed up to shake hands, and congratulate the glorious old mother and bid her God speed on her mission of 'testifying again concerning the wickedness of this 'ere people.' "

Mrs. Gage also in the same article relates the following:—

"Once upon a Sabbath in Michigan an abolition meeting was held. Parker Pillsbury was speaker, and criticized freely the conduct of the churches regarding slavery.[4] While he was speaking there came up a fearful thunder storm. A young Methodist arose, and interrupting the speaker, said he felt alarmed; he felt as if God's judgment was about to fall on him for daring to sit and hear such blasphemy; that it made his hair almost rise with terror. Here a voice, sounding above the rain that beat upon the roof, the sweeping surge of the winds, the crashing of the limbs of trees, the swaying of branches, and the rolling of thunder, spoke out: 'Chile, don't be skeered; you are not going to be harmed. I don't speck God's ever hearn tell on ye.' It was all she said, but it was enough."

She remained two years in the State of Ohio, going from town to town, attending conventions, and holding meetings of her own. Marius Robinson, of Salem, Ohio, editor of the *Anti-Slavery Bugle*, whose clarion notes never faltered in freedom's cause, was her friend and co-laborer.[5] She toiled on in this field perseveringly, sowing the seeds of truth in the hearts of the people, and patiently awaiting the time when she should help gather in the sheaves of a ripened harvest. At this time she attracted but little attention outside a charmed circle of reformers whose mighty moral power was the lever which eventually overthrew the institution of American slavery.

About the year 1856, she came to Battle Creek and bought a house and lot, since which time her home has been in Michigan. She still continued her itinerant life, spending much of her time in the neighboring States, especially in Indiana, which she felt needed her missionary efforts. An account of one of her meetings held in the northern part of that State has been kindly furnished us by her friend, Parker Pillsbury, accompanied by a note from himself.

"I inclose a communication from the Boston *Liberator*, of Oct. 5, 1858, relating to Sojourner Truth. The wondrous experiences of that most remarkable woman would make a library, if not indeed a literature, could they all be gathered and spread before the world. I was much in her company for several years in the anti-slavery conflict, and have often seen her engaged in what seemed most unequal combat with the defenders of slavery and foes of freedom; but I never saw her when she did not, as in the instance given below, scatter her enemies with dismay and confusion, winning more than victory in every battle.

"P. P."

"*Pro-Slavery in Indiana.*

> "*SILVER LAKE*, *Kosciusko Co., Ind.,*
> "*October 1, 1858.*

"**FRIEND W. L. GARRISON:**[6]—

"Sojourner Truth, an elderly colored woman, well known through-out the Eastern States, is now holding a series of anti-slavery meet-ings in Northern Indiana. Sojourner comes well recommended by H. B. Stowe,[7] yourself, and others, and was gladly received and wel-comed by the friends of the slave in this locality. Her progress in knowledge, truth, and righteousness is very remarkable, especially when we consider her former low estate as a slave. The border-ruf-fian Democracy of Indiana, however, appear to be jealous and sus-picious of every anti-slavery movement. A rumor was immediately circulated that Sojourner was an imposter; that she was, indeed, a man disguised in women's clothing. It appears, too, from what has since transpired, that they suspected her to be a mercenary hireling of the Republican party.*

"At her third appointed meeting in this vicinity, which was held in the meeting-house of the United Brethren, a large number of democrats and other pro-slavery persons were present. At the close of the meeting, Dr. T. W. Strain, the mouthpiece of the slave Democracy, requested the large congregation to 'hold on,' and stated that a doubt existed in the minds of many persons present respect-ing the sex of the speaker, and that it was his impression that a ma-jority of them believed the speaker to be a man. The doctor also affirmed (which was not believed by the friends of the slave) that it was for the speaker's special benefit that he now demanded that So-journer submit her breast to the inspection of some of the ladies present, that the doubt might be removed by their testimony. There were a large number of ladies present, who appeared to be ashamed and indignant at such a proposition. Sojourner's friends, some of whom had not heard the rumor, were surprised and indignant at such ruffianly surmises and treatment.

---

*In this era, the radical branch of the Republican Party was antislavery.

"Confusion and uproar ensued, which was soon suppressed by Sojourner, who, immediately rising, asked them why they suspected her to be a man. The Democracy answered, 'Your voice is not the voice of a woman, it is the voice of a man, and we believe you are a man.' Dr. Strain called for a vote, and a boisterous 'Aye,' was the result. A negative vote was not called for. Sojourner told them that her breasts had suckled many a white babe, to the exclusion of her own offspring;[8] that some of those white babies had grown to man's estate; that, although they had sucked her colored breasts, they were, in her estimation, far more manly than they (her persecutors) appeared to be; and she quietly asked them, as she disrobed her bosom, if they, too, wished to suck! In vindication of her truthfulness, she told them that she would show her breast to the whole congregation; that it was not to her shame that she uncovered her breast before them, but to their shame. Two young men (A. Badgely and J. Horner) stepped forward while Sojourner exposed her naked breast to the audience. I heard a democrat say, as we were returning home from meeting, that Dr. Strain had, previous to the examination, offered to bet forty dollars that Sojourner was a man! So much for the physiological acumen of a western physician.

"As 'agitation of thought is the beginning of wisdom,' we hope that Indiana will yet be redeemed.

"Yours, truly, for the slave,

"**WILLIAM HAYWARD.**"

The late lamented Josephine Griffing, whose loyal services in support of the Union, and untiring labors for the colored race, entitles her to a monument at the nation's cost, was often associated with Sojourner in anti-slavery times, and was invited to hold meetings with her in Angola and vicinity in the autumn of 1862. The slave-holding spirit was now fully aroused in Indiana, and very bitter toward the negro. A law had recently been passed forbidding their entering the State or remaining in it. This law was unconstitutional, nevertheless the democrats had enforced it and endeavored to enforce it in Sojourner's case. A warrant was made out and she was arrested for both offenses. Mrs. Griffing undertook her defense alone, outwitted and beat the enemy. Sojourner, nothing daunted, determined to remain and carry out the programme. For a time her meetings were much disturbed. When she arose to speak, the democrats would cry, "Down with you! We think the niggers have done enough! We will not hear you speak! Stop your mouth! &c., &c." She told them that the Union people would soon make them stop their mouths. The Union home guard took her into custody to protect her from being thrown into jail by the rebels.

A meeting was appointed at the town-house in Angola, but the democrats threatened to burn the building if she attempted to speak in it. To this she made answer, "Then I will speak upon the ashes." Describing this meeting, she says:—

"The ladies thought I should be dressed in uniform as well as the captain of the home guard, whose prisoner I was and who was to go with me to the meeting. So they put upon me a red, white, and blue shawl, a sash and apron to match, a cap on my head with a star in front, and a star on each shoulder. When I was dressed I looked in the glass and was fairly frightened." Said I, "It seems I am going to battle." My friends advised me to take a sword or pistol. I replied, "I carry no weapon; the Lord will reserve [preserve] me without weapons. I feel safe even in the midst of my enemies; for the truth is powerful and will prevail."

"When we were ready to go, they put me into a large, beautiful carriage with the captain and other gentlemen, all of whom were armed. The soldiers walked by our side and a long procession followed. As we neared the court-house, looking out of the window, I saw that the building was surrounded by a great crowd. I felt as I was going against the Philistines and I prayed the Lord to reliver [deliver] me out of their hands. But when the rebels saw such a mighty army coming, they fled, and by the time we arrived they were scattered over the fields, looking like a flock of frightened crows, and not one was left but a small boy, who sat upon the fence, crying, 'Nigger, nigger!'

"We now marched into the court-house, escorted by double files of soldiers with presented arms. The band struck up the 'Star Spangled Banner,' in which I joined and sang with all my might, while amid flashing bayonets and waving banners our party made its way to the platform upon which I went and advocated free speech with more zeal than ever before, and without interruption. At the close of the meeting, I was conducted to the house of the esquire for safety, as my friends feared the mob might return and make us trouble; but the day passed without farther annoyance.

"I spent some of the time at Pleasant Lake with Mr. Roby's family; but Mr. Roby was arrested for entertaining me, tried and acquitted. Another friend, Mr. Fox, was taken up for encouraging me to remain in the State and summoned to appear at the district court, but was found 'not guilty.'

"One day whilst I was at Mr. Roby's, two ladies drove up in haste and earnestly desired me to leave, saying the rebels were near by— coming to take me—whereupon I went home with them. But they, becoming more alarmed, advised me to seek safety in some woods not far away, by offering to go with me. This I positively refused to do, and told them I would sooner go to jail. I stood my ground and the rebel constable came with a warrant to take me; but a Union officer, following closely behind him, stepped up and read some papers showing that I was his prisoner. At this turn of affairs the rebel officer looked very much disgusted, and turning to go, said, 'I ain't going to bother my head with *niggers*, I'll resign my office first.' Then the home guard marched up to our house, playing upon the fife and drum, and gave loud cheers for Sojourner, Free Speech, and the Union.

"The last time I was arrested, the constable asked if I would appear at court, or if he should take me along with him. My friends assured him that they would be responsible for my appearance. When the day for my trial came, a great many went with me, some of the best families in the county, among whom were Dr. Gale, Dr. Moss and family, Thomas Moss and family, Mr. Roby, Mrs. Griffing,[9] and many other noble people whose names I cannot now recall, but the memory of whose friendship will be cherished whilst memory remains.

"My enemies, thinking I would probably run away, had made no preparation for the trial; but when they saw us come, hunted around and procured a shabby room into which I went with a few friends and waited for some one to appear against me. After a while, two half-drunken lawyers, who looked like the scrapings of the Democratic party, made their appearance, eyed us for a few moments, then left. Presently we saw them enter a tavern across the way, and this ended the trial.

"We now went to the house of a friend and had a grand picnic. I returned home after a month of hard labor in Indiana, which I believe did much for the cause of human freedom."

Mrs. Griffing, writing to the *Anti-Slavery Standard*, says, "Our meetings are largely attended by persons from every part of the county; especially by the most noble-hearted women, whose presence has produced a marked impression and has done more toward establishing a free government than would the killing of a hundred of Ellsworth's Zouaves. The lines are now being drawn as they never were by political maneuver, and as they cannot be by the cold steel alone, because it is a blow at slavery. 'Cannon balls may aid the truth, but thought's a weapon stronger.'

"Slavery has made a conquest in this county by the suppression of free speech, and freedom must make her conquest by the steadfast support of free speech. There was not manhood enough in the county last fall to protect an anti-slavery meeting at the county-seat; now there are a hundred men who would spill their blood sooner than surrender the right of even Sojourner. At all of our meetings we have been told that armed men were in our midst and had declared they would blow out our brains."

In the winter and spring of 1863, Sojourner was ill for many weeks and her finances becoming exhausted, she prayed the Lord to send an angel to relieve her wants. Soon after, a friend called bringing all needful supplies, to whom she said, "I just asked the Lord to send one of his chosen angels to me," and smiling added, "I knew he would think of you first."

Her case was made known to the public through the columns of the *Anti-Slavery Standard* and generous donations were forwarded to her. The following articles were published at the time:—

"*Sojourner Truth.*

"OLIVER JOHNSON:—

"*Dear Friend*—Again I would ask permission, through your paper, to return thanks to friends whose hearts have been moved to give aid and comfort to our 'venerable friend and teacher,' Sojourner Truth. She desires me to say that she cannot rest until *all* know how truly grateful she is for their kind assistance. She says her heart is full of praises and prayer, and sometimes she thinks her cup of happiness is about to run over, and she prays de Lord to pour it on to some of her friends. Would that some people had the power and goodness of heart to extract happiness from material surroundings in proportion to their possessions, as Sojourner has. A much better world would this be.

"When the kind and excellent letter reached her from Samuel May and wife, of Leicester, Mass., accompanied with donations from Ireland, she was greatly surprised, and expressions of deep gratitude came in rapid succession. Finally, she concluded that no mortal on earth was ever so blessed before, and she was quite sure 'de Lord never sent his angels from so great a distance, even in 'Lijah's day.' She wondered who ever heard of Sojourner way in Ireland, and when she thought that they were friends whom she had never seen, she was quite overcome with joy, and thought the goodness of the Lord was greater than she could understand.

"She wishes you to print the name of her grandson, James Caldwell, of the 54th,* thinking that some one may go and see him.

"She wishes her friends to know that her health is better than it was some time since. She says she has 'budded out wid de trees, but may fall wid de autumn leaves.'

"**Phebe H. M. Stickney.**"

"Names of Donors.

"Mrs. Edmundson,	Dublin, Ireland.
Mrs. Anne Allen,	" "
Richard D. Webb,	" "
Sarah R. May,	Leicester, Mass.
Samuel May, Jr.,	" "
Mrs. Goss,	New York.
W. H. Burleigh,	" "
George W. Bungay,	" "
Oliver Johnson,	" "

---

*Led by Col. Robert Gould Shaw, the 54th Massachusetts Regiment was the first Civil War regiment made up entirely of free blacks.

Theodore Tilton,   "   "
'Freedman's Relief Society,' Worcester, Mass.
Miss Ladd,
Mrs. Miller,
Mr. and Mrs. Twam,
Dr. Church and wife,
Mrs. John Hull,
Mrs. Maria Brown and Stillman,
Miss Laura Stebbins,
Mrs. Charles Hastings,
Mrs. Griffing,
Mrs. Samson and Mrs. Eliot,
Mrs. John Hamilton."

"**To the Editor of the National Anti-Slavery Standard:**

"This extraordinary woman still lives. When the letter of Phebe M. Stickney came to us at our home on the prairies in Iowa, suggesting pecuniary comfort for the blessed old saint in the sunset of her remarkable and useful life, I never remember to have regretted more that I had so little at command to bestow. *The Standard*, however, reports the names of a number of friends who were ready and willing to minister to her necessities. I hope others will do likewise. Few, if any, in the land are more worthy. Hers has been a life of pre-eminent devotion to the sacred cause of liberty and purity.

"The graphic sketch of her by the author of 'Uncle Tom's Cabin'[10] has doubtless been read with interest by thousands. No pen, however, can give an adequate idea of Sojourner Truth. This unlearned African woman, with her deep religious and trustful nature burning in her soul like fire, has a magnetic power over an audience perfectly astounding. I was once present in a religious meeting where some speaker had alluded to the government of the United States, and had uttered sentiments in favor of its Constitution. Sojourner stood, erect and tall, with her white turban on her head, and in a low and subdued tone of voice began by saying: 'Children, I talks to God and God talks to me. I goes out and talks to God in de fields and de woods. [The weevil had destroyed thousands of acres of wheat in the West that year.] Dis morning I was walking out, and I got over de fence. I saw de wheat a holding up its head, looking very big. I goes up and takes holt ob it. You b'lieve it, dere was *no* wheat dare? I says, God [speaking the name in a voice of reverence peculiar to herself], what *is* de matter wid *dis* wheat? and he says to me, "Sojourner, dere is a little weasel in it." Now I hears talkin' about de Constitution and de rights of man. I comes up and I takes hold of dis Constitution. It looks *mighty big*, and I feels for *my* rights, but der aint any dare. Den I says, God, what *ails* dis Constitution? He says to me, "Sojourner, dere is a little *weasel* in it."' The effect upon the multitude was irresistible.

"On a dark, cloudy morning, while she was our guest, she was sitting, as she often was wont to do, with her cheeks upon her palms, her elbows on her knees; she lifted up her head as though she had just wakened from a dream, and said, 'Friend Dugdale, poor old Sojourner can't read a word, will you git me de Bible and read me a little of de Scripter?' Oh, yes, Sojourner, gladly, said I. I opened to Isaiah, the 59th chapter. She listened as though an oracle was speaking. When I came to the words, None calleth for justice, nor any pleadeth for truth; your hands are defiled with blood, and your fingers with iniquity; they conceive mischief, and bring forth iniquity; they hatch cockatrice's eggs, and weave the spider's web; he that eateth of their eggs dieth, and that which is crushed breaketh out into a viper, she could restrain herself no longer, and, bringing her great palms together with an emphasis that I shall never forget, she exclaimed, '*Is dat thare?* "It shall break out into a viper." *Yes, God told me dat.* I never heard it read afore, *now* I know it *double!*' Of course her mind was directed to the heinous institution of American slavery, and she regarded these terrible words of the seer as prophetic concerning its fearful consequences.

"On one occasion, in a large reform meeting, where many able and efficient public speakers were present, Sojourner sat in the midst. One man, in defiance of propriety, was wasting the time of the meeting by distasteful and indelicate declamation. Some, in despair of his ending, were leaving the meeting. Others, mortified and distressed, were silently enduring, while the 'flea of the Convention,' continued to bore it, nothing daunted. Just at a point where he was forced to suspend long enough to take in a long breath, Sojourner, who had been sitting in the back part of the house with her head bowed, and groaning in spirit, raised up her tall figure before him, and, putting her eyes upon him, said, '*Child*, if de people has no whar to put it, what is de use? Sit down, child, *sit down!*' The man dropped as if he had been shot, and not another word was heard from him.

"A friend related the following anecdote to me: In that period of the anti-slavery movement when mobocratic violence was often resorted to, one of its most talented and devoted advocates, after an able address, was followed by a lawyer, who appealed to the lowest sentiments—was scurrilous and abusive in the superlative degree. Alluding to the colored race, he compared them to monkeys, baboons, and ourang-outangs. When he was about closing his inflammatory speech, Sojourner quietly drew near to the platform and whispered in the ear of the advocate of her people, 'Don't dirty *your* hands wid dat critter; let *me* 'tend to him!' The speaker knew it was safe to trust her. 'Children,' said she, straightening herself to her full hight, 'I am one of dem monkey tribes. I was born a slave. I had de dirty work to do—de scullion work. Now I am going to 'ply to dis critter'—pointing her long, bony finger with withering scorn at the petty lawyer. 'Now in de course of my time I has done a great deal of dirty scullion work, but of all de dirty work I ever done, dis is de scullionist and de dirtiest.' Peering into the eyes of the auditory with just such a look as *she* could give, and that no one could imitate, she continued: 'Now, children, don't you *pity* me?' She had taken the citadel by storm. The whole audience shouted applause, and the negro-haters as heartily as any.

"I was present at a large religious convention. Love in the family had been portrayed in a manner to touch the better nature of the auditory. Just as the meeting was about to close, Sojourner stood up. Tears were coursing down her furrowed cheeks. She said: 'We has heerd a great deal about love at home in de family. Now, children, I was a slave, and my husband and my children was sold from me.' The pathos with which she uttered these words made a deep impression upon the meeting. Pausing a moment, she added: 'Now, husband and children is *all* gone, and what has *'come* of de affection I had for dem? *Dat is de question before de house!*' The people smiled amidst a baptism of tears.

"Let food and raiment be given her. There are many in the land who will be made richer by seeing that this noble woman shares their bounty; and then, when her Lord shall come to talk with her, and take her into his presence chamber, and shall say, 'Sojourner, lacked thou anything?' she may answer, 'Nothing, Lord, either for body or soul.'

"J. A. D.
"Near Mt. Pleasant, Iowa, 1863."

In April, 1863, a lengthy account of Sojourner's life was published in the *Atlantic Monthly*, entitled, "Sojourner Truth, the Libyan Sibyl," written by Mrs. H. B. Stowe. This graphic sketch not only gave Sojourner greater notoriety, but added fresh laurels to Mrs. Stowe's increasing fame as an authoress. The description of her person and the portrayal of her character are so vivid that it finds a fitting place in her Book of Life, and is here fully given.

Sojourner Truth, the Libyan Sibyl.

Many years ago, the few readers of radical abolitionist papers must often have seen the singular name of Sojourner Truth, announced as a frequent speaker at anti-slavery meetings, and as traveling on a sort of self-appointed agency through the country. I had myself often remarked the name, but never met the individual. On one occasion, when our house was filled with company, several eminent clergymen being our guests, notice was brought up to me that Sojourner Truth was below, and requested an interview. Knowing nothing of her but her singular name, I went down, prepared to make the interview short, as the pressure of many other engagements demanded.

When I went into the room, a tall, spare form arose to meet me. She was evidently a full-blooded African, and though now aged and worn with many hardships, still gave the impression of a physical development which in early youth must have been as fine a specimen of the torrid zone as Cumberworth's celebrated statuette of the Negro Woman at the Fountain. Indeed, she so strongly reminded me of that figure, that, when I recall the events of her life, as she narrated them to me, I imagine her as a living, breathing impersonation of that work of art.

I do not recollect ever to have been conversant with any one who had more of that silent and subtle power which we call personal presence than this woman. In the modern spiritualistic phraseology, she would be described as having a strong sphere. Her tall form, as she rose up before me, is still vivid to my mind. She was dressed in some stout, grayish stuff, neat and clean, though dusty from travel. On her head she wore a bright Madras handkerchief, arranged as a turban, after the manner of her race. She seemed perfectly self-possessed and at her ease; in fact, there was almost an unconscious superiority, not unmixed with a solemn twinkle of humor, in the odd, composed manner in which she looked down on me. Her whole air had at times a gloomy sort of drollery which impressed one strangely.

"So this is *you*," she said.

"Yes," I answered.

"Well, honey, de Lord bless ye! I jes' thought I'd like to come an' have a look at ye. You's heerd o' me, I reckon?" she added.

"Yes, I think I have. You go about lecturing, do you not?"

"Yes, honey, that's what I do. The Lord has made me a sign unto this nation, an' I go round a-testifyin,' an' showin' on 'em their sins agin my people."

So saying, she took a seat, and, stooping over and crossing her arms on her knees, she looked down on the floor, and appeared to fall into a sort of reverie. Her great, gloomy eyes and her dark face seemed to work with some undercurrent of feeling; she sighed deeply, and occasionally broke out,

"O Lord! O Lord! Oh, the tears, an' the groans, an' the moans, O Lord!"

I should have said that she was accompanied by a little grandson of ten years—the fattest, jolliest woolly-headed little specimen of Africa that one can imagine. He was grinning and showing his glistening white teeth in a state of perpetual merriment, and at this moment broke out into an audible giggle, which disturbed the reverie into which his relative was falling.

She looked at him with an indulgent sadness, and then at me.

"Laws, ma'am, *he* don't know nothin' about it, *he* don't. Why, I've seen them poor critters beat an' 'bused an' hunted, brought in all torn—ears hangin' all in rags, where the dogs been a bitin' of 'em!"

This set off our little African Puck into another giggle, in which he seemed perfectly convulsed. She surveyed him soberly, without the slightest irritation.

"Well, you may bless the Lord, you *can* laugh; but I tell you, 't wa'n't no laughin' matter."

By this time I thought her manner so original that it might be worth while to call down my friends; and she seemed perfectly well pleased with the idea. An audience was what she wanted—it mattered not whether high or low, learned or ignorant. She had things to say, and was ready to say them at all times, and to any one.

I called down Dr. Beecher,[11] Professor Allen, and two or three other clergymen, who, together with my husband and family, made a roomful. No princess could have received a drawing-room with more composed dignity than Sojourner her audience. She stood among them, calm and erect, as one of her own native palm-trees waving alone in the desert. I presented one after another to her, and at last said—

"Sojourner, this is Dr. Beecher. He is a very celebrated preacher."

"*Is* he?" she said, offering her hand in a condescending manner, and looking down on his white head. "Ye dear lamb, I'm glad to see ye! De Lord bless ye! I loves preachers. I'm a kind o' preacher myself."

"You are?" said Dr. Beecher. "Do you preach from the Bible?"

"No, honey, can't preach from de Bible—can't read a letter."

"Why, Sojourner, what do you preach from, then?"

Her answer was given with a solemn power of voice, peculiar to herself, that hushed every one in the room.

"When I preaches, I has jest one text to preach from, an' I always preaches from this one. *My* text is, 'WHEN I FOUND JESUS!'"

"Well, you couldn't have a better one," said one of the ministers.

She paid no attention to him, but stood and seemed swelling with her own thoughts, and then began this narration:—

"Well, now, I'll jest have to go back an' tell ye all about it. Ye see we was all brought over from Africa, father, an' mother an' I, an' a lot more of us; an' we was sold up an' down, an' hither an' yon; an' I can 'member, when I was a little thing, not bigger than this 'ere," pointing to her grandson, "how my ole mammy would sit out o' doors in the evenin',' an' look up at the stars an' groan. She'd groan, an' groan, an' says I to her,

"'Mammy, what makes you groan so?'

"An' she'd say,

"'Matter enough, chile! I'm groanin' to think o' my poor children: they don't know where I be, an' I don't know where they be; they looks up at the stars, an' I looks up at the stars, but I can't tell where they be.

"'Now,' she said, 'chile, when you're grown up, you may be sold away from your mother an' all your old friends, an' have great troubles come on ye; an' when you has these troubles come on ye, ye jes' go to God, an' he'll help ye.'

"An says I to her,

"'Who is God, anyhow, mammy?'

"An' says she,

"'Why, chile, you jes' look up *dar*. It's him that made all *dem?*'

"Well, I didn't mind much 'bout God in them days. I grew up pretty lively an' strong, an' could row a boat, or ride a horse, or work round, an' do 'most anything.

"At last I got sold away to a real hard massa an' missis. Oh, I tell you they *was* hard! 'Peared like I couldn't please 'em nohow. An' then I thought o' what my old mammy told me about God; an' I thought I'd got into trouble, sure enough, an' I wanted to find God, an' I heerd some one tell a story about a man that met God on a threshin'-floor, an' I thought, well an' good, I'll have a threshin'-floor, too. So I went down in the lot, and I threshed down a place real hard, an' I used to go down there every day, an' pray an' cry with all my might, a-prayin' to the Lord to make my massa an' missis better, but it didn't seem to do no good; and so says I, one day,

"'O God, I been a-askin' ye, an' askin' ye, an askin' ye, for all this long time, to make my massa an' missis better, an' you don't do it, an' what *can* be the reason? Why, maybe you *can't*. Well, I shouldn't wonder if you couldn't. Well, now, I tell you, I'll make a bargain with you. Ef you'll help me to git away from my massa an' missis, I'll agree to be good; but ef you don't help me, I really don't think I can be. Now,' says I, 'I want to git away; but the trouble's jest here; ef I try to git away in the night, I can't see; an' ef I try to git away in the day-time, they'll see me an' be after me.'

"Then the Lord said to me, 'Git up two or three hours afore day-light, an' start off.'

"An' says I, 'Thank'ee Lord! that's a good thought.'

"So up I got about three o'clock in the mornin', an' I started an' traveled pretty fast, till, when the sun rose, I was clear away from our place an' our folks, an' out o' sight. An' then I begun to think I didn't know nothin' where to go. So I kneeled down, and says I,

"'Well, Lord, you've started me out, an' now please to show me where to go.'

"Then the Lord made a house appear to me, an' he said to me that I was to walk on till I saw that house, an' then go in an' ask the people to take me. An' I traveled all day, an' didn't come to the house till late at night; but when I saw it, sure enough, I went in, an' I told the folks that the Lord sent me; an' they was Quakers, an' real kind they was to me. They jes' took me in an' did for me as kind as ef I'd been one of 'em; an' after they'd giv me supper, they took me into a room where there was a great, tall, white bed; an' they told me to sleep there. Well, honey, I was kind o' skeered when they left me alone with that great white bed; 'cause I never had been in a bed in my life. It never came into my mind they could mean me to sleep in it. An' so I jes' camped down under it, on the floor, an' then I slep' pretty well. In the mornin', when they came in, they asked me ef I hadn't been asleep; an' I said, 'Yes, I never slep' better.' An' they said, 'Why, you havn't been in the bed!' An' says I, 'Laws, you didn't think o' sech a thing as my sleepin' in dat 'ar' *bed*, did you? I never heered o' sech a thing in my life.'

"Well, ye see, honey, I stayed an' lived with 'em. An' now jes' look here: instead o' keepin' my promise an bein' good, as I told the Lord I would, jest as soon as everything got a-goin' easy, *I forgot all about God.*

"Pretty well don't need no help; an' I gin up prayin'. I lived there two or three years, an' then the slaves in New York were all set free, 'an ole massa came to our house to make a visit, an' he asked me ef I didn't want to go back an' see the folks on the ole place. An' I told him I did. So he said, ef I'd jes' git into the wagon with him, he'd carry me over. Well, jest as I was goin' out to get into the wagon, *I met God!* an' says I, 'O God, I didn't know as you was so great!' An' I turned right round an' come into the house, an' set down in my room; for 'twas God all around me. I could feel it burnin', burnin', burnin' all around me, an' goin' through me; an' I saw I was so wicked, it seemed as ef it would burn me up. An' I said, 'O somebody, somebody, stand between God an' me! for it burns me!' Then, honey, when I said so, I felt as it were somethin' like an *amberill* [umbrella] that came between me an' the light, an' I felt it was *somebody*—somebody that stood between me an' God; an' it felt cool, like a shade; an' says I, 'Who's this that stands between me an' God? Is it old Cato?' He was a pious old preacher; but then I seemed to see Cato in the light, an' he was all polluted an' vile, like me; an' I said, 'Is it old Sally?' an' then I saw her, an' she seemed jes' so. An' then says I, '*Who* is this?' An' then, honey, for awhile it was like the sun shinin' in a pail o' water, when it moves up and down; for I begun to feel 'twas somebody that loved me; an' I tried to know him. An' I said, 'I know you! I know you! I know you!' An' then I said, 'I don't know you! I don't know you! I don't know you!' An' when I said, 'I know you, I know you' the light came; an' when I said, 'I don't know you, I don't know you,' it went jes' like the sun in a pail o' water. An' finally somethin' spoke out in me an' said, '*This is Jesus!*' An' I spoke out with all my might, an' says I, '*This is Jesus!* Glory be to God!' An' then the whole world grew bright, an' the trees they waved an' waved in glory, an' every little bit o' stone on the ground shone like glass; and I shouted an' said, 'Praise, praise, praise to the Lord!' An' I begun to feel sech a love in my soul as I never felt before—love to all creatures. An' then, all of a sudden, it stopped, an' I said, 'Dar's de white folks that have abused you, an' beat you, an' abused your people—think o' them!' But then there came another rush of love through my soul, an' I cried out loud—'Lord, Lord, I can love *even de white folks!*'

"Honey, I jes' walked round an' round in a dream. Jesus loved me! I knowed it—I felt it. Jesus was my Jesus. Jesus would love me always. I didn't dare tell nobody; 'twas a great secret. Everything had been got away from me that I ever had; an' I thought that ef I let white folks know about this, maybe they'd get *Him* away—so I said, 'I'll keep this close. I wont let any one know.'"

"But, Sojourner, had you never been told about Jesus Christ?"

"No, honey. I hadn't heerd no preachin'—been to no meetin'. Nobody hadn't told me. I'd kind o' heerd of Jesus, but thought he was like Gineral Lafayette, or some o' them. But one night there was a Methodist meetin' somewhere in our parts, an' I went; an' they got up an' begun for to tell der 'speriences: an' de fust one begun to speak. I started, 'cause he told about Jesus. 'Why,' says I to myself, 'dat man's found him, too!' An' another got up an' spoke, an' I said, 'He's found him, too!' An' finally I said, 'Why, they all know him!' I was so happy! An' then they sung this hymn" (Here Sojourner sang, in a strange, cracked voice, but evidently with all her soul and might, mispronouncing the English, but seeming to derive as much eleva-tion and comfort from bad English as from good):—

> "There is a holy city,
>   A world of light above,
> Above the stairs and regions,*
>   Built by the God of love.
>
> "An everlasting temple,
>   And saints arrayed in white,
> There serve their great Redeemer
>   And dwell with him in light.
>
> "The meanest child of glory
>   Outshines the radiant sun;
> But who can speak the splendor
>   Of Jesus on his throne?
>
> "Is this the Man of Sorrows
>   Who stood at Pilate's bar,
> Condemned by haughty Herod
>   And by his men of war?
>
> "He seems a mighty conqueror,
>   Who spoiled the powers below,
> And ransomed many captives
>   From everlasting woe.

---

*Starry regions.

"The hosts of saints around him
   Proclaim his work of grace,
The patriarchs and prophets,
   And all the godly race,

"Who speak of fiery trials
   And tortures on their way;
They came from tribulation
   To everlasting day.

"And what shall be my journey,
   How long I'll stay below,
Or what shall be my trials,
   Are not for me to know.

"In every day of trouble
   I'll raise my thoughts on high,
I'll think of that bright temple
   And crowns above the sky."

I put in this whole hymn, because Sojourner, carried away with her own feeling, sang it from beginning to end with a triumphant energy that held the whole circle around her intently listening. She sang with the strong barbaric accent of the native African, and with those indescribable upward turns and those deep gutturals which give such a wild, peculiar power to the negro singing—but above all, with such an overwhelming energy of personal appropriation that the hymn seemed to be fused in the furnace of her feelings and come out recrystallized as a production of her own.

It is said that Rachel was wont to chant the "Marseillaise" in a manner that made her seem, for the time, the very spirit and impersonation of the gaunt, wild, hungry, avenging mob which rose against aristocratic oppression; and in like manner, Sojourner, singing this hymn, seemed to impersonate the fervor of Ethiopia, wild, savage, hunted of all nations, but burning after God in her tropic heart, and stretching her scarred hands toward the glory to be revealed.

"Well, den ye see, after a while I thought I'd go back an' see de folks on de ole place. Well, you know de law had passed dat de culled folks was all free; an' my old missis, she had a daughter married about dis time who went to live in Alabama—an' what did she do but give her my son, a boy about de age of dis yer, for her to take down to Alabama? When I got back to de ole place, they told me about it, an' I went right up to see ole missis, an' says I,

"'Missis, have you been an' sent my son away down to Alabama?'

"'Yes, I have,' says she; 'he's gone to live with your young missis.'

"'Oh, Missis,' says I, 'how could you do it?'

"'Poh!' says she, 'what a fuss you make about a little nigger! Got more of 'em now than you know what to do with.'

"I tell you, I stretched up. I felt as tall as the world!

"'Missis,' says I, *I'll have my son back agin!*'

"She laughed.

"'*You* will, you nigger? How you goin' to do it? You ha'n't got no money.'

"'No, Missis—but *God* has—an' you'll see he'll help me!'—an' I turned round an' went out.

"Oh, but I *was* angry to have her speak to me so haughty an' so scornful, as ef my chile wasn't worth anything. I said to God, 'O Lord, render unto her double!' It was a dreadful prayer, an' I didn't know how true it would come.

"Well, I didn't rightly know which way to turn; but I went to the Lord, an' I said to him, 'O Lord, ef I was as rich as you be, an' you was as poor as I be, I'd help you—you *know* I would; and, oh, do help me!' An' I felt sure then that he would.

"Well, I talked with people, an' they said I must git the case before a grand jury. So I went into the town when they was holdin' a court, to see ef I could find any grand jury. An' I stood round the court-house, an' when they was a-comin' out, I walked right up to the grandest lookin' one I could see, an' says I to him:—

"'Sir, be you a grand jury?'

"An' then he wanted to know why I asked, an' I told him all about it; an' he asked me all sorts of questions, an' finally he says to me:—

"'I think, ef you pay me ten dollars, that I'd agree to git your son for you.' An' says he, pointin' to a house over the way, 'You go 'long an' tell your story to the folks in that house, an' I guess they'll give you the money.'

"Well, I went, an' I told them, an' they gave me twenty dollars; an' then I thought to myself, 'Ef ten dollars will git him, twenty dollars will git him *sartin.*' So I carried it to the man all out, an' said,

"'Take it all—only be sure an' git him.'

"Well, finally they got the boy brought back; an' then they tried to frighten him, an' to make him say that I wasn't his mammy, an' that he didn't know me; but they couldn't make it out. They gave him to me, an' I took him and carried him home; an' when I came to take off his clothes, there was his poor little back all covered with scars an' hard lumps, where they'd flogged him.

"Well, you see, honey, I told you how I prayed the Lord to render unto her double. Well, it came true; for I was up at ole missis' house not long after, an' I heerd 'em readin' a letter to her how her daughter's husband had murdered her—how he'd thrown her down an' stamped the life out of her, when he was in liquor; an' my ole missis, she giv a screech, an' fell flat on the floor. Then says I, 'O Lord, I didn't mean all that! You took me up too quick.'

"Well, I went in an' tended that poor critter all night. She was out of her mind—a cryin', an' callin' for her daughter; an' I held her poor ole head on my arm, an' watched for her as ef she'd been my baby. An' I watched by her, an' took care on her all through her sickness after that, an' she died in my arms, poor thing!"

"Well, Sojourner, did you always go by this name?"

"No, 'deed! My name was Isabella; but when I left the house of bondage, I left everything behind. I wa'n't goin' to keep nothin' of Egypt on me, an' so I went to the Lord an' asked him to give me a new name. And the Lord gave me Sojourner, because I was to travel up an' down the land, showin' the people their sins, an' bein' a sign unto them. Afterward I told the Lord I wanted another name, 'cause everybody else had two names; and the Lord gave me Truth, because I was to declare the truth to the people.

"Ye see some ladies have given me a white satin banner," she said, pulling out of her pocket and unfolding a white banner, printed with many texts, such as, "Proclaim liberty throughout all the land unto all the inhabitants thereof," and others of like nature. "Well," she said, "I journeys round to camp-meetin's, an' wherever folks is, an' I sets up my banner, an' then I sings, an' then folks always comes up round me, an' then I preaches to 'em. I tells 'em about Jesus, an' I tells 'em about the sins of this people. A great many always comes to hear me; an' they're right good to me, too, an' say they want to hear me agin."

We all thought it likely; and as the company left her, they shook hands with her, and thanked her for her very original sermon; and one of the ministers was overheard to say to another, "There's more of the gospel in that story than in most sermons."

Sojourner staid several days with us, a welcome guest. Her conversation was so strong, simple, shrewd, and with such a droll flavoring of humor, that the Professor was wont to say of an evening, "Come, I am dull, can't you get Sojourner up here to talk a little?" She would come up into the parlor, and sit among pictures and ornaments, in her simple stuff gown, with her heavy traveling shoes, the central object of attention both to parents and children, always ready to talk or to sing, and putting into the common flow of conversation the keen edge of some shrewd remark.

"Sojourner, what do you think of women's Rights?"

"Well, honey, I's ben to der meetins, an' harked a good deal. Dey wanted me fur to speak. So I got up. Says I, 'Sisters, I a'n't clear what you'd be after. Ef women want any rights more'n dey's got, why don't dey jes' *take 'em*, an' not be talkin' about it?' Some on 'em came round me, an' asked why I didn't wear bloomers. An' I told 'em I had bloomers enough when I was in bondage. You see," she said, "dey used to weave what dey called nigger-cloth, an' each one of us got jes' sech a strip, an' had to wear it width-wise. Them that was short got along pretty well, but as for me"——She gave an indescribably droll glance at her long limbs and then at us, and added, "Tell *you*, I had enough of bloomers in them days."

Sojourner then proceeded to give her views of the relative capacity of the sexes, in her own way.

"S'pose a man's mind holds a quart, an a woman's don't hold but a pint; ef her pint is *full*, it's as good as his quart."

Sojourner was fond of singing an extraordinary lyric, commencing,

> "I'm on my way to Canada,
>   That cold, but happy, land;
> The dire effects of slavery

I can no longer stand.

> O righteous Father,
> Do look down on me,
> And help me on to Canada,
> Where colored folks are free!"

The lyric ran on to state that, when the fugitive crosses the Canada line,

> "The queen comes down unto the shore,
> With arms extended wide,
> To welcome the poor fugitive
> Safe onto freedom's side."

In the truth thus set forth she seemed to have the most simple faith.

But her chief delight was to talk of "glory," and to sing hymns whose burden was,

> "O glory, glory, glory,
> Won't you come along with me?"

and when left to herself, she would often hum these with great delight, nodding her head.

On one occasion, I remember her sitting at a window singing and fervently keeping time with her head, the little black Puck of a grandson meanwhile amusing himself with ornamenting her red-and-yellow turban with green dandelion curls, which shook and trembled with her emotions, causing him perfect convulsions of delight.

"Sojourner," said the Professor to her, one day, when he heard her singing, "you seem to be very sure about Heaven."

"Well, I be," she answered, triumphantly.

"What makes you so sure there is any Heaven?"

"Well, 'cause I got such a hankerin' arter it in here," she said—giving a thump on her breast with her usual energy.

There was at the time an invalid in the house, and Sojourner, on learning it, felt a mission to go and comfort her. It was curious to see the tall, gaunt, dusky figure stalk up to the bed with such an air of conscious authority, and take on herself the office of consoler with such a mixture of authority and tenderness. She talked as from above—and at the same time, if a pillow needed changing or any office to be rendered, she did it with a strength and handiness that inspired trust. One felt as if the dark, strange woman were quite able to take up the invalid in her bosom, and bear her as a lamb, both physically and spiritually. There was both power and sweetness in that great warm soul and that vigorous frame.

At length, Sojourner, true to her name, departed. She had her mission elsewhere. Where now she is I know not; but she left deep memories behind her.

To these recollections of my own I will add one more anecdote, related by Wendell Phillips.[12]

Speaking of the power of Rachel to move and bear down a whole audience by a few simple words, he said he never knew but one other human being that had that power, and that other was Sojourner Truth.

He related a scene of which he was witness. It was at a crowded public meeting in Faneuil Hall, where Frederick Douglass was one of the chief speakers. Douglass had been describing the wrongs of the black race, and as he proceeded, he grew more and more excited and finally ended by saying that they had no hope of justice from the whites, no possible hope except in their own right arms. It must come to blood; they must fight for themselves and redeem themselves, or it would never be done.

Sojourner was sitting, tall and dark, on the very front seat, facing the platform; and in the hush of deep feeling, after Douglass sat down, she spoke out in her deep, peculiar voice, heard all over the house,

"Frederick, *is God dead?*"

The effect was perfectly electrical, and thrilled through the whole house, changing as by a flash the whole feeling of the audience. Not another word she said or needed to say; it was enough.

It is with a sad feeling that one contemplates noble minds and bodies, nobly and grandly formed human beings, that have come to us cramped, scarred, maimed, out of the prison-house of bondage. One longs to know what such beings might have become, if suffered to unfold and expand under the kindly developing influences of education.

It is the theory of some writers that to the African is reserved, in the later and palmier days of the earth, the full and harmonious development of the religious element in man. The African seems to seize on the tropical fervor and luxuriance of Scripture imagery as something native; he appears to feel himself to be of the same blood with those old burning, simple souls, the patriarchs, prophets, and seers, whose impassioned words seem only grafted as foreign plants on the cooler stock of the occidental mind.

I cannot but think that Sojourner with the same culture might have spoken words as eloquent and undying as those of the African Saint Augustine or Tertullian. How grand and queenly a woman she might have been, with her wonderful physical vigor, her great heaving sea of emotion, her power of spiritual conception, her quick penetration, and her boundless energy! We might conceive an African type of woman so largely made and moulded, so much fuller in all the elements of life, physical and spiritual, that the dark hue of the skin should seem only to add an appropriate charm—as Milton says of his Penseroso, whom he imagines

> "Black, but such as in esteem
> Prince Memnon's sister might beseem,
> Or that starred Ethiop queen that strove
> To set her beauty's praise above
> The sea-nymph's."

But though Sojourner Truth has passed away from among us as a wave of the sea, her memory still lives in one of the loftiest and most original works of modern art, the Libyan Sibyl, by Mr. Story, which attracted so much attention in the late World's Exhibition. Some years ago, when visiting Rome, I related Sojourner's history to Mr. Story at a breakfast at his house. Already had his mind begun to turn to Egypt in search of a type of art which should represent a larger and more vigorous development of nature than the cold elegance of Greek lines. His glorious Cleopatra was then in process of evolution, and his mind was working out the problem of her broadly developed nature, of all that slumbering weight and fullness of passion with which this statue seems charged, as a heavy thunder-cloud is charged with electricity.

The history of Sojourner Truth worked in his mind and led him into the deeper recesses of the African nature—those unexplored depths of being and feeling, mighty and dark as the gigantic depths of tropical forests, mysterious as the hidden rivers and mines of that burning continent whose life-history is yet to be. A few days after, he told me that he had conceived the idea of a statue which he should call the Libyan Sibyl. Two years subsequently, I revisited Rome, and found the gorgeous Cleopatra finished, a thing to marvel at, as the creation of a new style of beauty, a new manner of art. Mr. Story requested me to come and repeat to him the history of Sojourner Truth, saying that the conception had never left him. I did so; and a day or two after, he showed me the clay model of the Libyan Sibyl.[13] I have never seen the marble statue; but am told by those who have, that it was by far the most impressive work of art at the Exhibition.

A notice of the two statues from the London *Athenæum* must supply a description, which I cannot give.

"The Cleopatra and the Sibyl are seated, partly draped, with the characteristic Egyptian gown, that gathers about the *torso* and falls freely around the limbs; the first is covered to the bosom, the second bare to the hips. Queenly Cleopatra rests back against her chair in meditative ease, leaning her cheek against one hand, whose elbow the rail of the seat sustains; the other is outstretched upon her knee, nipping its forefinger upon the thumb thoughtfully, as though some firm, willful purpose filled her brain, as it seems to set those luxurious features to a smile as if the whole woman 'would.' Upon her head is the coif, bearing in front the mystic *uræus,* or twining basilisk of sovereignty, while from its sides depend the wide Egyptian lappels, or wings, that fall upon her shoulders. The *Sibilla Libica* has crossed her knees—an action universally held amongst the ancients as indicative of reticence or secrecy, and of power to bind. A secret-keeping looking dame she is, in the full-bloom proportions of ripe womanhood, wherein choosing to place his figure the sculptor has deftly gone between the disputed point whether these women were blooming and wise in youth, or deeply furrowed with age and burdened with the knowledge of centuries, as Virgil, Livy, and Gellius say. Good artistic example might be quoted on both sides. Her forward elbow is propped upon one knee; and to keep her secrets closer, for this Libyan woman is the closest of all the sibyls, she rests her shut mouth upon one closed palm, as if holding the African mystery deep in the brooding brain that looks out through mournful, warning eyes, seen under the wide shade of the strange horned (Ammonite) crest, that bears the mystery of the Tetragrammaton upon its upturned front. Over her full bosom, mother of myriads as she was, hangs the same symbol. Her face has a Nubian cast, her hair wavy and plaited, as is meet."

We hope to see the day when copies both of the Cleopatra and the Libyan Sibyl shall adorn the Capitol at Washington.

Near the close of the article Mrs. Stowe said, "Sojourner has passed away from among us as a wave of the sea." But as the wave describes larger circles in its outward bound course, so has her life become more significant as she has been borne forth into the ocean of life. Her work was then but just begun, and her record since that time shows a faith in the power of truth, a devotion in the cause of humanity, and a perseverance in the accomplishment of her purposes which command attention and respect. She had been around "a testifying," but now other duties were superadded. To the great work being done for the soldiers, she lent a helping hand, seeking every opportunity to aid them. The first colored troops that enlisted from Battle Creek encamped in Detroit. As the thanksgiving season approached, Sojourner proposed that the citizens of that city should send the "boys" a dinner, to which they cordially responded. In her soliciting rounds, she met a gentleman whom she invited to donate for the entertainment. He refused to do so, and made some severe remarks about the war, the nigger, &c. Much surprised, she asked him who he was. He replied, "I am the only son of my mother." "I am glad there are no more," said she, and passed on. Several large boxes, containing the luxuries of the season, not forgetting the fattened turkey, were dispatched by the generous people of the town with Sojourner as distributor. Detroit papers spoke of her efforts commendingly.

"Gala Day at Camp Ward.

"ADDRESS BY SOJOURNER TRUTH.—The colored soldiers at Camp Ward had a regular jubilee last Friday. About eleven o'clock a carriage drove up before Col. Bennett's quarters laden with boxes and packages containing all manner of delicacies for 'the boys,' sent from Battle Creek. Sojourner Truth, who carries not only a tongue of fire, but a heart of love, was the bearer of these offerings. The Colonel ordered the regiment into line 'in their best' for the presentation, which was made by Sojourner, accompanied by a speech glowing with patriotism, exhortation, and good wishes, which was responded to by rounds of enthusiastic cheers. At the close of the ceremony, Sojourner spent an hour or two among the soldiers in motherly conversation, and assisting in opening the boxes and distributing their contents, which the recipients disposed of with hearty good-will.

"Sunday afternoon, according to appointment, Sojourner went up to the camp to deliver another address to the soldiers, but so large a crowd of white citizens were gathered to hear that her inspirations were devoted almost exclusively to their ears, with a promise of a future discourse for the soldiers. At the close of the lecture, a handsome collection was volunteered for the benefit of the speaker.—*Advertiser and Tribune*."

In the spring of 1864, a brief article in the same journal mentioned her having gone to Washington to see Mr. Lincoln.

"TO THE EDITOR OF THE ADVERTISER AND TRIBUNE.

"Many of our citizens are doubtless acquainted with the name of Sojourner Truth, have seen racy anecdotes of her from time to time in the newspapers, read Harriet Beecher Stowe's narrative of her in the *Atlantic Monthly*, and remember her stay of several months in this city five or six years ago. Those who called upon her at that time, were richly entertained by her original remarks, her ready wit, and the stories of her wonderful life. She was then full of intense interest in the war, and foresaw its result in the emancipation of her race. It was touching to see her eager face when the newspapers were read in her presence. She would never listen to Mrs. Stowe's 'Libyan Sibyl.' 'Oh!' she would say, 'I don't want to hear about that old symbol; read me something that is going on *now*, something about this great war.' She had utter faith in Abraham Lincoln. To a friend who was impatient with his slow movements she said, 'Oh, wait, chile! have patience! It takes a great while to turn about this great ship of State.' Toward spring she made ready for a journey to Washington, to see Mr. Lincoln. 'I shall surely go,' she said, 'I never determined to do anything and failed.' And she did go—the brave-hearted, indomitable old woman—despite her light purse and heavy burden of seventy-seven years."

She left Battle Creek in June, but did not immediately go to Washington. A New York paper says of her:—

"Sojourner has been some months in New York, speaking in many places with great acceptance, and is now in this city, where she will speak this evening in the lecture room of the Unitarian Church, corner of Lafayette Avenue and Shelby Street. Let those who enjoy an original entertainment hear her. She is trying to pay off a mortgage on her little house in Battle Creek. Give her a full house, and a generous contribution. Remember that here in the North, in the State of New York, she was robbed, by our race and by our laws, of FORTY YEARS of her life. Do we not owe her, from abundant fullness, some compensation for those years with their entailed sorrow?

> "'There is that scattereth and yet increaseth.'
> "'The soul of the liberal man waxeth fat.'
> "'The Lord loveth the cheerful giver.'

"C. E. C."

From New York she went to Brooklyn, and spoke in Plymouth Church, where a collection of $100 was taken up for her. A Brooklyn paper speaks of her as follows:—

"Sojourner Truth, whom the newspapers lately described as dying, reported herself in person to us last week, a living contradiction of the false rumor. The old lady says that, so far from being at the point of death, she has not experienced for many months any symptom of sickness. Her age is now eighty, but her spirit continues as youthful as ever. On Sunday morning she heard Mr. Beecher's opening sermon of the season, which she called 'a feast for her poor old soul.' Sojourner's conversation is witty, sarcastic, sensible, and oftentimes profound. Her varied experience during a long life gives her a rich and deep fountain to draw upon for the entertainment and instruction of her friends, and her reminiscences and comments are equally interesting both to grown folks and children. She looks and acts as if she might live to be a hundred years old. She has uplifted her voice to two generations of mankind, and may yet become sibyl and prophetess to a third."

Sojourner reached Washington during the autumn, and in due time made her long-contemplated visit to the president.

The Story of Her Interview with the President.

The following letter from Sojourner Truth, written by a friend at her dictation, was addressed to Rowland Johnson, who has kindly handed it to us for publication. Our readers will be glad to see Sojourner's own account of her visit to the president.

"FREEDMAN'S VILLAGE, VA., Nov. 17, 1864.

"DEAR FRIEND:—

"I am at Freedman's Village. After visiting the president, I spent three weeks at Mrs. Swisshelm's, held two meetings in Washington, at Rev. Mr. Garnet's Presbyterian Church, for the benefit of the Colored Soldiers' Aid Society. These meetings were successful in raising funds. One week after that I went to Mason's Island, and saw the freedmen there, and held several meetings, remained a week and was present at the celebration of the emancipation of the slaves of Maryland, and spoke on that occasion.

"It was about 8 o'clock A.M., when I called on the president. Upon entering his reception room we found about a dozen persons in waiting, among them two colored women. I had quite a pleasant time waiting until he was disengaged, and enjoyed his conversation with others; he showed as much kindness and consideration to the colored persons as to the whites—if there was any difference, more. One case was that of a colored woman who was sick and likely to be turned out of her house on account of her inability to pay her rent. The president listened to her with much attention, and spoke to her with kindness and tenderness. He said he had given so much he could give no more, but told her where to go and get the money, and asked Mrs. C——n to assist her, which she did.

"The president was seated at his desk. Mrs. C. said to him, 'This is Sojourner Truth, who has come all the way from Michigan to see you.' He then arose, gave me his hand, made a bow, and said, 'I am pleased to see you.'[14]

"I said to him, Mr. President, when you first took your seat I feared you would be torn to pieces, for I likened you unto Daniel, who was thrown into the lion's den; and if the lions did not tear you into pieces, I knew that it would be God that had saved you; and I said if he spared me I would see you before the four years expired, and he has done so, and now I am here to see you for myself.

"He then congratulated me on my having been spared. Then I said, I appreciate you, for you are the best president who has ever taken the seat. He replied: 'I expect you have reference to my having emancipated the slaves in my proclamation. But,' said he, mentioning the names of several of his predecessors (and among them emphatically that of Washington), 'they were all just as good, and would have done just as I have done if the time had come. If the people over the river [pointing across the Potomac] had behaved themselves, I could not have done what I have; but they did not, which gave me the opportunity to do these things.' I then said, I thank God that you were the instrument selected by him and the people to do it. I told him that I had never heard of him before he was talked of for president. He smilingly replied, 'I had heard of you many times before that.'

"He then showed me the Bible presented to him by the colored people of Baltimore, of which you have no doubt seen a description. I have seen it for myself, and it is beautiful beyond description. After I had looked it over, I said to him, This is beautiful indeed; the colored people have given this to the head of the government, and that government once sanctioned laws that would not permit its people to learn enough to enable them to read this book. And for what? Let them answer who can.

"I must say, and I am proud to say, that I never was treated by any one with more kindness and cordiality than were shown to me by that great and good man, Abraham Lincoln, by the grace of God president of the United States for four years more. He took my little book, and with the same hand that signed the death-warrant of slavery, he wrote as follows:

"'For Aunty Sojourner Truth,

"'Oct. 29, 1864.   A. LINCOLN.'

"As I was taking my leave, he arose and took my hand, and said he would be pleased to have me call again. I felt that I was in the presence of a friend, and I now thank God from the bottom of my heart that I always have advocated his cause, and have done it openly and boldly. I shall feel still more in duty bound to do so in time to come. May God assist me.

"Now I must tell you something of this place. I found things quite as well as I expected. I think I can be useful and will stay. The captain in command of the guard has given me his assistance, and by his aid I have obtained a little house, and will move into it to-morrow. Will you ask Mrs. P., or any of my friends, to send me a couple of sheets and a pillow? I find many of the women very ignorant in relation to house-keeping, as most of them were instructed in field labor, but not in household duties. They all seem to think a great deal of me, and want to learn the way we live in the North. I am listened to with attention and respect, and from all things, I judge it is the will of both God and the people that I should remain.

"Now when you come to Washington, don't forget to call and see me. You may publish my whereabouts, and anything in this letter you think would interest the friends of Freedom, Justice, and Truth, in the *Standard* and *Anglo-African*, and any other paper you may see fit.

"Enclosed please find four shadows [carte de visites]. The two dollars came safely. Anything in the way of nourishment you may feel like sending, send it along. The captain sends to Washington every day. Give my love to all who inquire for me, and tell my friends to direct all things for me to the care of Capt. George B. Carse, Freedman's Village, Va. Ask Mr. Oliver Johnson to please send me the *Standard* while I am here, as many of the colored people like to hear what is going on, and to know what is being done for them. Sammy, my grandson, reads for them. We are both well, and happy, and feel that we are in good employment. I find plenty of friends.

"**YOUR FRIEND, SOJOURNER TRUTH.**"

"The colored population of Baltimore have procured the most beautiful Bible ever manufactured in this country, to be presented to the

President of the United States. The cover bears a large plate of gold, representing a slave with his shackles falling from him in a cotton field, stretching out his hands in gratitude to President Lincoln for the freedom of the slave. At the feet of the freedman there is a scroll bearing upon its face the word 'Emancipation,' in large letters. On the reverse cover is another gold plate containing the following inscription: 'To Abraham Lincoln, President of the United States, the friend of universal freedom, by the loyal colored people of Baltimore, as a token of respect and gratitude. Baltimore, July 4th, 1864.' The book is enclosed in a walnut silver-mounted box. The entire affair cost $5,800."

Although in Sojourner's estimation Abraham Lincoln was the "foremost man of all this world," yet no idle curiosity prompted her to ask this interview. From the head of the nation she sought that authority which would enable her to take part in the awful drama which was enacting in this Republic, and that being obtained, she at once entered upon her work.

When we follow her from one field of labor to another, her time being divided between teaching, preaching, nursing, watching, and praying, ever ready to counsel, comfort, and assist, we feel that, for one who is nobody but a woman, an unlettered woman, a black woman, and an old woman, a woman born and bred a slave, nothing short of the Divine incarnated in the human, could have wrought out such grand results.

In December she received the following commission from the National Freedman's Relief Association:—

"New York, Dec. 1, 1864.

"This certifies that The National Freedman's Relief Association has appointed Sojourner Truth to be a counselor to the freed people at Arlington Heights, Va., and hereby commends her to the favor and confidence of the officers of government, and of all persons who take an interest in relieving the condition of the freedmen, or in promoting their intellectual, moral, and religious instruction.

"On behalf of the N. F. R. Association,
"F. C. Shaw, *President*,

"Charles C. Leigh,
"Chairman of Home Com."

Sojourner spent more than a year at Arlington Heights, instructing the women in domestic duties, and doing much to promote the general welfare. She especially deprecated their filthy habits, and strove to inspire them with a love of neatness and order. On the Sabbath she preached to large and attentive congregations, and was once heard to exclaim, "Be clean! be clean! for cleanliness is godliness."

Liberty was a stranger to these poor people. Having but lately been introduced to the goddess, they had never yet so much as touched the tips of her lovely fingers, and dared not raise their bowed heads to steal even a sidelong glance at her radiant face. Thus, being wholly unfamiliar with her divine attributes, they often submitted to grievous wrongs from their old oppressors, not presuming to expostulate. The Marylanders tormented them by coming over, seizing, and carrying away their children. If the mothers made a "fuss," as these heartless wretches called those natural expressions of grief in which bereaved mothers are apt to indulge, they were thrust into the guard-house. When this was made known to Sojourner, she told them they must not permit such outrages, that they were free, and had rights which would be recognized and maintained by the laws, and that they could bring these robbers to justice.

This was a revelation indeed, for they had never known that freedom meant anything more to them than being no longer obliged to serve a master, and at liberty to lounge about in idleness. But her electrifying words seemed to inspire them with new life and to awaken the latent spirit within them which, like fire in flint, had lain torpid for ages, but, unextinguished and unextinguishable, awaited only favorable conditions to escape in freedom. The manhood and womanhood of these crushed people now asserted itself, and the exasperated Marylanders threatened to put Sojourner into the guard-house. She told them that if they attempted to put her into the guard-house, she "would make the United States rock like a cradle."

Soon after the Freedmen's Bureau was established, Sojourner was appointed to assist in the hospital,[15] as the following letter will show:—

"WAR DEPARTMENT,
"BUREAU OF REFUGEES, FREEDMEN, AND ABANDONED LANDS.

"Washington, September 13, 1865.

"Sojourner Truth has good ideas about the industry and virtue of the colored people. I commend her energetic and faithful efforts to Surgeon Gluman, in charge of Freedmen's Hospital, and shall be happy to have him give her all facilities and authority so far as she can aid him in promoting order, cleanliness, industry, and virtue among the patients.

"JOHN EATON, JR.,
"Col. and Assistant Commissioner."

While Sojourner was engaged in the hospital, she often had occasion to procure articles from various parts of the city for the sick soldiers, and would sometimes be obliged to walk a long distance, carrying her burdens upon her arm. She would gladly have availed herself of the street cars; but, although there was on each track one car called the Jim Crow car, nominally for the accommodation of colored people, yet should they succeed in getting on at all they would seldom have more than the privilege of standing, as the seats were usually filled with white folks. Unwilling to submit to this state of things, she complained to the president of the street railroad, who ordered the Jim Crow car to be taken off. A law was now passed giving the colored people equal car privileges with the white.

Not long after this, Sojourner, having occasion to ride, signaled the car, but neither conductor nor driver noticed her. Soon another followed, and she raised her hand again, but they also turned away. She then gave three tremendous yelps, "I want to ride! *I want to ride!!* I WANT TO RIDE!!! Consternation seized the passing crowd—people, carriages, go-carts of every description stood still. The car was effectually blocked up, and before it could move on, Sojourner had jumped aboard. Then there arose a great shout from the crowd, "Ha! ha! ha!! She has beaten him," &c. The angry conductor told her to go forward where the horses were, or he would put her out. Quietly seating herself, she informed him that she was a passenger. "Go forward where the horses are, or I will throw you out," said he in a menacing voice. She told him that she was neither a Mary-lander nor a Virginian to fear his threats; but was from the Empire State of New York, and knew the laws as well as he did.

Several soldiers were in the car, and when other passengers came in, they related the circumstance and said, "You ought to have heard that old woman talk to the conductor." Sojourner rode farther than she needed to go; for a ride was so rare a privilege that she deter-mined to make the most of it. She left the car feeling very happy, and said, "Bless God! I have had a ride."

Returning one day from the Orphan's Home at Georgetown, she hastened to reach a car; but they paid no attention to her signal, and kept ringing a bell that they might not hear her. She ran after it, and when it stopped to take other passengers, she succeeded in overtak-ing it and, getting in, said to the conductor, "It is a shame to make a lady run so." He told her if she said another word, he would put her off the car, and came forward as if to execute his threat. She replied, "If you attempt that, it will cost you more than your car and horses are worth." A gentleman of dignified and commanding man-ner, wearing a general's uniform, interfered in her behalf, and the conductor gave her no further trouble.

At another time, she was sent to Georgetown to obtain a nurse for the hospital, which being accomplished, they went to the station and took seats in an empty car, but had not proceeded far before two ladies came in, and seating themselves opposite the colored woman began a whispered conversation, frequently casting scornful glances at the latter. The nurse, for the first time in her life finding herself in one sense on a level with white folks and being much abashed, hung her poor old head nearly down to her lap; but Sojourner, noth-ing daunted, looked fearlessly about. At length one of the ladies called out, in a weak, faint voice, "Conductor, conductor, does nig-gers ride in these cars?" He hesitatingly answered, "Ye-yea-yes," to which she responded, "'Tis a shame and a disgrace. They ought to have a nigger car on the track." Sojourner remarked, "Of course col-ored people ride in the cars. Street cars are designed for poor white, and colored, folks. Carriages are for ladies and gentlemen. There are carriages [pointing out of the window], standing ready to take you three or four miles for sixpence, and then you talk of a nigger car!!!"

Promptly acting upon this hint, they arose to leave. "Ah!" said Sojourner, "now they are going to take a carriage. Good by, ladies."

Mrs. Laura Haviland,[16] a widely known philanthropist, spent several months in the same hospital and sometimes went about the city with Sojourner to procure necessaries for the invalids. Returning one day, being much fatigued, Mrs. Haviland proposed to take a car although she was well aware that a white person was seldom allowed to ride if accompanied by a black one. "As Mrs. Haviland signaled the car," says Sojourner, "I stepped one side as if to continue my walk and when it stopped I ran and jumped aboard. The conductor pushed me back, saying, 'Get out of the way and let this lady come in.' Whoop! said I, I am a lady too. We met with no further opposition till we were obliged to change cars. A man coming out as we were going into the next car, asked the conductor if 'niggers were allowed to ride.' The conductor grabbed me by the shoulder and jerking me around, ordered me to get out. I told him I would not. Mrs. Haviland took hold of my other arm and said, 'Don't put her out.' The conductor asked if I belonged to her. 'No,' replied Mrs. Haviland, 'She belongs to humanity.' 'Then take her and go,' said he, and giving me another push slammed me against the door. I told him I would let him know whether he could shove me about like a dog, and said to Mrs. Haviland, Take the number of this car.

"At this, the man looked alarmed, and gave us no more trouble. When we arrived at the hospital, the surgeons were called in to examine my shoulder and found that a bone was misplaced. I complained to the president of the road, who advised me to arrest the man for assault and battery. The Bureau furnished me a lawyer, and the fellow lost his situation. It created a great sensation, and before the trial was ended, the inside of the cars looked like pepper and salt; and I felt, like Poll Parrot, 'Jack, I am riding.' A little circumstance will show how great a change a few weeks had produced: A lady saw some colored women looking wistfully toward a car, when the conductor, halting, said, 'Walk in, ladies.' Now they who had so lately cursed me for wanting to ride, could stop for black as well as white, and could even condescend to say, 'Walk in, ladies.'"

The city of Washington was now literally swarming with a class of people who had by the war been thrown upon the surface of society like mud from a volcano, and who were not unlike that article in respect to being dirty and entirely unfitted by a want of contact with refining and favorable influences to obtain and maintain a hold upon civilization. A report from the superintendent of police will help to explain their condition:—

"Condition of the Destitute Colored People of the District.

"In the Senate, on Tuesday, while the bill reported by Senator Morrill appropriating $25,000 for the relief of destitute colored people of the District was under consideration, the following letter from Superintendent of Police Richards was read:—

"Department of Metropolitan Police.

"Office of Sup't, 483 Tenth st., West,
"*Washington, March 6, 1866.*

"Gentlemen:—

"I have the honor at this time to submit a report, based mainly upon personal inspection, of the sanitary condition of certain localities in the city of Washington, inhabited by colored people, mostly known as 'contrabands,' together with certain other facts connected with the condition of these people.

"The first locality visited is known as 'Murder Bay,' and is situated between Thirteenth and Fifteenth Streets west, below Ohio Avenue, and bordering on the Washington Canal. Here crime, filth, and poverty seem to vie with each other in a career of degradation and death. Whole families, consisting of fathers, mothers, children, uncles, and aunts, according to their own statements, are crowded into mere apologies for shanties, which are without light or ventilation. During the storms of rain or snow their roofs afford but slight protection, while from beneath a few rough boards used for floors the miasmatic effluvia from the most disgustingly filthy and stagnant water, mingled with the exhalations from the uncleansed bodies of numerous inmates, render the atmosphere within these hovels stifling and sickening in the extreme. Their rooms are usually not more than six or eight feet square, with not a window or even an opening (except a door) for the admission of light. Some of the rooms are entirely surrounded by other rooms, so that no light at all reaches where persons live and spend their days and nights. In a space about fifty yards square I found about one hundred families, composed of from three to ten persons each, living in shanties one story in hight, except in a few instances where tenements are actually built on the tops of others. There is a distance of only three or four feet separating these buildings from each other—not even as convenient as an ordinary three-feet alley. These openings lead in so devious a course that one with difficulty finds his way out again. Thus pent up, not even these paths are purified by currents of fresh air. In one building visited, seventeen families were found upon the ground floor, consisting of from two to seven persons each, one restaurant, and one boarding-house. The second story is a large dance hall, where these people nightly congregate for amusement.

"Nearly all of these people came from Virginia during the rebellion, and some of them propose to return whenever they are assured that they can find work to do there, and will be well treated. It was found that from five to eight dollars per month are paid for the rent of these miserable shanties, except in some instances, where a ground rent of three dollars per month is paid for a little spot covering a few square feet—there some of the more enterprising have erected cabins of their own. These, also, are in equally close proximity to each other, so that it is with difficulty that one can crowd between them.

"On the west side of Fourteenth Street near the same locality, are a large number of small buildings, which, however, are kept in a somewhat more cleanly condition, and are opened to light and ventilation. Here some of the occupants of houses boast of small back yards, but so low and wet are their surfaces that they are a curse rather than a benefit. Filthy water here accumulates, from which, with the advent of warm weather, the seeds of disease must spread among and destroy these wretched people.

"In each of these localities there are no proper privy accomodations, and those that exist are in a leaky and filthy condition generally. Nor can the sanitary laws be properly enforced against delinquents, for they have no means wherewith to pay fines, and a commitment to the work-house is no punishment. I can see no efficient mode of remedying this evil except that scavengers be em-

ployed at the public expense, to visit these localities; though by far
the best remedy would be to require that these buildings be razed to
the ground.

"Under the best sanitary laws that can be enacted, and stringently
enforced, these places can be considered as nothing better than
propagating grounds of crime, disease, and death; and in the case of
a prevailing epidemic, the condition of these localities would be
horrible to contemplate.

"A similarly crowded lot of shanties exists on Rhode Island Avenue, between Tenth and Eleventh Streets, though as to fresh air
and cleanliness, a somewhat better condition of things exists. Here,
in a space some two hundred feet square, two hundred and thirteen
persons reside, mostly known as 'contrabands.' There are several
other places equally crowded within the city limits, which I have not
yet had time to visit and inspect personally; for which purpose I respectfully ask for further time.

"A. C. RICHARDS, SUP'T

"To the Board of Police."

Sojourner, witnessing the afflictions of her people, and desiring
to mitigate their sufferings, found homes and employment for many
in the Northern States, government furnishing transportation for
all. In the winter of 1867, she made three trips from Rochester to a
town about 200 miles south of Richmond, to obtain laborers for
those localities left destitute by the war; but she soon came to see
that this was not the best mode of procedure, as it cost a great
amount of labor, time, and money to locate the young and strong,
leaving the aged and little children still uncared for.

The imagination can scarcely conceive a more harrowing spectacle than the vast multitude, composed of both sexes, and all ages
from helpless infancy to tremulous senility, roaming about, having
no possessions but the bodies which had recently been given them
by a dash of Abraham Lincoln's pen. Surging to and fro, this motley crowd could claim no more of mother earth than sufficed for
standing room, and were liable at any time to be ordered, like Joe,
"to move on."

Thus they were borne upon the waves of society as a wrecked

ship upon the sea, stripped of spar and sail, rudder and compass, tempest tossed upon the black and sullen deep, with no ray of light to illumine its pathway of gloom. The heads of government, seeing and commiserating their hapless state, established what was called the Freedman's Bureau as a measure of relief, and by its orders each ward daily furnished to the refugees 700 loaves of bread, which served to sustain life, but was inadequate to meet the emergency; for civilization has needs which cannot be supplied by bread alone.

It was sad to see the hungry mass stretch forth its hand, seize the proffered loaf, seek a spot where it might be devoured, and idle away the time till another loaf was due. And could the Bureau have ministered to all their wants, would not this mode of life become productive of enormous evils, since the habits it fostered, having been engendered by the system of slavery, needed no such encouragement? This institution was emphatically the necessity of the hour, but neither wisdom nor prudence would advise its continuance.

The race was increasing at a rapid rate, and the drain upon the national treasury would become exhaustive. Still, justice demanded that government take efficient legislative action in the interest of these people, whom the genius of General Butler had denominated contrabands, as some reward for years of uncompensated services. Nations anxiously watching the scales in which this government and its dependent millions must be weighed, waited to render their verdict. Advancement moves with slow and feeble pace. The new hinges upon the old. In obtaining freedom, these people were separated from many things, for which, as yet, they had received no equivalent. Those who had not where to lay their heads thought of the rude cabin once their home, in pleasant contrast with the present couch of earth, canopied by the over-arching sky. Languishing with homesickness, the worst of ailments, they were a striking counterpart of those sorrowing captives who, sitting by the rivers of Babylon, hung their harps upon the willows and wept for remembered joys.

Their coarse food and clothing cost them no thought while in slavery. But in a moment comes a change. Now, all thought and action must be bent upon self support. But from transmitted habits many were powerless to exercise the functions of the brain in planning for the future, and, though they had arrived at man's estate, must be cared for like children. As Sojourner went about the city, she soon came to distinguish these contrabands. They had a dreamy look, taking no note of time; it seemed as if a pause had come in their lives—an abyss, over whose brink they dared not look. 'With so few resources, with beclouded minds, with no education from books or contact with the world, aside from plantation life— strangers in a strange land, hungry, thirsty, ragged, homeless, they were the very impersonation of Despair, humbly holding out her hands in supplication.

Sojourner had known the joys of motherhood—brief joys, for she had been cruelly separated from her babes, and her mistress' children given to occupy the place which nature designed for her own. She had tasted its sorrows, too—such sorrows as Rachel, weeping for her children because they were not, could never feel. She had drained the cup of woe to the very dregs, and its fumes, like liquid fires, had dried the fountain of tears till there were none to flow.

But many years had passed since that season of affliction. The shackles had been removed from her body, and spirit also. Time dissolves the hardest substance—'tis called the great destroyer—it reconstructs as well. As the divine aurora of a broader culture dispelled the mists of ignorance, love, the most precious gift of God to mortals, permeated her soul, and her too-long-suppressed affections gushed from the sealed fountains as the waters of an obstructed river, to make new channels, bursts its embankments and rushes on its headlong course, powerful for weal or woe. Sojourner, robbed of her own offspring, adopted her race. Happy for the individual, good for humanity, when high aspirations emanate from sad experiences!

The forlorn and neglected children who prowled about the city excited her commiseration; for they had neither homes nor employment, and as idleness is the parent of crime, they were becoming exceedingly vicious. As a punishment for misdemeanors, they were sent to the station house, from which, after serving their time, they were released, only to continue the same destructive course. Slavery's teachings had bedimmed their perceptions of right, and rendered them incapable of continued moral effort; for her blighting influence, worse than a millstone about their necks, tended to drag them downward forever and forevermore.

Intelligently appreciating the law of transmitted tendencies, Sojourner looked upon them as sinned against as well as sinning. Knowing that the children were the future nation, and that those of her race would play no unimportant part in that future, she felt the need of enlisting sympathy, either human or superhuman, in their behalf. Aided by Gen. Howard,[17] she held meetings in one of the largest churches of the city, to urge the establishment of industrial schools, remote from the city, where they might be placed and taught to become useful members of community. Had she possessed the power and influence of the humane and philanthropic Gov. Bagley, institutions such as he has recently been instrumental in establishing would have sprung into being, till homeless, neglected children would have been no more.

The past she abhorred, with its coffles, its loaded whips, auction blocks, brutal masters, overseers, and all the fearful horrors accruing from the ownership of man by his fellow-man; the sufferings of the present called out her deepest sympathies; but as she peered toward the future with sibyl eyes, her heart beat loud and fast; for she saw in it all grand possibilities. The angel of emancipation had rolled the stone away from the door of the sepulcher of slavery, and the resurrected millions, bound hand and foot in the grave-clothes of ignorance, bewildered and uncertain, awaited guidance in this transition hour.

Would a Moses appear to remove the bands from wrist and ankle, and with uplifted finger pointing to the pillar of cloud and of promise, lead them forth from this sea of troubles and plant their weary feet upon the Canaan of their desires? Would manna descend from heaven to feed this multitude, who were morally, physically, and intellectually destitute? As neither man nor miracle appeared, Sojourner said, "Lord, let me labor in this vineyard."

But how begin the work of establishing right relations where chaos reigns? Justice must constitute the bottom round in this ladder of progress, up which the race must mount in the struggle to reach higher conditions. How can justice be secured?

As she looked about upon the imposing public edifices that grace the District of Columbia, all built at the nation's expense, she said, "*We helped* to pay this cost. We have been a source of wealth to this republic. Our labor supplied the country with cotton, until villages and cities dotted the enterprising North for its manufacture, and furnished employment and support for a multitude, thereby becoming a revenue to the government. Beneath a burning southern sun have we toiled, in the canebrake and the rice swamp, urged on by the merciless driver's lash, earning millions of money; and so highly were we valued there, that should one poor wretch venture to escape from this hell of slavery, no exertion of man or trained blood-hound was spared to seize and return him to his field of unrequited labor.

"The overseer's horn awoke us at the dawning of day from our half-finished slumbers to pick the disgusting worm from the tobacco plant, which was an added source of wealth. Our nerves and sinews, our tears and blood, have been sacrificed on the altar of this nation's avarice. Our unpaid labor has been a stepping-stone to its financial success. Some of its dividends must surely be ours."

Who can deny the logic of her reasoning? The prophet* of the nineteenth century said, many years ago, that "our nation will yet be obliged to pay sigh for sigh, groan for groan, and dollar for dollar, to this wronged and outraged race." Ah, me! what an awful debt when we consider that every mill of interest will surely be added! Did mothers and wives whose husbands and sons languished and died in Libby and Andersonville ever think of that prophecy? Does this nation realize that the debt is still unpaid? the note not taken up yet?

She knew that the United States owned countless acres of unoccupied land, which by cultivation would become a source of wealth to it. She also saw that it was given to build railroads, and that large reservations were apportioned to the Indians. Why not give a tract of land to those colored people who would rather become independent through their own exertions than longer clog the wheels of government?

It seemed to Sojourner that the money expended upon officials, in just this District alone, to convict and punish these vagabond children, would be ample to provide for them homes with the accessories of church and school-house and all the necessary requirements of civilization. With God's blessing, they might yet become an honor to the country which had so cruelly wronged them. This scheme presented itself to her mind as a divine revelation, and she

---

*Parker Pillsbury.

made haste to lay her plan before the leading men of the government. They heard her patiently, expressed themselves willing to do the people's bidding; but manifested no enthusiasm. She regretted now, as ever, that women had no political rights under government; for she knew that could the voice of maternity be heard in the advocacy of this measure, the welfare, not only of the present generation, but of future ones, would be assured.

As it requires both the male and female element to propagate and successfully rear a family, so the State, being only the larger family, demands both for its life and proper development. As those who had the power to legislate for the carrying out of this measure, regarded it indifferently, and those who would gladly work for its accomplishment lacked political opportunity, some other measure must be adopted. She thought that whatever else had been denied to woman, she had ever been allowed to stand on praying ground, and that through petition she might be able to reach the head and heart of the government, or rather half the head and half the heart, as only in this proportion have they ever been represented in our country's legislation. She therefore dictated the following petition:—

"TO THE SENATE AND HOUSE OF REPRESENTATIVES,
IN CONGRESS ASSEMBLED:—

"*Whereas*, From the faithful and earnest representations of Sojourner Truth (who has personally investigated the matter), we believe that the freed colored people in and about Washington, dependent upon government for support, would be greatly benefited and might become useful citizens by being placed in a position to support themselves: We, the undersigned, therefore earnestly request your honorable body to set apart for them a portion of the public land in the West,[18] and erect buildings thereon for the aged and infirm, and otherwise legislate so as to secure the desired results."

The vitalizing forces of her nature were now fully aroused and deeply earnest. She felt that her life culminated at this point, and that all her previous experiences had been needful to prepare her for this crowning work. Being convinced of the feasibility and justice of this plan, she hastened to present her petition to the public, and solicit signatures. Her first lecture for this object was delivered in Providence, R. I., in Feb., 1870, to a large and appreciative audience.

The Voice of the Press.

"The renowned Sojourner Truth spoke in the town hall last evening, and gave one of her peculiar and forcible appeals, distinguished for native wit, eloquence, and religious pathos. The burden of her message was the urgent necessity for colonizing in the West, on land which she calls upon government to give them, the large number of freed people collected in and around Washington. During the war, at the request of President Lincoln, Sojourner spent much time among these people to do them good. With that clear insight and native good sense for which she is remarkable, she saw that the course pursued by government, in supporting them by charity instead of putting them in the way of sustaining themselves, was working immense mischief. True statesmanship demands that government give them lands in the West, thus paying a little of the great debt we owe this long-oppressed people, while at the same time leading them to support themselves, to enrich the nation, and become useful citizens. Sojourner wants the people to petition Congress to do this work at once. At this very time, as appears by a letter read at the meeting last evening, some of the freedmen are dying of starvation, right in sight of our national capitol. Petitions have been placed in the hands of friends of this movement, and it is hoped every person will sign as soon as opportunity is offered." —S. H., *in Northampton (Mass.) paper.*

From Fall River Papers.

"Sojourner Truth—the colored American Sibyl—is spending a few days in our city, and will gladly welcome any of her old or new friends at the house of Robert Adams, Esq., on Rock Street. She bears her four-score years* with ease, showing no signs of decay, but

---

*Often those who met Truth believed her to be as much as twenty years older than she was; at this time, she was probably in her mid-sixties.

conversing on all familiar topics with a clearness of apprehension that would hardly be expected of one who has passed through the varied unpleasant experiences which have fallen to her lot. Give her a call, and enjoy a half hour with a ripe understanding, and don't forget to purchase her photograph."

"Sojourner Truth—the colored American Sibyl—will speak in the vestry of the Franklin Street Church, on Monday evening. Come and hear an *original*."

"SOJOURNER TRUTH.—Sojourner Truth had a good audience at the Christian Church, last evening, and delivered a very unique and interesting address. Many more would have attended had they been aware how pleasantly the evening would have been spent in company with the aged philosopher. Her theme was the duty of the North to the emancipated negroes. Many of her photographs were purchased. It is not impossible that she may speak again during her stay here."

"Sojourner Truth will speak at the vestry of the First M. E. Church, to-morrow evening, Friday, Oct. 14th, at a quarter before 8 o'clock. This will probably be the last opportunity, at least for some time, that our citizens will have of hearing this interesting and decidedly original character."

"Sojourner Truth had a large audience in the vestry of the First M. E. Church, last evening, and was listened to with interest for somewhat more than an hour. She will remain here a few days longer, at Mr. Robert Adams'."

"SOJOURNER TRUTH.—Your readers will notice that this eminent colored lady will discourse this evening, at the vestry of the First Methodist Church, on Main Street, on various topics. Her utterances at the Franklin Street Church, on Monday evening last, drew out quite an audience, which was exceedingly entertained by her instructive remarks; but as very limited notice was previously given, there was not the attendance from the male sex which she wished to see, as her talk is on a matter that peculiarly interests tax-payers. This ancient saint has given largely of her time to the bettering of

the condition of the freedmen at Washington, and in that capacity
has discovered certain abuses which should be rectified. All who
come to listen will learn how some of the public money goes that is
nominally appropriated to feed the black paupers in Washington.
Her scheme for their improvement is practical, and should be put in
operation at once.

"We hope our friend James Buffington, who has a voice in the
administration of the money of the people, will be present and take
note of her points on this matter. As a nomination here amounts to
an election, he may consider himself in for the next two years, and
can aid immensely in straightening out this abuse. No gang of paupers should be allowed to huddle together like pigs anywhere, and
be fed out of the public funds. Go and hear on the subject.

"Everybody, of course, knows of Sojourner Truth, of her sad early
life as an abject slave under the old laws of New York, until she was
forty years old; of her growth in wisdom which seemed born in her
as an inheritance; of her active benevolences in all directions; of her
shrewd repartees and wise sayings which will go down as proverbs
among the intelligent for coming ages; of her goodness as a nurse to
our sick and wounded soldiers when at an advanced age; of her sharp
logic and pointed satire when warmed up on subjects of interest.

"All these have been set forth by pens of power in description,
and will live in story for coming generations. 'The Lord never hearn
tell on ye,' was her comforting remark to a young clergyman very
much afflicted for fear the women would get their rights. 'Is God
dead, Frederick?' to Douglas, when forecasting the sad fate of his
race in the old slave days. Don't come expecting fine rhetoric, finished grammar, or dictionary pronunciation; but if you want to hear
an earnest soul of eighty or more years, on the borders of the coming world, still young in the graces of Christian charity, and ardent
in the work assigned her, talk of right and justice, and set them forth
with a spirit and skill that learned men might well envy, turn out to-
night. Don't forget that she has photographs of herself for sale—her
only means of support for expenses of travel, livelihood, and a humble home in Michigan—and that while she 'sells the shadow to support the substance,' it will probably be the last time we shall see the
lady among us. Don't forget the hour—one-quarter before 8 o'clock
this evening."

From New Jersey Papers.

"Springfield, Union County, New Jersey, and its Presbyterian Church were honored on Wednesday night by the presence of that lively old negro mummy, whose age ranges among the hundreds—Sojourner Truth—who fifty years ago was considered a crazy woman; who was wont to address street meetings and Garrison abolition conventicles. She was smuggled into the church by some pious radical to give her religious experience; and she did it—rather to the confusion and disgust of the audience. When respectable churches consent to admit to the houses opened for the worship of God every wandering negro minstrel or street spouter who may profess to have a peculiar religious experience, or some grievance to redress, they render themselves justly liable to public ridicule. The effects of our late civil war, which brought many of our divines upon the political rostrum, and converted many of our pulpits into recruiting stations, we fear will not soon be removed.

"Our Springfield correspondent writes of the visit of Sojourner Truth:—

> "'Mislike me not for my complexion,
> The shadowed liv'ry of the burnished sun.'

"'Thus Shakespeare. But we do most decidedly dislike the complexion and everything else appertaining to Mrs. Truth, the radical—the renowned, saintly, liberated, oratorical, pious slave. The superintendent of the Presbyterian Sunday-school, hearing such glowing accounts of her, invited her to speak to his charge. She spoke on the 1st inst., not on religion, but at random, on copperhead Jersey, hypocrites, freemen, woman's rights, etc., till the superintendent was forced to call her to order. She is a crazy, ignorant, repelling negress, and her guardians would do a Christian act to restrict her entirely to private life.'"

"SOJOURNER TRUTH DEFENDED.—Whenever I have heard the State of New Jersey stigmatized, I have always resented its being used as a mark of derision and a jest for scoffers; but a circumstance that occurred last week has proved it a fit land for missionaries to enter with books to enlighten the inhabitants, and purifiers with scourges to correct the people. The village of Springfield, that prides itself on its great age, had the honor of a visitor (no less a personage than Sojourner Truth)—a dear creature, one of the Lord's true servants, who has worked in his vineyard for forty years, and who, at the great age of eighty, instead of taking her ease during the infirmities of old age, feels that as long as the Lord gives her the breath of life she must work for his glory. Her fame went through all the land many years ago, and she numbers among her dearest friends the most intellectual, renowned, and gifted men and women of our land, and many are the weeks she has spent in the homes of those dear to our people. She has held happy converse with our lamented president, and our present one; has spoken in Beecher's Church to thousands, in many of our State capitol buildings, and our nation's senate chamber. Turn from these happy greetings and behold her welcome in New Jersey!—no, not there, but in a small, benighted corner, where the people pride themselves on their being and remaining as a century ago. They were so ignorant a people they knew not they had a great guest, and many had not even heard of Sojourner Truth. Then they had so little good breeding they left during her remarks, interrupting and showing disrespect to old age, which always commands respect. Then to show their ignorance, their lilliputian minds, they write of her as being a crazy woman, an old mummy that ought to be enclosed in an asylum. That is the testimony of Springfield, N. J., to be placed by the side of beautiful letters of cheer, volumes full of well-wishes and blessings from such personages as Lincoln, Gen. Grant, Henry Ward Beecher, Gen. Howard, Sumner, Phillips, Anna Dickinson, Lucretia Mott, &c., &c.,—men and women we all long to meet and take by the hand, and would be rejoiced to call our friends.

> "'By ignorance is pride increased;
> Those most assume who know the least;
> Their own self-balance gives them weight,
> But every other finds them light.'—*Gay's Fables.*

"A New Springfield Correspondent."

"SOJOURNER TRUTH.—Sojourner Truth, now about fourscore years, who has devoted the whole of her time during the last twenty years of her life to the interests of the colored race, and during the late rebellion gave her personal service to the important work of educating the freed men and women in the moral, social, and domestic duties of life, without fee or reward, is now engaged in getting signatures to a petition to Congress for the benefit of a large class of dependent freedmen who may be found around Washington and other places in the South.

"Sojourner Truth is now at her home at Battle Creek, in Michigan, and writes us a letter under date of November 29. She has just returned from an extensive tour through Ohio, Indiana, Illinois, Michigan, Wisconsin, Iowa, Missouri, and Kansas, and wishes to carry her petition, to which she has obtained many signatures, to Washington this winter, and present it personally to Congress. She makes an appeal for a little pecuniary aid to defray the expenses of her journey, and gives information that a narrative of her life will soon be published which will undoubtedly be full of interest, as her life has been an eventful one.

"R. J.
"Orange, N. J."

"Sojourner Truth addressed a good-sized audience at the Unitarian Church on Wednesday evening, Jan. 12. Mr. Clute, in introducing her, said that he had a three-fold pleasure in doing so. First, he was sure the audience would be entertained by her varied experience of more than eighty years. Secondly, the lecturer was a negro, and her presence on the platform was a living argument for the admission of her race to all the privileges of society. Thirdly, the lecturer was a woman who has for many years affirmed that woman's humanity gives her claim to education, labor, and the ballot.

"The lecturer spoke for more than an hour in her usual, humorous, common-sense style. She gave some account of her thoughts when she was a heathen, and said there was no little heathenism in the very heart of the churches to-day. She spoke of the Fatherhood of God, and of his loving care for all his children; of the brotherhood of man and of the duty of men to labor for each other. Her remarks were interspersed with anecdotes fitly illustrating the subject, and had such point and pungency as carried the truth home."

From a Williamsburgh (L. I.) Paper.

"LECTURE OF A COLORED WOMAN.—The female lecturer, styling herself 'Sojourner Truth,' who was for many years a slave, delivered a lecture last evening in the Congregational Church, corner of South Third and Eleventh Streets, Williamsburgh. The lecturer, who is quite aged, commenced by saying that she was born a slave in this State, and resided on the banks of the North River, near Albany, until the time of her emancipation, which took place when she was—twenty-five years of age. During that time she had five different masters, some of whom were very severe, and she related with tears in her eyes the manner in which she had been tied up in the barn, with her clothes stripped from her back, and whipped until the blood stood in pools upon the floor; and scars upon her back were undeniable proofs of her assertion. She had been twice married, and had five children, the oldest being forty years of age. Her husbands and children were torn from her and sold into bondage, the youngest at the age of five years having been taken to Alabama. She said that she never had any learning, and while in bondage was not allowed to hear the Bible or any other books read. Her mother often told her of God, and her impressions were that God was a very large human being, who sat in the skies.

"'About a year previous to my emancipation, I ran away from my master, and went to live with Mr. Wagner; it was here that a change first came over my heart, and I felt that I was a sinner. I prayed to God, and he answered my prayers, and I have experienced his blessings. I said, I really believe I am a sinner, and that Jesus died for me. I had never been to church, and never heard any one say this. I believe my only sin consisted in wishing harm to the white folks; but now I love everybody.'

"After speaking of the condition of the colored race, she spoke of the white people, and their holding human beings in bondage, and asked how it would be with them when summoned before the bar of Judgment to answer for their deeds upon earth. The speaker also narrated the history of her mother-in-law, who was stolen from her native land in Africa and brought to this country and sold into bondage. The lecture was delivered in a simple yet affecting manner."

From Boston Papers.

"EMANCIPATION MEETING.

"Commemoration of the Eighth Anniversary of Negro Freedom in the United States—A Large Gathering and Eloquent Speeches in Tremont Temple, Jan, 1, 1871.

"The eighth anniversary of the emancipation of negro slaves in the United States was commemorated in Tremont Temple last evening by a large gathering and eloquent speeches, under the auspices of the National Association for the Spread of Temperance and Night Schools among the Freed People of the South. The admission was free, and at a comparatively early hour the Temple began to be filled, for 7 o'clock was the time announced for the services to commence, and seldom is there an occasion of more attraction or greater general interest. Every available space of sitting or standing room was crowded. Professor Gardiner was present.

"The platform was occupied by the Tremont Temple choir, the distinguished personages of the evening, such as Rev. J. D. Fulton, Rev. Gilbert Haven,[19] and Rev. L. A. Grimes,[20] and many others, not omitting to mention Sojourner Truth, of Jersey, and William Wells Brown, M. D.,[21] who has in numerous instances taken a leading position among New England's orators, and who has done a great deal to elevate the colored race a grade higher in the strata of civilization. Mr. Brown is president of the National Association above alluded to, and as a matter of course he officiated as chairman of the meeting. The services were opened with the singing of a hymn by the choir, after which Mr. Brown read a portion of the Scriptures. Prayer was then offered by Rev. Mr. Grimes, the choir sang another hymn, and Mr. Brown made a half-hour's address.

"The Rev. J. D. Fulton was the next speaker. He congratulated the meeting upon the work of ennobling and elevating the black race, but while he did so he could not forget the perils which surrounded it in a city like Boston. This emancipation was but the beginning of a big job. Mental emancipation from the chains of ignorance was a felt necessity, and education must be given the black men now. The freedmen of the South without education will be cursed rather than blessed by the ballot. 'I do not believe,' he said, 'in anybody casting a vote in this land that cannot read and write.' (The meeting applauded.) 'Now don't you cheer me,' said Mr. Fulton, 'this is God's night, and I don't want to be cheered.'

"At this juncture there was a movement at the left end of the platform, and Rev. Gilbert Haven and Sojourner Truth appeared. Mr. Fulton turned around to the good old lady and said, indicating the seat he had occupied previous to taking the floor, 'Now, Aunty, you take this easy chair.' (Laughter and applause.) Mr. Fulton— 'Now I do wish you wouldn't do that.' The speaker then concluded his remarks by an earnest advocacy of temperance, and further observations upon education; and at a quarter before eight o'clock left the Temple to take the train for New York."

"Remarks by Rev. Gilbert Haven.

"A collection was then taken up, a hymn sung by the choir, and Rev. Gilbert Haven introduced. He had the misfortune, he said, of coming after the king (referring to Mr. Fulton) and before the queen (referring to Sojourner Truth), and of course a person in that position was of very little account except to get out of the way. But such things were matters of necessity, and he would endeavor to do his best. He dwelt at some length upon the emancipation proclamation and spoke particularly of the happiness manifested by Frederick Douglass upon the occasion of its declaration. The time of this anniversary meeting had been most appropriately chosen. It was fitting that we celebrate this great event upon a Sabbath evening, for in the Bible itself we find that the most sacred festival was on account of the deliverance from the land of bondage. The present situation of affairs must be accepted with all our hearts. If we do not so accept it, there is more danger in ourselves than we are aware of. As to our duty to the South and to the colored people, Mr. Haven said there must be a brotherly feeling everywhere. First, we must assist in Christianizing our emancipated brethren, both white and black, in the South. By so doing we shall be disarmed of our predjudice and hostility. Secondly, we must give them education. There is a passion of thirst for it there, and there are a great many ways of working it out. There's the Institute of Instruction in Washington, and freedmen's societies. But, some way or other, we must put ourselves in connection with the teacher of the South. We need the school system. Thirdly, we must add to churches and schools prohibition. Mr. Haven spoke of the terrible system of intemperance which prevails, and called for the immediate and unconditional extirpation of it by a rigid prohibitory law. They have got to have prohibition down South. The black men are becoming terribly demoralized by rum; and America has got to meet this issue or America goes to ruin. Boston is fast becoming a Sodom and a hell; on every side this demoralization is occurring. There is also work to be done in Boston. We must have a national education and a national prohibition; and one thing more we need, and that is homes, lands for the freedmen. That I shall let my good friend chiefly dwell upon.

"Thus introduced, Sojourner Truth took the stand. She spoke about half an hour, substantially as follows, the piquancy of her remarks being greatly hightened by the inimitable patois, if it may be so called, of her expression:—

"Truths from Sojourner Truth.

"'Well, chilern, I'm glad to see so many together. Ef I am eighty-three years old, I only count my age from de time dat I was 'mancipated. Then I 'gun ter live. God is a fulfillin', an' my lost time dat I lost bein' a slave was made up. W'en I was a slave I hated de w'ite pepul. My mother said to me when I was to be sole from her, "I want to tole ye dese tings dat you will allers know dat I have tole you, for dar will be a great many tings tole you after I sta't out ob dis life inter de world to come." An' I say dis to you all, for here is a great many pepul dat when I step out ob dis existence, dat you will know what you heered ole Sojourn' Truth tell you. I was boun' a slave in the State of Noo Yo'k, Ulster County, 'mong de low Dutch. W'en I was

ten years old, I couldn't speak a word of Inglish, an' hab no eddi-
cati'n at all. Dere's wonder what dey has done fur me. As I tole you
w'en I was sole, my master died, an' we was goin' to hab a auction.
We was all brought up to be sole. My mother, my fader was very ole,
my brudder younger 'en myself, an' my mother took my han'. Dey
opened a canoby ob ebben, an' she sat down an' I an' my brudder sat
down by her, en she says, "Look up to de moon an' stars dat shine
upon you father an' upon you mother when you sole far away, an'
upon you brudders an' sisters, dat is sole away," for dere was a great
number ob us, an' was all sole away befor' my membrance. I asked
her who had made de moon an' de stars, an' she says, "God," an' says
I, Where is God? "Oh!" says she, "chile, he sits in de sky, an' he hears
you w'en you ax him w'en you are away from us to make your
marster an' misteress good, an' he will do it."

   "'When we were sole, I did what my mother told me; I said, O
God, my mother tole me ef I asked you to make my marster an' misteress good, you'd do it, an' dey didn't get good. [Laughter.] Why,
says I, God, mebbe you can't do it. Kill 'em. [Laughter and applause.] I didn't tink he could make dem good. Dat was de idee I
had. After I made such wishes my conscience burned me. Then
I wud say, O God, don't be mad. My marster make me wicked; an'
I of'm thought how pepul can do such 'bominable wicked things an'
dere conscience not burn dem. Now I only made wishes. I used to
tell God this—I would say, "Now, God, ef I was you, an' you was me
[laughter], and you wanted any help I'd help ye;—why done you
help me?" [Laughter and applause.] Well, ye see I was in want, an' I
felt dat dere was no help. I know what it is to be taken in the barn
an' tied up an' de blood drawed out ob yere bare back, an I tell you
it would make you think 'bout God. Yes, an' den I felt, O God, ef I
was you an' you felt like I do, an' asked me for help I would help
you—now why won't you help me? Trooly I done know but God has
helped me. But I got no good marster ontil de las' time I was sole,
an' den I found one an' his name was Jesus. Oh, I tell ye, didn't I fine
a good marster when I use to feel so bad, when I use to say, O God,
how ken I libe? I'm sorely 'prest both widin and widout. W'en God
gi' me dat marster he healed all de wounds up. My soul rejoiced. I
used to hate de w'ite pepul so, an' I tell ye w'en de lobe come in me
I had so much lobe I didn't know what to lobe. Den de w'ite pepul

come, an' I thought dat lobe was too good fur dem. Den I said, Yea, God, I'll lobe ev'ybuddy an' de w'ite pepul too. Ever since dat, dat lobe has continued an' kep' me 'mong de w'ite pepul. Well, 'mancipation came; we all know; can't stop to go troo de hull. I go fur adgitatin'. But I believe dere is works belong wid adgitatin', too. On'y think ob it! Ain't it wonderful dat God gives lobe enough to do Ethiopins to lobe you?

" 'Now, here is de question dat I am here to-night to say. I been to Washin'ton, an' I fine out dis, dat de colud pepul dat is in Washin'tun libin on de gobernment dat de United Staas ort to gi' 'em lan' an' move 'em on it. Dey are libin on de gov'ment, an' dere is pepul takin' care of 'em costin' you so much, an' it don't benefit him 'tall. It degrades him wuss an' wuss. Therefo' I say dat these people, take an' put 'em in de West where you ken enrich 'em. I know de good pepul in de South can't take care of de negroes as dey ort to, case de ribils won't let 'em. How much better will it be for to take them culud pepul an' give 'em land? We've airnt lan' enough for a home, an' it would be a benefit for you all an' God would bless de hull ob ye for doin' it. Dey say, Let 'em take keer of derselves. Why, you've taken dat all away from 'em. Ain't got nuffin lef'. Get dese culud pepul out of Washin'tun off ob de gov'ment, an' get de ole pepul out and build dem homes in de West, where dey can feed themselves, and dey would soon be abel to be a pepul among you. Dat is my commission. Now adgitate them pepul an' put 'em dere; learn 'em to read one part of de time an' learn 'em to work de udder part ob de time.'

"At this moment a member in the audience arose and left, greatly to the disturbance of the lady, who could with difficulty make herself heard.

" 'I'll hole on a while,' she said. 'Whoever is agoin' let him go. When you tell about work here, den you have to scud.* [Laughter and applause.] I tell you I can't read a book, but I can read de people. [Applause.] I speak dese tings so dat when you have a paper come for you to sign, you ken sign it.'

"This was the last speech, and the services of the eighth anniversary concluded at half-past nine o'clock with the pronouncing of the

---

*To run quickly and easily.

benediction by Rev. Mr. Haven, a general hand-shaking and con-
gratulating on the platform, and a discussion with Sojourner Truth,
whom her questioners found as apt and keen at repartee as she had
proved herself to be while in attendance upon the Woman's Bazar
last week."—*Boston Post.*

For many years she has been blessed with the friendship and
sympathy of the widely known and justly revered Rev. Gilbert
Haven, whom she met during her last visit in Boston. At this time
he made her a present of *Zion's Herald*, a paper of extensive circulation, to the reading of which she listens with great pleasure.

"WOMAN'S SUFFRAGE ASSOCIATION.—This morning's session of
the Woman's Right's Convention was opened at ten o'clock. After
the transaction of some business, Col. T. W. Higginson, of Newport, was introduced to the audience, mostly composed of ladies,
whose number increased as the hour advanced. The main object of
the speaker was to rally the women of our State and induce them to
come forward in the defense of their own rights. As one result of female eloquence, he said, Mrs. Lucy Stone[22] had succeeded in melt-
ing the heart of the chairman of the judiciary committee in our
general assembly. At the conclusion of Col. Higginson's address a
string of resolutions was introduced bearing on the question of
Woman's Suffrage. Sojourner Truth, who was sitting on the platform, was invited to speak, and made one of her characteristic addresses, favoring a grant of land to the freedmen of Washington, and
such a provision of educational privileges as will tend to the elevation of this unfortunate class.

"The great speech of the morning was made by Mrs. Livermore,[23] of Boston, whose statement of facts was better than any labored argument. Her account of the restricted female suffrage in
Kansas was highly interesting and instructive. The women in that
State are allowed to vote in matters pertaining to public schools, and
they use their privileges for the promotion of good education, and
really out-wit the men in carrying their points. In the territory of
Wyoming, where female suffrage is secured, the women have joined
en masse in favor of temperance and morality, defeating the vile
demagogues who strove for office, and electing persons whose character and principles are a guaranty of public order and security."

Another journal speaks of Sojourner Truth's presence at this meeting thus:—

"Mrs. Paulina W. Davis[24] said they had a venerable lady on the platform who commenced her life a slave, was forty years in that condition, and since that time had labored for the emancipation of her race.

"Sojourner Truth, who seems to carry her weight of years very heartily, said she was somewhat pleased to come before them to bear testimony, although she had a limited time—only a few minutes— but as many friends wanted to hear Sojourner's voice, she thought she would accept the offer. She spoke when the spirit moved her— not when the people moved her, but when the spirit moved her— for when she was limited to a few minutes, the people moved her. She was in the woman movement, for she was a woman herself. The Friend said that woman ought to have her rights for her own benefit, she ought to have them, not only for her own benefit, but for the benefit of the whole creation, not only the women, but all the men on the face of the earth, for they were the mothers of them. Therefore she ought to have her God-given right, and be the equal of men, for she was the resurrection of them. There was another question which lay near her heart, and that was the condition of the poor colored people around Washington, remnants of the slavery which was ended by the war. Sojourner earnestly urged that land be given to these poor people in order that they might be made self-supporting, and concluded her remarks by saying, in her naive way, that she would stop before she was stopped."

"THE AMERICAN SIBYL.—Sojourner Truth, whom Mrs. Stowe has honored with the title of 'The American Sibyl,' is spending a few days in our city, and we hope our citizens will have the pleasure of listening to her graphic descriptions of the condition of the freedmen of the city of Washington, where she spent three years during the war in nursing and teaching the poor soldiers and the emancipated people who followed the army. She has been there again recently, endeavoring in her zeal and goodness of heart to help the aged colored people to find comfortable homes in some rural district. She has spoken in nearly all the cities, and has just come from Fall River, where she spoke in two of the churches to large and enthusiastic audiences, who listened with delight to the words of wit and wisdom which fell from the lips of the ancient colored philosopher. She was, as is well known, a slave in New York the first forty years of her life, and since her emancipation and remarkable conversion to Christianity, she has labored unceasingly for the good of her race and for oppressed humanity everywhere."

"PERSONAL.—'Sister Sojourner Truth' was in town yesterday and visited the Woman Suffrage Bazaar, where she could not resist the movings of the spirit to say a few words upon her 'great mission,' which now is to 'stir up the United States to give the colored people about Washington, and who are largely supported by charity, a tract of land down South, where they can support themselves.' She don't believe in keeping them paupers, and thinks they have earned land enough for white people in past days to be entitled to a small farm apiece themselves. She says she is going to accomplish her mission in this respect before she dies, and she wants an opportunity to address the people of Boston and to get up petitions to Congress in its favor. She means to 'send tons of paper down to Washington for them spouters to chaw on.' Sojourner believes in women's voting, and thinks the men are very pretentious in denying them the right. Still she thinks there has been a great change for the better in this respect the last few years. She is rather severe on the sterner sex, and asks, by way of capping her argument in favor of her sex: 'Did Jesus ever say anything against women? Not a word. But he did speak awful hard things against the men. You know what they were. And he knew them to be true. But he didn't say nothing 'gainst de women.' And solacing herself with this reflection the old heroine retired to admire the beautiful bouquets in the flower department of the Fair."

"Sojourner Truth, now in her eighty-third year, gave a thrilling address at the Fair—in the Phillips' Street Church (Rev. Mr. Grime's) on Monday evening. It was unique, witty, pathetic, sensible; and, aged as she is, was delivered with a voice that, in volume and tone, was equally remarkable and striking.

"Rev. Norwood Damon[25] succeeded her in a speech of great eloquence and power. The subject was the dependent condition and the hinderances to education of the blacks in Washington and the South, and the duty of the government to open avenues and furnish inducements to a better civilization and manhood. The venerable Sojourner will renew the subject at a public meeting in Rev. Mr. Grime's church this evening."

"The first forty years of her life were spent in slavery in the State of New York. She became free when slavery was abolished in that State, and has devoted the remainder of her life to the cause of the freedom of her race. She is now at this advanced age engaged in a mission for their welfare. She wants the government, instead of feeding them as now, to put them on land of their own, as it does the Indians, and teach them to work for themselves. Unless this be done, she thinks the jails and penitentiaries will have to be increased. It is the only way to prevent a large amount of misery, degradation and crime in the present and future generations. She carries with her three small books in which she has inscribed the autographs of nearly all the eminent people in America. This she proposes sometime to have printed in *fac similes*. She calls them the 'Book of Life.'"

From N.Y. and Philadelphia Papers.

"SOJOURNER TRUTH.—Sojourner Truth was born a slave in the family of Colonel Hardenburgh, near Swatakill, in Ulster County, New York, and sold away from her family when about ten years old. She remained in Ulster County forty years, a slave, and had, during that time, numerous owners. She obtained her freedom under the Act of Emancipation in the State of New York. After her freedom she lived in the city of New York a number of years, and in Massachusetts, at Northampton, about twenty years. During all this time she traveled through every section of the country, laboring to promote the welfare of her race. She worked without fee or reward. She then went to Michigan, where she has resided since that time. She has devoted her life to the interest of her suffering race. During the war, under President Lincoln's administration, she spent her time among the freedmen in and around Washington, teaching the women how to perform their domestic duties. She is now over eighty years, and has secured a little home at Battle Creek, in

Michigan. The past summer she purchased a barn, and had it converted into a comfortable dwelling-house. It is encumbered with a mortgage of nine hundred dollars, and to clear this place of debt, she is now on a visit to her friends, and proposes to visit President Grant, at Washington. Sojourner is remarkably active and bright for a person of her age. She has endured much hardship, and deserves the aid of her friends."

—Frank Leslie's Illustrated Paper.

"SOJOURNER TRUTH.—This remarkable colored lady addressed rather a small audience in the Methodist Church on Tuesday evening. It was small because it had not been sufficiently advertised; hence, comparatively few knew of her presence. Sojourner is a perfect type of her race, uneducated, but possessed of strong common sense. She was a slave forty years of her life, and when liberated, and an attempt was made to educate her, she declares she could never get beyond her a, b, abs. She is now eighty-three years old, and has been a public speaker for a great many many years. She spoke in Phœnixville some twenty years ago, in the old M. E. Church, and has ever since been anxious to do so again. In her address that evening she stated that she had in her wanderings inquired now and then concerning her friend Elijah F. Pennypacker,[26] because she knew so long as he lived she would if she visited this section have a place wherever she could 'put the sole of her foot.' She spoke in high terms of the Methodist people of West Chester, and especially of their minister, the Rev. Mr. Best, and said he wasn't like the majority of preachers, who wasn't in their element unless they were 'spouting,' but he was satisfied to sit at her feet and to learn the truth as she knew it. Sojourner was in the anti-slavery movement in its palmiest days, and was associated with the shining lights of that struggle, and now that the wildest dreams of those she considered enthusiastic have been abundantly realized, she has turned her attention to the amelioration of her race, and considers her mission to be the establishment of a home for old and feeble colored people in the far West, for which purpose she is endeavoring to arouse public sentiment and to interest the government.

"On Thursday afternoon she addressed the ladies of the neighborhood in the Friends' meeting-house, at the corner stores."

"SOJOURNER TRUTH.—Earnest, self-sacrificing devotion to principle, especially when its scope is to benefit humanity, is always an object of the deepest interest, whatever the race, color or condition of the individual exemplifying it. This fact explains why a large and highly respectable audience assembled last night in the Friends' Meeting House, on Lombard Street, and listened with the deepest attention to the utterances of an old colored woman, who was a slave for forty years. That old colored woman was so earnest, so fearless and untiring a laborer for her race during the long contest between freedom and slavery that she is known and loved by thousands in every State in the Union. Very black, and without much education, she has remarkable faith in God, wonderfully clear perceptions of moral right and wrong, the most devoted love for the poor and needy, and the most untiring determination to carry forward plans for the amelioration of the condition of her race.

"She last night gave startling pictures of the degradation and suffering among the colored people at Washington and elsewhere; showed that it would pay the nation to transform those paupers into industrious, moral citizens, and concluded by detailing her plan for doing that work, and stating the objections made to it. She stated that she desired to hold a number of meetings here to induce the colored people who are in better circumstances to do something to further the best interests of the unfortunate of their race.

"When she had concluded, Mr. John Needles stated that the old lady paid her expenses in her present work by selling her photograph, whereupon a number of persons went forward and bought copies.

"Sojourner Truth jocularly denies that she ever nursed General Washington, but she says she 'has done quit' telling people how old she is. 'Sometimes folks just quit growing and stop as they is, and I specs that I has jis quit growing old and keeps on de same all de time.' This is Sojourner's explanation of her remarkable longevity."

A Pennsylvania paper thus mentions another of her meetings:—

"Old Sojourner Truth was here last Thursday night and preached a good sermon in the Methodist Church. A tremendous crowd assembled to hear and see her, and were all pleased with her address and the manner in which it was delivered."

From Rochester Papers.

"A LECTURE BY SOJOURNER TRUTH.—This aged negress lectured in Rochester, N. Y., recently, and the *Democrat and Chronicle* gives this account of her effort:—

"'Her appearance reminds one vividly of *Dinah* in "Uncle Tom's Cabin." A white handkerchief was tied closely about her head and she wore spectacles, but this was the only indication of her extreme age. Her voice is strong, has no touch of shrillness, and she walked about as hale and hearty as a person of half her years. She said her object was to arouse attention to the wants of the freedmen. Their condition at Washington was pitiful. No work could be found for them, and their children were growing up in ignorance. She described the treatment they had received during the war, even after they were freed. "The poor creeters were heaped together" with no food but a ration of bread. Children were taken away from their mothers, and when the latter complained, they were thrust into the guard-house. She went among them, and when she told them they were free, they did not understand her. After drawing a vivid picture of the sufferings of the freedmen and their unfortunate condition, even at the present time, she said: "You ask me what to do for dem? Do you want a poor old creeter who do' no how to read to tell edecated people what to do? I give you de hint, and you ought to know what to do. But if you don't, I kin tell you. De government hab given land to de railroads in de West; can't it do as much for these poor creeters? Let 'em give 'em land and an outset, and hab teachers learn 'em to read. Den they can be somebody. Dat's what I want. You owe it to dem, because you took away from dem all dey earned and made 'em what they are. You take no interest in de colored people. I was forty years a slave in de State of New York, and was 'mancipated 'long wid de odder culered people of the State.

"'You are de cause of de brutality of these poor creeters. For you're de children of those who enslaved dem. Dat's what I want to say. I wish dis hall was full to hare me. I don't want to say anything agin Anna Dickinsin because she is my friend, but if she come to talk here about a woman you know nothing about, and no one knows whether there was such a woman* or not, you would fill dis

---

*Miss Dickinson's lecture upon Joan of Arc.

place. You want to hear nonsense. I come to tell something which you ought to listen to. You are ready to help de heathen in foreign lands, but don't care for the heathen right about you. I want you to sign petitions to send to Washington. Dey say there dey will do what de people want. The majority rules. If dey want anything good dey git it. If dey want anything not right dey git it too. You send these petitions, and those men in Congress will have something to spout about. I bin to hear 'em; could make nothing out of what dey said, but if dey talk about de colored people I will know what dey say. Send a good man wid de petitions, one dat will not turn de other side out when he gits to Washington. Let de freedmen be emptied out in de West; gib 'em land an' an outset; teach 'em to read, an' den dey will be somebody. Dat's wat I want to say.'"

"SOJOURNER TRUTH.—Let no one fail to hear the lecture of this re-markable woman in Corinthian Hall, on Thursday evening of this week. Her subject is the condition of the freed colored people de-pendent on the government. Having spent several years among them, she knows whereof she speaks. She was for forty years a slave in the State of New York. Wholly uneducated, her eloquence is that of nature, inspired by earnest zeal in her Heaven-appointed mission. She speaks to crowded houses everywhere; let Rochester give her a cordial reception."

"SOJOURNER TRUTH.—The lecture of this remarkable colored woman comes off at Corinthian Hall, on Thursday evening, 4th inst. The lecturer is a child of nature, gifted beyond the common measure, witty, shrewd, sarcastic, with an open, broad honesty of heart, and unbounded kindness.

"Wholly untaught in the schools, she is herself a study for the philosophers, and a wonder to all. Her natural powers of observa-tion, discrimination, comparison, and intuition are rare indeed, and only equaled by her straightforward common sense and earnest practical benevolence. She is always sensible, always suggestive, al-ways original, earnest, and practical, often eloquent and profound. Her lecture will be in behalf of her people, and whoever would be edified, entertained, and even amused, without frivolity, would do well to be present."

"SOJOURNER TRUTH.—This celebrated colored woman spoke at Lyceum Hall, Sunday evening, to an audience of several hundred people. Her subject was her own experience, more particularly her religious experience. She is now about eighty-three years old, though she looks much younger. She is unable to read or write, and in her manner and style is perfectly natural and original. She acts and speaks with the simplicity and innocence of a child, and seems to have nothing to conceal. Her motives she speaks out without hesitation. Her religious experience was very beautiful, and was told in a style that defies imitation. To be appreciated it must be heard, for nobody can repeat it. Her religion is of an exceedingly practical character, and consists in doing good to others. 'How can you expect to do good to God,' she asked, 'unless you first learn to do good to each other'? In regard to God, she says she feels that he is all around her; that we live in him as the fishes live in the sea.

"Speaking of death, she compared it—her countenance fairly lighting up with emotion—to stepping out of one room into another, stepping out into the light. 'Oh,' said she, 'won't that be glorious!'"

"Sojourner Truth Talks to Ladies.

"Sojourner spoke to a company of ladies at Association Hall, on Wednesday afternoon. She portrayed in forcible language the vice and degradation in which the war has left the poor blacks. Ignorant and debased, they cannot be made to understand that they are responsible human beings, but continue the debased practices that marked their slave life. She endeavored to enlist the sympathies of her hearers in behalf of the black women of the South, and related many incidents connected with her efforts to find homes for them in the West. She had succeeded in providing for a hundred in this manner. At the conclusion of her address the ladies present took Sojourner by the hand and gave her pecuniary aid as well as words of encouragement."

From a Syracuse Paper.

"Sojourner Truth.

"To the Editor of the Syracuse Journal:—

"It affords me great pleasure to announce to the Christian people of Syracuse that Sojourner Truth is in this city, and will address the people upon the 'Condition of the South,' to-morrow (Friday) evening, at 7½ o'olock.

"This remarkable woman at the age of eighty years is as eloquent as ever, and all who desire to see and hear her should take this opportunity, which will probably be the last one afforded in this city.

"The officers and pastor of the Fourth Presbyterian Church have kindly proffered their fine audience room, which is so central that it will doubtless be filled very early in the evening.

"Sojourner Truth is too well known to need any endorsements, but I was greatly pleased yesterday to read that of the martyr president—so characteristic of Lincoln—'For Aunty.'

"Sojourner Truth—let the Christian people hear her.

"Yours, truly, A. F. B."

From Battle Creek Papers.

"First of August.—The colored people of Battle Creek and vicinity will observe the 39th anniversary of the emancipation of the slaves of the British West Indies by a picnic at St. Mary's Lake, interspersed with boat riding, 'swinging in the lane,' &c. W. Sweeney has been invited to deliver the oration of the day, followed by 'Aunt Sojourner Truth' and others. The festivities of the day will be concluded by a grand Grant and Wilson club ball, at Stuart Hall, under the immediate supervision of the officers of the club. G. Long is the chairman of the committee of arrangements.

"Sojourner Truth asserts that if ever the Augean stables* of our political temple are to be cleared, it must be done by woman, and

---

*In Greek mythology, the filthy stables that King Augeas commanded Hercules to clean, which he did by diverting two rivers to flow through them.

that it never will be clean until she is admitted to full fellowship therein.

"This well-known and venerable old lady called to see us Thursday afternoon and to subscribe for the *Journal*. She leaves for Ohio in a few days to lecture upon her favorite topic, that of providing a home for the colored people in and about Washington by granting them a tract of land in the West. Sojourner has been stumping for Grant, and says that if such a strange occurrence as the election of Greeley should happen, she will remove to Canada."—*Battle Creek Journal*.

"Republican Meeting—Sojourner Truth.

"On Tuesday evening, Sojourner Truth addressed the people of Hillsdale upon political topics at the court-house. The attendance was immense, not half the throng were able to get seats, and hundreds went away without even gaining admittance. The old lady was somewhat 'scattering in her remarks but she kept firing away, and occasionally a winged duck went out of the crowd, shrieking. The principal points touched were the slanders against President Grant, the inconsistent relations assumed by Greeley,[27] Sumner, Blair, and others, and the duties of the colored voters. The audience, in the best humor, applauded and cheered the speaker.

"Sojourner Truth, on the Saturday before the recent election, appeared before the Board of Registration, in the third ward where she resides, and claimed the right to have her name entered upon the list of electors. Upon being refused, she repaired to the polls on election day in the same ward and again asserted her right to the ballot. She was politely received by the authorities in both instances, but did not succeed in her effort, though she sustained her claim by many original and quaintly put arguments. Sojourner states that she learned one thing by her visit to the polls on the 5th inst. She verily thought before that day that a literal pole was erected to designate the voting place, and she asked the bystanders to point it out. Her astonishment on being undeceived, as described to us by her own lips and in her characteristic style, is peculiarly amusing. It is Sojourner's determination to continue the assertion of her right, until she gains it."—*Battle Creek Journal*.

From Detroit Papers.

"SOJOURNER TRUTH.

"A veteran worker—her 'mission'—the colored paupers about Washington and what to do with them.

"For several days past, Sojourner Truth—the 'Libyan Sibyl,' as Mrs. Stowe has aptly termed her—has been the guest of Mrs. Nanette B. Gardner, on Howard Street, where many friends, and strangers as well, have called to see and converse with this veteran worker in the cause of her own race. Already past fourscore years and ten, she yet maintains a constitution and mind unimpaired, and has an amount of vigor that betokens a 'green old age' indeed. Those who have before heard her lectures, will doubtless remember well the strong, and yet well-modulated voice, and the characteristic expressions in which she delivers her addresses, as well as the pith and point of her spicy sentences.

"To all calling upon her, she asks the question, 'Don't you want to write your name in de Book of Life?' to which query, the counter one in relation to the same 'Book of Life,' is generally put, and Sojourner is usually gratified by the chirography of her visitor, in some manner, according to the pleasure of the writer. The book in question contains scores on scores of names, of different individuals throughout the country, including many persons of note, senators, authors, politicians, etc. Foremost in the list is Lucretia Mott's,[28] who signs herself a 'co-laborer in the cause of our race.' Also that of Senator Revel, of Mississippi, of Senators Morrill, Pomeroy, Henry Wilson, of Massachusetts, Patterson, of New Hampshire, and numerous others.

"Among the first and most treasured is that of the late President Lincoln, who has inscribed in his hurried style, 'For Aunty Sojourner Truth. A. Lincoln, October 29, 1864.' From President Grant, who, she declares, 'was in a most drefful hurry to put down his name,' on being asked to write in the 'Book of Life;' written in his hurried manner, are the lines, 'Sojourner Truth. U. S. Grant, March 31, 1870.' There are letters from Gerritt Smith, Wm. Lloyd Garrison, *et id genus omne*, and also a few lines each from Vice President Colfax, Theodore Tilton,[29] Mrs. Elizabeth Tilton, and many others. Sojourner has 'views' as well as others, and does not hesitate to promulgate them. She is in most respects radical, and believes in the temperance movement, woman suffrage, and has no faith whatever in the 'New Departure' movement, as announced of late in the main plank in the Democratic platform. The constant and repeated inquiry made by visitors, as to her age, she considers as somewhat trying, as it is what she has done and is to do, that she considers of the most importance. In connection with this, she mentions that when in Brooklyn last spring Theodore Tilton called upon her, and in the course of conversation proposed that he should write her life, a proposition which did not meet her views, and which she did not accordingly accept, but replied in effect that she expected to live a long time yet, and was going to accomplish 'lots' before she died, and didn't want to be 'written up' at present.

"Sojourner calls Battle Creek her home, but as she is constantly on the move, she visits that place but seldom. Her great object, she says, in visiting this city and others, is to 'stir up' the people and interest them in her long-desired object of procuring a home for the aged and infirm—particularly colored people—who are now in and around Washington, and wholly dependent upon the government for support.

"Sojourner is to remain a short time only in Detroit, going from here westward on the same mission which induced her to come here. In the course of her travels she intends visiting Kansas, in order to prospect the land."

"About a year ago, Sojourner commenced her lectures in behalf of this object, in Providence, since which time she has lectured in many towns and cities throughout the country. Concerning this, she says that not much encouragement is given her, except the constant adjuration to talk to the people, and 'stir 'em up,' and adds, 'why don't you stir 'em up? as tho' an old body like myself could do all the stirring.'

"In relation to the subject, she states that there are hundreds of colored people in the city of Washington, who, from being cared for, and clothed, and fed by the government, have become apathetic and indifferent, and all they care for is to lead the hum-drum, hand-to-mouth existence that calls for no action on their part. Hundreds of children are brought up in a shiftless manner, and, believing that the government will provide for them, they help swell the constantly increasing number of paupers. Without friends or homes, they are sent to some of the numerous asylums in Washington which are provided for them, and thus manage to exist, but have no thought or care as to how they are to do hereafter. When urged to go North, away from Washington, the invariable reply, at least of nearly all of the able-bodied men in particular is, 'What fo' I go way? gubernment feed me, gib me close, I's doin' well enuff,' and so say they all, or at least a great part of them.

"That a new order of things may be established, Sojourner proposes to excite such an interest as shall not fail in the end to accomplish her purpose.

"As showing what a large number are fed at government expense during the winter, at least when there is little or no work, she states that last season there were from 600 to 700 loaves of bread given daily in each ward, to the colored people, who had in many cases only this to depend upon for sustenance. The following extract from a letter written by Mrs. C. A. F. Stebbins, to the editor of the *National Standard*, shows the condition of things then existing, and which is no better at the commencement of each winter, and, as Sojourner claims, is even growing worse:—

"To the Editor of the National Standard:—

" 'There could be no wider possible gulf between Dives and Lazarus, in the day when the impoverished and despised craved the crumbs which fell from the rich man's table, than here this very day in the court center of the republic, where women are starving for bread, while after all the regular nourishing meals of the day, evening tables are heaped high with luxuries from every clime, and hundreds are invited to share, but they are the hundreds who have plenty upon their own boards at home. . . . .

" 'I am thankful, dear *Standard*, that I do not believe the Dives of Washington city will ever go to the burning gulf as did Dives in the parable; or that they will ever lack for a kind and tender hand to administer the cup of cold water in the future world; but I cannot say, in the turning and constant revolutions of the wheel, that I believe all will be so fortunate in this, for experience in the valley of humility saves, no doubt, some bitter regret, and necessitates reflections on wasted opportunities which may lead to the realization that all are brothers, and human wants are ever the same.'

"Sojourner proposes to solicit government aid, in the way of having some portion of the as yet unoccupied lands of the West donated for the purpose as set forth in the petition first mentioned, and there to have suitable buildings erected, and schools established where the now dependent thousands of colored people may go, and not only attain an independence for themselves, but become educated and respectable citizens, instead of the 'trash'—as she denominates the humbug idlers in Washington—which their dependence on government aid and bounty renders them.

"Sojourner intends remaining in Detroit several days longer, during which time, if a hall or suitable place can be provided, she will give a lecture on the subject described, and will doubtless attract even more than on the occasion of her last appearance in Detroit, in '68."—*Detroit Post.*

"Sojourner Truth.

"This remarkable woman, born a slave in the State of New York more than eighty years ago, and emancipated in 1827, will speak in the lecture room of the Unitarian Church, corner of Shelby Street and Lafayette Avenue, on Monday evening, to any who will choose to hear her. Her lecture will be highly entertaining and impressive. She is a woman of strong religious nature, with an entirely original eloquence and humor, possessed of a weird imagination, of most grotesque but strong, clear mind, and one who, without the aid of reading or writing, is strangely susceptible to all that in thought and action is now current in the world. At the antislavery and women's-rights meetings she has been one of the chief attractions, and her shrewd good sense, mixed with oddities of speech and whimsical illustrations, never fail of producing a sympathetic interest as well as exciting the curiosity of the audience. Her life has been one of extreme vicissitudes, and a great portion of it full of hardship. She has been a true and eloquent friend of her race, and a practical and efficient counselor and assistant in their moral and religious training.

Her work in the freedmen's camps at Washington and in Virginia, during the war, was very valuable and much esteemed. She was a staunch friend of Mr. Lincoln, and he gave her many words of encouragement and praise. We advise our friends to attend her 'lecture,' at the Unitarian Church, if they desire to be instructed, amused, and gratified by one of the most original, if, indeed, not one of the most marvelous, persons of the time. All she does and says is, as she believes, inspired by the Almighty, and she connects with his direct agency the events and circumstances which surround and control her. She now resides at Battle Creek, Michigan."—*Detroit Post.*

In a notice of the lecture the *Post* said:—

"Sojourner mentioned that the Rev. Gilbert Haven, of Boston, had volunteered to take charge of all the petitions signed and forward them to Congress in due form, that they might be presented before Congress in such a way as to demand both attention and action. She hoped to find some one, among those assembled to hear her lecture, who would also aid her in this respect. The Rev. Charles Foote, chaplain of the house of Correction, thereupon offered to collect and forward all petitions which should be signed, to Washington, which offer was thankfully accepted by the lecturer.

"After the lecture several of those interested went upon the platform and interviewed Sojourner, to all of whom she gave a cordial welcome, and conversed in her characteristic style."

From the N.Y. Tribune

"SOJOURNER TRUTH AT WORK.

"TO THE EDITOR OF THE TRIBUNE:—

"SIR: Seeing an item in your paper about me, I thought I would give you the particulars of what I am trying to do, in hopes that you would print a letter about it and so help on the good cause. I am urging the people to sign petitions to Congress to have a grant of land set apart for the freed people to earn their living on, and not be dependent on the government for their bread. I have had fifty petitions printed at my own expense, and have been urging the people of the Eastern States for the past seven months. I have been crying out in the East, and now an answer comes to me from the West, as you will see from the following letter. The gentleman who writes it I have never seen or heard of before, but the Lord has raised him up to help me. Bless the Lord! I made up my mind last winter, when I saw able men and women taking dry bread from the government to keep from starving, that I would devote myself to the cause of getting land for these people, where they can work and earn their own living in the West, where the land is so plenty. Instead of going home from Washington to take rest, I am traveling around getting it before the people.

"Instead of sending these people to Liberia, why can't they have a colony in the West? This is why I am contending so in my old age. It is to teach the people that this colony can just as well be in this country as in Liberia. Everybody says this is a good work, but nobody helps. How glad I will be if you will take hold and give it a good lift. Please help me with these petitions. Yours truly,

"Sojourner Truth.
"Florence, Mass., Feb. 13, 1871.

"P. S. I should have said that the Rev. Gilbert Haven of Boston is kindly aiding me in getting petitions signed, and will receive all petitions signed in Massachusetts and send them to Congress. S. T."

"Topeka, Kansas, Dec. 31, 1870.

"Sojourner Truth.—*Dear Madam:* I know so much of you by reputation, and venerate and love so much your character, that I am induced to write this. I say I know so much of you, which is true, but it is only by report, as I have never had the pleasure of meeting you yet. My object in writing this is to ask and earnestly request that you make our town a visit. I would very much like to have you come to my house and make it your home as long as you can be contented. If you will say you will come, I will send you the price of your railroad fare and enough to pay additional expenses. Please let me hear from you, and, if possible, convey the good intelligence that you will come and see us. Yours, very respectfully,

"B. M. S."

"Sojourner Truth in Springfield.

"Those who remember Mrs. Stowe's graphic sketch of 'Sojourner Truth, the Libyan *Sibyl*,' in the *Atlantic* some years ago, will be interested to see and hear her. She is now visiting at Dr. Church's on Elm Street, for a few days, and will address an audience at Institute Hall, to-night, on her chosen subject, the sufferings of the old colored people and children in Washington, and how to relieve them. She is one of the most original and effective speakers, though an unlettered woman, and all her early life a slave in New York. She is now between seventy and eighty years old, and has outlived many of her thirteen children, but her eye is not dim nor her natural force abated in proportion to her years, and her deep, powerful voice has the same effect as formerly in moving an audience. She says, however, that this is the last time she shall speak in Massachusetts; she is now on her way to a friend of hers and her cause in Kansas, and at her age she never expects to return here. Her object in holding meetings is, not to raise money, but to stir up the people to petition Congress to show humanity to the old and helpless of her race. She has spent much time in Washington, and knows by observation the misery of the colored people there, and she wants Congress to provide a tract of land for them in some Western State and remove them to it, where they can live frugally and support themselves, instead of depending upon charity at Washington. We hope our citizens will avail themselves of this opportunity to see and hear one of the most remarkable women of our time—a true sibyl, as Mrs. Stowe calls her, but a Christian sibyl, and more devoted to good words and works than to obscure predictions. Her book of autographs contains those of Abraham Lincoln, Gen. Grant, Mr. Garrison, and a great many other eminent men and women, living or dead, and is a curious memento of her life."

"Sojourner Truth's Lecture

"At Franklin Hall, last evening, was in the main an exhortation to all interested in the elevation of the blacks to petition the authorities at Washington for land out West whereon to locate the surplus freedmen, and let them earn their own living, which she argued would be cheaper and better for the government than to care for them in any other way. Her matter and manner were simply indescribable, often straying far away from the starting point; but each digression was fraught with telling logic, rough humor, or effective sarcasm. She thought she had a work to do, and had considerable faith in what she was accomplishing; but she said to her audience, 'With all your opportunities for readin' and writin', you don't take hold and do anything. My God, I wonder what you are in the world for!' She had infinite faith in the influence which the majority had with Congress and believed that whatever they demanded, good or bad, Congress would grant; hence she was working to make majorities. She leaves the East soon never to return, and goes to Kansas where the Lord had plainly called her by prompting a man whom she had never seen or heard of to invite her and pay her expenses. Her enthusiasm over the prospect was unbounded, and she said that, like the New Jerusalem, if she didn't find the West all she had expected, she would have a good time thinking about it. A good deal of sound orthodox theology was mingled with her discourse, as well as a description of her visit to the White House, and the reformation she effected in the Washington horse-car system. The whole was followed by a valedictory song in true plantation style. A large and interested audience was present to get the benefit of her remarks."

"Her views on the question of woman's dress and the prevailing fashions are interesting. They are substantially these: 'I'm awful hard on dress, you know. Women, you forget that you are the mothers of creation; you forget your sons were cut off like grass by the war, and the land was covered with their blood; you rig yourselves up in panniers and Grecian-bend backs and flummeries; yes, and mothers and gray-haired grandmothers wear high-heeled shoes and humps on their heads, and put them on their babies, and stuff them out so that they keel over when the wind blows. O mothers, I'm ashamed of ye! What will such lives as you live do for humanity? When I saw them women on the stage at the Woman's Suffrage Convention, the other day, I thought, What kind of reformers be you, with goose-wings on your heads, as if you were going to fly, and dressed in such ridiculous fashion, talking about reform and women's rights? 'Pears to me, you had better reform yourselves first. But Sojourner is an old body, and will soon get out of this world into another, and wants to say when she gets there, Lord, I have done my duty, I have told the whole truth and kept nothing back.'"

In another issue the Tribune says:—

"Mrs. Sojourner Truth, a venerable colored woman, who has been heard before, gave her testimony the other day, in Providence, against the flummery and folly of 'feminine vestments,' and specially did she rebuke the 'women on the stage at the Woman's Suffrage Convention.' Hark to her!

"'When I saw them women on the stage at the Woman's Suffrage Convention, the other day, I thought, What kind of reformers be you, with goose wings on your heads, as if you were going to fly, and dresses in such ridiculous fashion, talking about reform and women's rights? 'Pears to me you had better reform yourselves first.'"

"Just before this, Mrs. Sojourner had freed her mind respecting 'panniers and Grecian-bend backs, high-heeled shoes, and humps on the head.' We should earnestly join in Mrs. Truth's protest against the manifold absurdities of woman's clothing, if we thought reform possible; but we don't. There has been no simplicity of attire since our grandmother Eve made her first apron of fig-leaves."

"The Fashions.

"Sojourner says that 'the women wear two heads on their shoulders with but little if any brains in either.' She knew of a young woman who had her hair cut on account of an impotency in her head and eyes. After the hair was cut, she put it into a net and wore it for a waterfall—getting rest for the head only during the night. Her hair grew again but still she continued to wear the extra hair with the addition of several skeins of stocking or other sort of yarn. Her impotencies of course *'grew no better'* very fast. Perhaps there is no truer saying than that 'folly is a fund that will never lose ground while fools are so rife in the nation.' The trouble of the thing is, or the reason why we have the trouble is, that the priests are dumb dogs and dare not bark or bring out the truths of the gospel against such gigantic evils, as *war, slavery,* and the *prided fashions.* We leave Sojourner Truth with her intuitiveness and without the letter, to battle almost alone these world-wide evils. May Heaven bless and sustain her in her humanitarian work and 'God-like mission.'

"SELAHOMMAH."

Accompanied by her grandson, Samuel Banks, she left Battle Creek in Sept., 1871, for her western trip to Kansas. Frequently stopping by the way to hold meetings, they at length reached Kansas, where she was cordially received by her new friend, Mr. Smith, as well as by friends of earlier date, whom she had known in Massachusetts and Michigan. Her stay in this State was rendered most agreeable by the attentions of kind and sympathizing people, who spared no pains to make her visit both pleasant and profitable. The newspaper reporters did not neglect her, as the following extracts will show:—

From Kansas Papers.

"'Sojourner Truth' is the name of a man now lecturing in Kansas City. He could only be called a 'sojourner' there, for truth could not abide in that place long as a permanent resident."—*St. Louis Dispatch.*

"Considerable ignorance is displayed in the first sentence, and an unusual regard for truth in the last."—*Leavenworth Times, Jan. 18, 1872.*

"Ignorance of the sex of this noted personage, Sojourner Truth, by the writer of the above, is proof of wonderful lack of general information. Certainly, knowledge does not sojourn in that head, and truth without knowledge has but poor dispatch in the affairs of men and women."—*Kansas City Journal, Jan. 19, 1872.*

"SOJOURNER TRUTH'S TALK.—There was a large attendance at the Opera House last night to listen to Sojourner Truth. Her mission, although not very intelligently stated by her, is to secure petitions to Congress to set apart a portion of the public domain for the occupation of such of the blacks as are still living on the bounty of the government in and around Washington. Sojourner's plan seems to be to have this class of 'contrabands' dealt with much in the same way as are the various tribes of Indians who occupy reservations and are being taught to support themselves.

"As the lecturer announced her intention of speaking again and again in Topeka, we will not prestate her arguments but permit them to be brought out by her in her own way.

"That she is a remarkable woman, all who have kept pace with the history of the past thirty years know, and being known, her persistent efforts will undoubtedly secure thousands of names to her pet petition.

"She also gave her views upon temperance, favoring prohibition. As to woman suffrage she declared that the world would never be correctly governed until equal rights were declared, and that as men have been endeavoring for years to govern alone, and have not yet succeeded in perfecting any system, it is about time the women should take the matter in hand."

A Topeka, Kansas, paper says:—

"SOJOURNER TRUTH:—The Temperance Society of this village have secured this remarkable colored woman to lecture here on Monday evening, Feb. 24, 1872. None should fail to hear her. For years she has been widely known. As the companion and peer of the great antislavery leaders during the dark days of the nation's struggle for freedom, she has made for herself a national reputation. Born in slavery, with no opportunities for improvement save those which come of poverty and wretchedness, she is with her rich imagination and shrewd good sense but what the oppressed race might become under circumstances fitted to develop their peculiar gifts. The music which greeted her childish ears was the imperious voice of her pretended master and the crack of the driver's whip; but it failed to crush out the spirit of eloquence and poetry with which nature had endowed her. Says Harriet Beecher Stowe concerning her: 'I never knew a person who possessed so much of that subtle, controlling personal power, called presence, as she.' Wendell Phillips says of her that he has known a few words from her to electrify an audience and affect them as he never saw persons affected by another party.

"Come and see and hear this peculiar, imaginative, yet strong and stalwart, daughter of the tropics. The lecture will be given in the

Congregational Church, and upon the subject of temperance. We hope to see a full house."

She left Kansas in Feb., 1872, and traveled through Missouri, Iowa, and Wisconsin, making many friends, from whom she received tokens of respect and affection. Her "Book of Life," which she always carries with her, contains autograph letters from the most influential and intelligent people residing in those places through which she journeyed. She returned to Michigan with scrolls of signatures as trophies of success, over which she felt as jubilant as "great Cæsar bringing captives home to Rome." The time was nearing when these petitions might be presented in due form to Congress; accordingly, she left Battle Creek in the spring of 1874, and joining her grandson in Ohio, proceeded once more toward our national capital. They stopped on their way thither in Orange, New Jersey, being entertained in the beautiful home of her much-endeared friends, Rowland Johnson[30] and wife. There she met the prominent and highly gifted preacher, George Truman, with whom she held meetings. One meeting is thus noticed by one of the New Jersey papers:—

"George Truman and Sojourner Truth in Orange.

"The little company of Friends in Orange held a very interesting meeting yesterday morning in Association Hall, where they were addressed by two noted preachers, one a man, the other a woman, the former white and the latter colored. These were George Truman and Sojourner Truth. The former was the first speaker.

"At the conclusion of Mr. Truman's address there was a short interval of silent meditation, after which Sojourner Truth, the venerable preacher and missionary, rose to speak. Her tall form was slightly bent with age, and as she faced her audience, clad in the simple garb of a Quakeress, she looked like an aged sibyl pleading the cause of her people. At first her voice was somewhat husky, and a few words were scarcely intelligible at the other end of the room, but as she warmed up with her subject all signs of weakness disappeared. She said that she felt that she was called to her work, and that if we are inheritors of the kingdom of God there must be some work that is to be done by us. That was what she had been trying to do for twenty or thirty years. When she was enlightened by God's love and truth she wanted to know, 'Lord, what wilt thou have me to do? Now I want to go to work. Well, it came to me in the anti-slavery cause. I knew slavery was a curse. I had been a slave and a chattel, and I went to work then. After that there seemed to be a call for me to go to work for the poor and outcast, for they are as poor as any one on God's foot-stool.' She said she had tried for years to get the government to help her and give the old destitute people, left destitute by the war, and the young growing up in wickedness, a home.

"She spoke of the misery and degradation she had seen among the colored people in the South, of the Black Maria* full of them driving up to the Washington police court, of their being thrown into jails, and of their children growing up in vice and ignorance, and said that it was a shame and an abomination, and that the people did not know these things simply because they did not see them. She had heard it said that these evils would die out in time, but they would not die out, 'they must be learned out.' God looks down on these things and sees them, and we all ought to feel that the world should be better because we are in it. She believed in being doers of the word, not hearers only, and in doing something to show we are workers in the vineyard. She lectured four years on this matter, and had got up a petition to Congress to set aside a portion of the public lands in the West, and put buildings thereon for a home for the destitute. People would sign her petition, but they would say that the plan could not be carried out. It was not so, it can be carried out. She said she wished the women of the place would get up a meeting and give her a hearing, as she wanted to tell them things she could not tell the men. The venerable preacher then wandered from sacred to secular matters, stating her opinion that the national government needed the administration of women to become cleaner. In conclusion she spoke of the aid she had received from General O. O. Howard, and caused her grandson to read a letter written by the general favoring the object she was working for.

---

*Police van.

"Sojourner Truth will address a woman's meeting in Association Hall, on Wednesday afternoon at 3 o'clock. It is hoped that there will be a large attendance, as she proposes to fully present the condition and needs of her race at the South to the ladies of Orange."

"Washington, June 3, 1874.

"GEN. B. F. BUTLER, M. C.,

"WASHINGTON, D.C.

"MY DEAR SIR:—Sojourner Truth began her labors for her people many years ago. Under the operations of our laws with reference to the indigent there is constant change. The government did lend a helping hand for a time, and many think no more should be done by the general government for the classes rendered helpless by the war and by slavery.

"Sojourner finds many people living in comparative beggary, and many children growing up without education in either books, or industry, or honesty, whom she believes can be properly aided by the general government into better conditions. It struck me that the number of totally disabled soldiers, &c., would grow less as time goes on, and that possibly the income for your Asylum would soon render it practicable to try an experiment in the direction that Sojourner indicates. Without much thought and without consulting with any one, I have indicated by the enclosed papers what you may be able to put into some good, practical shape.

"It is hard to steer clear of very serious objections which arise against the exercise of benevolence or charity by the general government. Yet, as in cases of sudden overflow or famine, I believe the exercise deepens this feeling of regard for our already renovated Republic. Yours truly,

"(Signed,)

"O. O. HOWARD."

The year '74 brought many vicissitudes to Sojourner. Sammie Banks, her dutiful and beloved grandson, began to decline in health soon after they reached Washington, which obliged them to leave that city and return to Battle Creek, where he lingered till Feb., 1875; when he passed away from amongst us. Sojourner also suffered from serious illness during that winter, and her life was despaired of for many long weeks. But her friends now rejoice to see her convalescing. She feels that for some special purpose her life has been spared, comparative health restored, and her mind brought back from the shadowy realm where it wandered during the days and nights when that red-lipped demon, Fever, with insatiate thirst, sucked the juices from life's fountain. She says, "My good Master kept me, for he had something for me to do."

She has no means of support. The ulcer upon her limb, from which she has so severely suffered, is partially healed. She says the "Lord has put new flesh on to old bones," which is proof to her mind that he requires more work of her. She hopes to go to Washington again and get her petition before Congress. Anna Dickinson says, "I hope every one will buy the pictures I gave her, and do all they can to help the woman, poor and old, who in her prime and strength helped so many." Another earnest woman asks the people to buy her book, and by so doing make her independent in her last days. No faithful servant of the divine Master should be accounted a burden while on earth, for the earth is the Lord's and the products are doubtless designed to sustain the creatures he has placed upon it. Especially should those who have borne the burden and heat of the day of life trustfully receive every comfort.

A friend not long ago offered to write her life. She told him she was "not ready to be writ up yet, for she had lots to accomplish first." She is now ready to be written up to this date, hoping thereby to complete the great enterprise she has undertaken. Born far back in the eighteenth century, and working for nearly a hundred years for the good of humanity, we see her ready to enter the last quarter of the nineteenth century with eye of faith undimmed and strength of spirit unabated. She has sought to promote every reform that has been agitated during this century. Most of those who were associated with her have gone from "works to rewards." But few survive to witness the flowering of those free institutions which they labored so industriously to plant.

Sojourner yet lingers on the verge of time, presenting to the world the extraordinary spectacle of a woman who, by native force, arose from the dregs of social life, like a phoenix from its ashes, to become the defender of her race; and she has for years struggled faithfully to extricate it from the doom of perpetual slavery, to which it seemed to have been committed by the despotism of a great nation, the gigantic atrociousness of whose laws surpassed any other in the annals of the ages. Her parallel exists not in history. She stands by the closing century like a twin sister. Born and reared by its side, what it knows she knows, what it has seen, she has seen. Her memory is a vast storehouse of knowledge, the shelves of which contain a history of the revolutions, progressions, and culmination of the great ideas which have been a part of her life purpose. She continues to keep guard over the rights of her race, to the interests of which she has so long been devoted. True to the character of sibyl, which genius has awarded her, she, while working in the present, points to the future for the fulfillment of her longings and her hopes.

Cosmopolitan in her nature, she calls the world her home, and says she could never apply to a town for aid, but would sooner appeal to the whole United States, for the welfare of which she has labored and which is more her home than any single locality of town or State. She loves her country with truest love. After the emancipation of her people, when passing the capitol buildings, she would often pause to contemplate the ensigns of liberty displayed upon them, which then admitted a new interpretation. She devoutly thanked her God that the flag proudly floating over the dome at last afforded protection to such as she, and that the stars and stripes no longer symbolized the "scars and stripes" upon the negro's back. Instinctively her soul claimed kinship with the emblematic eagle, whose glittering eye seemed to pierce the clouds, and the span of whose wings was ample to hover over four million freemen, upon whose limbs the clanking chain would drag no more. And when her free black hands were raised to heaven, invoking blessings upon her country, it was a fairer sight to see and a surer guarantee of its permanence and glory than was the imposing spectacle of that beauteous "queen of the East," upon whose snowy, perfect hands the golden chains of slavery shone, as she entered the gates of the eternal city, leading the triumphant procession of a Cæsar.

The nineteenth century towers above all preceding ones. Numberless inventions and improvements are embraced within its circle. Mechanics, agriculture, commerce, science, and arts, the world of matter and the world of mind, have budded and blossomed, so to speak, as never before. The contemplation of its achievements is at once sublime and overwhelming, and not alone for what it has done, but for what it prophecies of the coming time. The century is a sibyl, too. Upon the foundation it has laid, a superstructure may arise more symmetrical than prophet has yet dared foretell. "It builded better than it knew," can truly be averred of it. But the century has nearly run its course. Already are the "fateful Spinners" coiling the strands with which to ring its funeral knell. Its plumed hearse and sable mourners loom up like ghosts in the dim horizon of the near future. The grave-digger, sharpening spade and pick, prepares to do his part. Representatives from many nations and races hasten to join the pageant, to pay the last honors in the "City of Brotherly Love," where the obsequies are to be celebrated.

Let us accept the name as a happy omen, foreshadowing the time when brotherly love shall so abound that the relation of each to all will be so plain that "he who runs may read." The century's history is nearly written up, and Sojourner's lacks but another chapter in which she hopes to chronicle the accomplishment of her heart's desire. May her longevity transcend the century with which she has so long kept pace.

She has ever listened to the still, small voice within her soul, and followed where it led. She has clothed the naked, and fed the hungry; been bound with those in bondage, and remembered her less fortunate brother when released from chains herself. She has upheld the right and true, denouncing wrong in high places as well as low. Her barque has been carried far out to sea, and now it nears the port. May she encounter no more storms upon her homeward course, but, wafted by soft, sweet winds through placid waters, peacefully enter the harbor of the "King Eternal." And when she glides from ship to shore, may she hear the welcome, "Come unto me all ye that labor and are heavy laden, and *I* will give you rest."

Sojourner Truth's Correspondence.

But few of the autograph letters contained in her "Book of Life" will be published, as it is beyond her limited means to give *all* to the public. She trusts her scribe to make the selections. She holds all in dear and precious remembrance. The light emanating from their true friendship pierces the darkest clouds that obscure her horizon, and sheds its blessed rays across the path she treads. She hopes and believes that all their names are written in the "*Lamb's Book of Life*," and that the sweet communion begun in time will continue when time shall be no more.

LETTERS AND SIGNATURES.

"Boston, Aug. 6, 1870.

"Having been long acquainted with Sojourner Truth, and familiar with her eventful life and marvelous experience, I heartily commend her to the respect, hospitality, and, generous good-will of those among whom her lot may be cast for the time being: first, because of the cruel wrongs and sufferings endured by her while held for so many years in slavery; secondly, because of her disinterested, timely, and self-sacrificing labors among the wounded colored soldiers and destitute freedmen at the national capitol during the late rebellion; thirdly, because of her worthy character, and her many inspirational public testimonies in the cause of truth and righteousness; and, fourthly, because of her venerable age and necessarily increasing infirmities.

"WM. LLOYD GARRISON."

"Sojourner Truth, with the best wishes of her friend,

"HELEN E. GARRISON."

––––––––

"About twenty years ago my acquaintance began with this great and truly estimable woman, Sojourner Truth, since which time I have never ceased to feel myself stronger in spirit, and more earnest for justice and right for knowing her. We have dwelt together under the same roof weeks at a time; we have traveled together, holding meetings, myself a silent companion, and to-day I rejoice to subscribe my name with her chosen friends, in her 'Book of Life.'

"AMY POST.[31]

"Rochester, N. Y., May 3, 1871."

"May God bless, elevate, and enlighten the colored race, is the humble wish of their friend. We have met and conversed with their representative, Sojourner Truth, and are very much struck with her experience, as proving the principle that God reveals himself in other ways excepting that of his word.

"JAMES E. WALLACE.
"Rochester, N. Y."

"God speed thee in the right, Sojourner.

"Thy friend,
STEPHEN ARCHER.
"Dobb's Ferry, N. Y."

"Anti-Slavery Office, New York, July 29, 1863.

"DEAR SOJOURNER:—

"Yours by the hand of J. M. Peebles came promptly. I thank you for the photographs, though they are poor compared with the one you sent me first. It is a pity you did not preserve the negative of that instead of this. Not only is the likeness better, but the work also.

"The mob did not disturb the Anti-Slavery office, nor me. The fact is, the *Standard* is scarcely known to the vile class composing the mob, having but a small circulation in the city. But it would have taken only a hint to direct their attention to us, and then my life would have been in danger, and the office would probably have been destroyed. A good Providence seems to have watched over us. Mr. Leonard, the colored clerk, was obliged to hide, but no harm came to him. Many of the colored people were dreadfully abused, but a very healthful reaction has already set in; and I believe the condition in this city will be better than it was before. Upwards of $30,000 has been raised for the relief of the sufferers, and they will get pay from the city government for the property they lost. I shall send the *Standard* as you request.

"With sincere regard for you, and earnest prayers for your welfare, I subscribe myself,

"Yours faithfully,
OLIVER JOHNSON."[32]

"Boston, Oct. 21, 1867.

"DEAR MADAM:—

"I inclose my check for ten dollars ($10), a donation from the Rev.
Photius Fiske, for Sojourner Truth. Please acknowledge the receipt
of same. Yours very truly,

WENDELL PHILLIPS."

———

"The first time that Sojourner addressed a public meeting in Orange,
some years since, she said that the first shall be last and the last first,
and that she believed the colored race would yet lead the people out
of darkness and ignorance. It now seems likely that the colored voters of New Jersey will redeem the State from the grasp of the ignorant and depraved democratic party. Sojourner is now laboring to
consummate that glorious work. May Heaven grant her success.

ROWLAND JOHNSON.
"Orange, N. J., 1870."

———

A LETTER OF INTRODUCTION.

"Syracuse, Oct. 9, 1868.

"DEAR FRIENDS:—

"The bearer of this note will be Sojourner Truth, a worthy and remarkable woman. She is going to Courtland, to visit Miss Mary E.
Mudge and other friends. I shall be obliged to any persons who, on
the arrival of the train at the Courtland depot, will help her to find
her friend's house.

"SAMUEL J. MAY."[33]

———

"Washington, D. C., March 22, 1865.

"MY DEAR SOJOURNER:—

"I have made an arrangement for a meeting at the Union Baptist
Church for next Sunday evening. I want you to come, if possible.
Let me know if you can.

"Yours truly,
JOHN DUDLEY."

"TO MY FRIEND, SOJOURNER TRUTH:—

"The nearly thirty years' acquaintance I have had with you, all confirm your title to the name you have chosen, and its record in humanity's 'Book of Life.'

"Yours,

SAMUEL L. HILL.[34]

"Florence, Mass., Feb. 14, 1871."

––––––––

"After a wearied pilgrimage of over eighty years, she is a sojourner among us, witnessing the culmination and fulfillment of those great truths which she has humbly foretold oft-times within the last four decades. Her pilgrimage is nearly over. Sojourner Truth is resting. She quietly and proudly awaits her time to pass over among those who have performed their part. Good-by, aged friend.

"RICHARD LAMBERTH, OF SAN FRANCISCO.

"Washington, D. C., 1870."

––––––––

"Philadelphia, Tenth Month, 21st, 1869.

"I hope people will buy her pictures, which I have given to Aunt Sojourner, and so help her. And indeed I hope every one will do all they can to help the woman, poor and old, who in her prime and strength has helped so many. I will write for you, aunty, the Arabic blessing, 'May you live to be a thousand years old, and may your shadow never grow less.'

"ANNA E. DICKINSON."

"Amen to all dear Anna has said.

"A. C. HARRIS."

––––––––

"I have very pleasant memories of Sojourner Truth. She has been a faithful worker in the cause of freedom and of right. She can truly say, with Paul, 'I have fought a good fight, . . . I have kept the faith; henceforth there is laid up for me a crown of righteousness, which the Lord, the righteous Judge shall give me.' With my sincerest good wishes,

"ROBERT F. WALCUT."

"The wisest, wittiest woman I know is Sojourner Truth. Wiser and wittier, of course, than any man. I am glad to have enjoyed many years of acquaintance with her. I hope to enjoy many ages. May she and all her friends believe on her divine Jesus, and be with him where he is.

GILBERT HAVEN."

———

"DEAR SOJOURNER:—

"Love is the light, life, and central attraction of the universe, and will, if men yield to it, bring selfishness and misrule into harmony and law. May you ever feel its blessing.

"C. A. F. STEBBINS.
"Washington, D. C."

"With earnest best wishes, your friend,

"GILES B. STEBBINS."[35]

———

"May the Lord Jesus, who met you in the way, ever be your friend, companion, and guide.

"Your friend,
HENRY FOSTER."

———

"SOJOURNER, as you are crowning earth's children with bright and beautiful truths, so the angels will crown you, when you enter the bright Spirit Land.

"RENINO, THE LITTLE INDIAN SQUAW."

———

"Anthony Village, R. I., Ninth Month, 16th, 1870.

"God hath many aims to compass,
Many messages to send,
And his instruments are fitted
Each to some distinctive end.

"PERES PECK. AGED 84 YEARS."

"SOJOURNER TRUTH.

"Arisen from the degradation of slavery to be one of the most noble reformers of the age. Long may her star illumine the pathway of the progressive world.

MRS. M. GALE.
"East Medway, Mass."

"May the Lord bless and preserve you through life. Yours,

J. MCMILLEN.
"Brooklyn, N. Y."

"That Sojourner Truth has ennobled human nature by her life, is the firm conviction of her friend,

"ALFRED E. GILES.
"Boston, Mass."

"Syracuse, N. Y., March 25, 1871.
"Sojourner Truth was in Syracuse, laboring in the cause of Christ and humanity. Although over eighty, she still has plans for future usefulness which she seems happy to contemplate. Her life testifies to her faith in God's words that 'no man putting his hand to the plough and looking back is fit for the kingdom of God.'

J. S. LEONARD."

"With ever kind and ever loving remembrance of my dear old friend of more than thirty years' acquaintance.

JAMES BOYLE, M. D.
"No. 20 W. Broadway, N. Y., July 13, 1870."

"P. S. All the years during which we have known each other, we were co-laborers in the anti-slavery movement, and now we see our wishes accomplished in the overthrow of that horrid wall of crimes and cruelties which Church and State combined to perpetuate. The great God is leading the bondmen and bondwomen through a Red

Sea to their freedom, and writing their deed of enfranchisement with the point of the sword, in the blood of their oppressors North and South.

J. B."

James Boyle made Sojourner a present of the stereotype portion of her "Narrative," which includes the first 128 pages of this volume.

"I have conversed with Aunt Sojourner, and believe her to be a child of God.

"MRS. LEWIS FAIRBROTHER.
"Pawtucket, R. I."

"DEAR AUNT SOJOURNER:—

"I thank the 'King Eternal' that he is no respecter of persons, and that we are all his children.

HENRY C. L. DORSEY.
"Pawtucket, Sept. 6, 1870."

"Slavery has gone over the battlements, thanks be to God.

JOSEPH A. DUGDALE.[36]
"Mt. Pleasant, Iowa."

"Dear Sojourner Truth, a holy woman doing a godlike work—May she prosper in her noble undertakings.

M. L. IVES.
"Detroit, Mich."

"Rochester, N. Y., May 3, 1871.

"MY DEAR SOJOURNER TRUTH:—

"I rejoice to find you strong in health, vigorous in mind, warm in heart, and, as usual, full of noble purposes, looking to the welfare of suffering men and women. May you long live to bless, cheer, and enlighten, and to lift up the oppressed, and smooth the pathway of the lowly, and may you see the fruit of your labors multiply more than sixty or an hundred fold.

"**Frederic Douglass**."

"**Dear Mother in Israel:**—

"You are called of the Lord and anointed by his Holy Spirit to bind up the broken-hearted, and to sway the hearts of men by a power greater than that which resides in thrones and scepters. May God bless you, and give you success in your divine mission.

Daniel Steele.
"Genesee College, Lima, N. Y., May 12, 1871."

"Iola, Kan., Nov. 5, 1871.

"How easy it is to detect the spirit, however humble its garb, freed from the trammels of the world, party, or sectarianism. In you, good old Sojourner, we see it far removed above all clogs. Once a slave, now, in the highest sense a freedwoman; desiring nothing, hoping for nothing, but the truth as revealed by the Spirit, not killed by formalism. We thought we saw afar off a true spirit, and desired to meet you. At our request and invitation, you honored us with your presence at our house. We hope you have enjoyed the visit as well as ourselves. The best room, the best bed, and the best seat, we have intended to reserve for you, hoping to make you feel free and at home. Be assured, good friend, we feel grateful to you, and benefited by your counsel, and words of wisdom and truth. May your labors for the promotion of your race and our common humanity meet with abundant success, and, finally, great reward, is the earnest desire of your friends and well-wishers,

"**Byron M. Smith,**[37]
"**Eliza S. Smith.**"

"May God's blessing rest on thy labors for the elevation of thy race and the general good of mankind.

"**G. Knowles.**
"Leavenworth, Kan."

"Dear Friend Sojourner:—

"I hope that you will live to see the day when the people of this land shall be wise, and through their government care for the poor and ignorant, both black and white, as a wise parent cares for his children.

Eliza R. Morgan.
"Leavenworth, Kan."

"53 Broadway, New York, Jan. 17, 1868.

"Sojourner Truth:—

"Dear Madam—I had the pleasure of meeting you several years ago, at my uncle's, Mr. Richard Mott's, in Toledo. I saw Mr. Mott a few days ago, and he told me where you reside. I send one dollar, inclosed, for which please send me, by mail, as many of your photographs as the money will pay for. If you have two or three different ones, please send one of each. Perhaps you may have heard of the death of Uncle James Mott, brother of Richard Mott and husband of Lucretia Mott. He died last Sunday. Mrs. Mott is quite feeble and feels her great loss very much. I shall be glad to see you again when you come to New York, and shall try to do so.

"Very truly yours,

Walter Brown."

"Brooklyn, Sept. 8, 1869.

"Your letter of the 12th inst. has just reached me. I take pleasure in seconding my husband's invitation to you for a visit at our house. He will, no doubt, be away most of the winter, therefore, if your health will permit, as soon as you can come it will be best. We live at 136 Livingstone St., Brooklyn. Write to Mr. Tilton the day of your arrival, and he will meet you at the depot.

"I am yours sincerely,

"Elizabeth R. Tilton."

"Providence, R. I., Sept. 14, 1870.

"To Sojourner Truth:—

"May your last days be your best. May your sun set in glory. Having followed in the footsteps of Jesus all the way, he will now guide your feeble steps up the mount of ascension, and when the opening heavens receive you, you shall hear his sweet voice saying, 'Well done, good and faithful servant.'

Rachel C. Mather,[38]
"Teacher of Freedmen in Beaufort, S. C."

"To Sojourner Truth, the Libyan Sybil:—

"I give thee joy, my noble friend and true,
Thou who, but yesterday, a scorned slave,
Bearing the cross within thy great, brave heart,
Wert scourged and scoffed at by the heartless crew,
And only pitied by the Christ-like few
Who seek—like Christ—the sorrowing to save,
To-day, forevermore enshrined in art!
Honor and joy be thine! How few like thee
Wear the saints' aureole on an earthly brow.
So thy wronged race, long trodden beneath the feet
Of tyrant lords, and wearing the brand of shame,
Shall yet in manhood's majesty complete
Stand proudly in the sacred halls of fame.

"Mrs. C. L. Morgan.
"Mt. Pleasant, Wis., May 2, 1863."

———

"Again are we privileged in having Sojourner with us. 'Tis very pleasant for us that she feels our house is her home. She speaks this evening in the Congregational Church.

Mrs. A. Montague.
"Kalamazoo, Mich., Aug. 26, 1871."

"That the evening of your life may be as calm and peaceful as the morning was dark and stormy, is the earnest wish of your sincere friend,

"LUCINDA WALLING.
"Mt. Pleasant, Wis., Sept., 1871."

––––––––

"May our friendship of many years continue for long ages after the close of this short life.

"THOMAS CHANDLER.
"Raisin, Mich., 1871."

––––––––

"MY DEAR GRANDMOTHER:—

"As the present is your first visit to Missouri, I want to put it on record in your 'Book of Life,' that there is at least one native Missourian who entertains no prejudice against colored people, but, on the contrary, values all alike according to their worthiness. Your noble labors for the freedom of the colored race are among my earliest remembrances, and your beautiful ideas of life, death, and God, will be among the last things I shall forget.

"W. H. MILLER, JOURNAL OF COMMERCE.
"Kansas City, Mo., June 15, 1872."

––––––––

"OUR VETERAN FRIEND,

Sojourner Truth—We have known thee for a quarter of a century, heard thy clarion voice in the day when the slave power rioted in the land and trod with its iron heel upon the hearts of its victims. God has blessed the labors of his servants in a signal manner, and slavery by his mighty power has gone over the battlements and is destroyed. May thy old age be crowned by his presence, and thy trumpet join with Gabriel's in the jubilee, when the countless multitudes shall surround the throne of God.

JOSEPH A. DUGDALE.
"Mt. Pleasant, Iowa, Second Month 7th, 1872."

"Nov. 17, 1868.

"Sojourner Truth commenced her advocacy of the rights of her race during our war with Mexico, since which her travels and labors have been wide-spread, constant, and arduous. God has given her remarkable native sagacity, a ready command of strong, expressive language, and a vein of sharp wit and rich humor with which to combat the falsities and delusions among the people of her time. May God give her length of days, and free utterance on the side of right and justice.

W. L. CHAPLIN."

"To SOJOURNER TRUTH:—

"You say you wish to leave the world better than you found it. Posterity will give you the credit of having done so.

"R. B. TAYLOR, EDITOR GAZETTE.
"Wyandotte, Kansas, Dec. 25, 1871."

"AUNTY:—

"Accept this book to collect the scraps of your eventful life, which has accomplished so much, and is now so entirely devoted to the interests of the poor colored people in Washington and elsewhere.

"ROBERT ADAMS.
"Fall River, Oct. 16, 1870."

"Mendota, Ill., April 22, 1872.

"To THE METHODIST MINISTRY OF THE PARK RIVER CONFERENCE:—

"Dear Brethren—Allow me to introduce to you Sojourner Truth, and bespeak for her your friendly attentions. If her religious experience, as narrated a few years ago in the *Atlantic Monthly*, by Mrs. H. B. Stowe, affected you as it did me, you will feel it an honor to receive her in the Lord with all gladness.

"Your brother in Christ,
D. F. HOLMES."

A short sermon inserted in Sojourner's 'Book of Life,' and one which she appreciates:—

> "Our ingress in life is marked and bare,
> Our progress through life is trouble and care,
> Our egress out of it we know not where,
> But doing well here, we shall do well there.
>
> "C. P. Morgan.
> *"Leavenworth, Kan., Jan. 31, 1872."*

"Springfield, Mass., Feb. 28, 1871.

"Sojourner Truth:—

"Dear Friend—In writing my name in your 'Book of Life,' it gives me great pleasure to say that our acquaintance of some twenty years has made me largely your debtor. Your steady devotion to the cause of suffering humanity has always commanded my esteem, admiration, and reverence. As you have spent a long and laborious life for the good of others, may you always find troops of friends to minister to your comfort while you sojourn among mortals. And when at last you pass on to the higher life, I trust you will be met by a host of immortal friends on the shores of the summer land, who will welcome you to the blest abodes.

E. W. Turing."

"Your life, commencing in the depths of slavery, opens grandly and brightly even there, and who can tell of the glorious angelhood into which it is unfolding? The 'Well done' awaits you, Sojourner, and all earnest workers for humanity.

"Martha L. Gale.
"East Medway, Mass., 1871."

"Aunty Sojourner Truth:—

"We have been greatly pleased and edified by a visit from you. Having known you for about thirty years, it is with pleasure we add our testimony to your self-sacrificing labors in behalf of your despised and oppressed race, and the cause of humanity every-where. Although far advanced in years, may you be spared to see your efforts for the elevation of your people crowned with suc-cess.

"N. B. Spooner,

"L. H. Spooner.
"Plymouth, Mass., 1871."

––––––––

"May she who patiently hath wrought
Through years of earnest toil and thought,
Find her best hopes fulfilled at last,
And when her wanderings are past,
To crown her work of love be given
Sweet peace on earth and rest in Heaven.

"J. Walter Spooner.
"Plymouth, Mass."

––––––––

"James N. Buffum, Ruth Buffum, Abby B. Buffum—all good friends of Sojourner Truth.

"Lynn, Mass., 1870."

––––––––

"Go on, Sojourner, God speed you.

"J. A. B. Stone.
"Kalamazoo, Mich."

––––––––

"Blessings on thee, my good old friend.

"Wendell Phillips.
"Boston, Mass."

Visits President Grant—Letter of Introduction from Gen. Howard.

"BUREAU OF REFUGEES, FREEDMEN,
AND ABANDONED LANDS.

"Washington, D. C., March 17, 1870.

"GEN. U. S. GRANT:—

"President U. S.—Sojourner Truth, quite an aged and distinguished colored woman, earnestly working for years for her people, desires to see the president. She will pray for him surely; but more heartily if she sees him.

"Yours respectfully,

O. O. HOWARD."

Sojourner says: "I went in company with several ladies and gentlemen to see the president. While waiting in the ante-room with other visitors, a gentleman called, to whom I was introduced. During a short conversation with him, he said, 'I recollect having seen you at Arlington Heights. How old do you call yourself now?' I had felt very much annoyed by people's calling to me in the street and asking that question. I mentioned it to Dr. Howland, and he advised me to charge five dollars for answering that question; so I said to the gentleman, A friend told me to ask five dollars for telling my age. He smiled pleasantly, and invited me to call upon him at the city hall. After he left, my friends told me that that gentleman was Mayor Bowen,[39] one of the best men in the city. Presently, a man came in, a free-and-easy sort of fellow, and asked to see the president. We were now ushered into the presence room. A very elegant lady and gentleman shook hands with the president, and after a few pleasant words were passed, took their leave.

"Then the 'hail fellow' stepped up and offered his hand, saying, 'This is President Grant, is it? You ain't as old as I thought you was. I've seen your picter, and your picter looks older than you do.' The president smilingly said, 'I am not so very old.' 'Wall, how old do you call yourself, anyhow?' The president replied that he was 49 years of age. 'Ain't you no older than that?' said the fellow. 'No, sir,' patiently answered the president. 'You look older than that,' said he, and waited to see if the president had anything more to say, but, finding that the interview was ended, turned to go, saying, 'Good-by.' 'Good-by, sir,' said the president, and the fellow walked off.

"I felt very much mortified because I had asked Mayor Bowen five dollars for inquiring of me how old I was, when I saw how kindly and politely the president treated that clownish fellow. I will here add that I subsequently called upon the mayor and apologized for my rudeness to him. He said he ought to be the one to ask an apology, for it was improper to ask a lady her age. He invited me to spend a day with his family, which invitation I accepted and was cordially entertained by his lovely wife and interesting family. It was now our turn to be presented to the president. He shook my hand, and said he was pleased to see me. After a little pleasant conversation, I expressed my gratification that the colored people had gained the right of suffrage. This he cordially indorsed. I now showed him my 'Book of Life,' which contains the autographs of Lincoln and other distinguished persons. He took the book and wrote his name in it. 'To Sojourner Truth. U. S. Grant, March 31, 1870.' I then handed him two of my photographs, which he took, and putting one in his pocket-book, he laid the other on the table and gave me a five dollar bill, for which I thanked him.

"We now left, carrying with us a pleasant impression of the president, and the memory of a delightful hour spent in the White House."

"Washington, April 14, 1867.

"My Dear Sojourner:—

"I am so thronged with work, and applications for colored people, from all parts, that I cannot finish any day's work. I always go to bed tired, leaving much work undone. As to sending you people, it is impossible to promise anything. We have been trying to get some people to go the last week, but all who go incline to go to Providence, Battle Creek, or some place where already several have gone.

"One thing now you may do—send the names and residences of those who have applied to you for help, and we will make one desperate effort. We send our men to Brockport this coming week. The Bureau requires that the names of employers be sent; so if you send on the names, I will do the best I can. You need not promise any till you see whether they can be obtained. I wish much we could send a hundred men, they stand idle everywhere and will not go in any considerable numbers till after the first of June, when they will vote. With love and best wishes,

"Your friend,

JOSEPHINE S. GRIFFING."[40]

"*Oct. 16, 1874.*

"MRS. F. W. TITUS:—

"Can you inform me who wrote out (or otherwise compiled) and edited the narrative of Sojourner Truth's life? I shall be much obliged to you if you can give me this information; it is desired for the library of a public institution. If you can tell me where Sojourner Truth is now, and as to her health and circumstances, I shall be glad and further obliged to you.

"Respectfully,

"SAMUEL MAY.
"*Leicester, Mass.*"

Extract from a Letter.

"*Leeds, Mass., Jan. 17, 1870.*

"SOJOURNER TRUTH:—

"*My Dear Friend*—A line from my brother received this afternoon, speaks of your being at Vineland, so I must send you a few lines to say how much pleased I was to hear from you through friend Amy Post, of Rochester, New York. Hope you have been successful in your present journey with such kind and efficient friends as Mr. and Mrs. Theodore Tilton to help you. Was very glad your mind was set at rest about your son Peter. How strange are the events of our lives. How little we know of the world we live in, especially of the spiritual world by which we are surrounded. But we may see enough to know that it is at least marvelously interesting. You and I seem to move around as easily as soap bubbles—now here—now there—making our mark, I suppose, everywhere, though mine is a very quiet mark compared to yours. I get a glimpse of you often through the papers, which falls upon my spirit like bright rays from the sun. There is a wee bit of a chapel here, pulpit supplied by a Mr. Merritt, and one evening last fall he repeated something that 'Sojourner Truth' had said. I was not there, so I cannot tell what it was. I did not think you were laying the foundation of such an almost worldwide reputation when I wrote that little book for you, but I rejoice and am proud that you can make your power felt with so little bookeducation.

"**OLIVE GILBERT.**"

Another Letter from the Same Person.

"**MY DEAR FRIEND:**—

"I may not be able to make you sensible of the heart-felt pleasure I experienced on receiving your kindly greetings once more, but hasten to thank you sincerely for them, and for your address which I have long wished for; and I assure you I am most happy in thus being enabled to return you my own greeting, fervent, fresh, and warm from the heart. It is a very long time since we have had any opportunity of communicating with each other directly, though I have been enabled to find traces of you and your labors, from time to time, which was more, I think, than you have been able to do of your old friend; for I am not so public a personage as yourself.

"Your call upon Mrs. Stowe, and our dear, sainted president, and your labors connected with the army, and the Freedmen's Bureau, gave you a publicity that enabled me to observe you at your old vocation of helping on and doing good to your fellow-creatures, both physically and mentally. I was much pleased with Mrs. Stowe's enthusiasm over you. You really almost received your apotheosis from

her. She proposed, I think, that you should have a statue and sym-
bolize our American Sibyl.

I have written more than a sheet, and have not spoken of what
has been in my mind all the time, of the great deliverance of your
people from the house of bondage, the wonderful work of the Lord,
accomplished only through a cruel and bloody war, as was so often
predicted by friend Garrison and others in days gone by. You may
have witnessed many of its terrors. And oh! it makes me almost
speechless when I contemplate the hosts of men, and those the
flower of their country, that were thus sacrificed to Moloch. There
is but one reconciling thought, and that is, The Lord is all-wise and
reigneth over all. He sees and knows what we observe, and not a
sparrow falls to the ground without his notice. Of the little book I
wrote for your benefit, some of the copies I took are sold; others I
gave to my friends as keepsakes, &c.

"Get some one to write for you soon, and believe me to be your
true friend and well-wisher, now and forevermore.

O. G."

———

"The company of our estimable friend, Sojourner Truth, will ever be
cherished with feelings of love.

"Sarah T. Rogers.
"No. 323, North Eleventh St., Philadelphia."

———

"3 Exeter Street, Boston, Mass., Apr. 25, 1875.

"Dear Friend:—

"We are sorry to hear that you are suffering from ill health, and hope
you may be getting better by this time. My mother, Mary May, who
was one of the earliest abolitionists, with Mr. Garrison and Wendell
Phillips, wishes me to send her remembrances to you, and her best
wishes, and wants you to accept ten dollars from her. Perhaps you
have seen her, either here in Boston, or at the house of my brother,
Samuel May, in Leicester. She is eighty-seven years of age and
rather feeble, though her mind is bright, and she is able to read a lit-

tle and knit a good deal. I inclose a post-office order for fifteen dollars. Please accept five from me.

"I should be glad to hear that the money reaches you safely, so I inclose a card addressed to us, for reply. I am, with very great respect, dear madam,

"Yours,

ABBY W. MAY."

"*Richmond, Ind., April 15, 1875.*

"SOJOURNER TRUTH:—

"*My Good Sister*—Mrs. Dr. Thompson and myself, on hearing of your afflictions in the death of your grandson and your own sickness, have been trying to raise some funds for you, but I am sorry to be obliged, after waiting so long, to send you so small a sum as two dollars. For this you will find inclosed a money order. In reply I wish you would tell me all about your situation and wants, and if possible I will send you more. Have you received anything from the Julians? Have your wants been supplied? Tell me all the facts. How are you getting along with your sickness?

"Mrs. Dudley sends with me our hearty good wishes, and we only regret that we cannot send you something more substantial to supply your needs. You are remembered in our poor prayers in our family. We shall never forget the light and cheer which your presence and words gave us when here. The good Lord, whom you have so faithfully served in labor for your poor race, will take you through and give you, a weary old pilgrim, a home of rest and reward. Let me hear from you soon.

"Your fellow-pilgrim and sojourner,

"JOHN DUDLEY."

"With earnest respect for your constant effort to help humanity, and to make the world better for your being in it, I want you, dear friend, to think of me in this life and the higher one as your friend and sympathizer.

ELIZA S. LEGGETT.
"*Detroit, Mich., June 20, 1871.*"

"Grand Rapids, March, 1873.

"God bless Sojourner Truth, who spoke so grandly at the Second Street M. E. Church, last night, and who has been our honored guest for a few days.

"L. H. Pearce."

———

"Equality of rights is the first of rights.

"Charles Sumner.[41]
"Senate Chamber, April 26, 1870."

———

"Orange, Feb. 10, 1875.

"Aunt Sojourner:—

"Dear Friend—I learned last evening that thee is dangerously ill, and that it is paralysis which has prostrated thee. I spent the evening with Mrs. McKinn and learned it from her. Most sincerely do I hope she has been misinformed, and that thy illness is something from which thee may recover, and that we may see thee again in the flesh; but if this cannot be I know that thee is prepared to enter that beautiful world of spirits which has seemed so near thee while here.

"Dear Aunt Sojourner, may I among the many who love thee here, be remembered by thee on that beautiful shore of the river of everlasting life, and if thee is permitted to return to the children of earth, receive from thee some token of thy presence and continued affection.

"Thee left a trunk here which we will fill and send thee as soon as we learn what will be most useful. I do not doubt but that thee has kind friends who are not only willing but anxious to make thee comfortable in every respect, I mean in Battle Creek. But those of thy friends who have not the privilege of relieving thy wants in person, would like to add their mite toward returning the kindness which thee, for so many years, has shown others. May the Infinite Love sustain thee, and that faith which has ever been thy support in the trials of life become stronger and purer as thee nears the golden gates, is the prayer of thy loving friends,

"H. W. Johnson & Rowland Johnson."

"Standard Office, New York, Jan. 13, 1866.

"MY DEAR FRIEND:—

"I know you will be glad to put your mark to the inclosed petition, and get a good many to join it, and send or take it to some member of Congress to present. Do you know there are three men, Schench, Jenkes, and Broomall, who have dared to propose to amend the United States Constitution by inserting in it the word 'male,' thus shutting all women out by constitution from voting for president, vice-president, and congressmen, even though they may have the right to vote in the State for State officers. It is a most atrocious proposition, and I know Sojourner Truth will say, No, to it. God bless you, and help you to do the good work before you, is the wish of your friend,

SUSAN B. ANTHONY."[42]

———

"Biddle House, Detroit, Jan. 29, 1869.

"SOJOURNER TRUTH:—

"*My dear Grandmother in Israel*—I am sorry I cannot get time to take you once again by the hand before I leave Detroit, but I herewith inclose to you a five-dollar bill to keep you in mind of

"Your dutiful grandson,

"THEODORE TILTON."

———

"MY DEAR FRIEND, SOJOURNER TRUTH:—

"If we never meet on earth again, my prayer is that we may meet on the other shore.

"E. DICKINSON.
"Brodhead, Wis."

———

"SOJOURNER TRUTH:—

"You want the government to give land to the freed people. This would be true statesmanship, as by so doing we should be paying a little of the great debt we owe the freedmen, and at the same time putting them in the way of supporting and educating themselves, and enriching the nation.

"SETH HUNT.
"Northampton, Mass., 1871."

"Boston, March 18, 1875.

"MRS. F. W. TITUS:—

"Dear Madam—I have your prompt reply to my note of inquiry, and hasten to inclose a check for twenty-five dollars for the benefit of Sojourner Truth. It is the contribution of Mr. Phillips, father, and myself.

"W. L. GARRISON, JUN."

"SOJOURNER TRUTH:—

"Dear Friend—Your life is a living epistle known and read of all men. You surely are a sojourner, laboring for the truth. Your life has been one of sorrow and toil, bearing in your own body and your own family the bitter injustice and cruelty that has sent you a missionary to the learned and unlearned alike for many years. You and I have cause of sympathy, each with the other. God bless and keep you ever.

CALVIN FAIRBANKS.*
"Florence, Mass., March 20, 1871."

"North Topeka, Kan., Nov. 20, 1871.

"It has gratified me much, Sojourner, to see your face once more, and welcome you to my home and my church. It is a dozen years since we first met, and, possibly, we may meet again in this world; if not, we will in the next. Our meeting in this far West has brought to my mind the beautiful words of Phœbe Carey:—

---

*Calvin Fairbanks was confined for 12 years in Frankfort prison, Kentucky, for aiding a slave to escape.

'As ships from far and distant ports
    To distant harbors hurrying on,
Meet with each other on the deep,
    And hail, and answer, and are gone,

'So we upon the sea of life,
    Have met as mortals often will,
One from the prairies of the West,
    One from the land of rock and rill.

'So we shall pass on separate ways,
    As vessels parting on the main,
And in the years to come, our paths
    May never meet or cross again.

'Yet when life's voyage all is done,
    Where'er apart our paths may tend,
We'll drop our anchors side by side
    In the same harbor at the end.'

"THOMAS W. JONES.
"Pastor of Cong. Church."

"SOJOURNER:—

"The words of my husband are warmly echoed from my heart, and I feel more than gratified to have had the opportunity of entertaining you in my own home. Be sure you will always be held in loving remembrance by us all.

HELEN M. JONES."

"DEAR SOJOURNER:—

"At your request I record the fact that I succeeded in registering my name in the First Precinct of the Ninth Ward, and on Tuesday, the 4th of April, cast the first vote for a state officer deposited in an American ballot-box by a woman for the last half century. After the vote was deposited, I presented a vase of flowers to the inspectors, and also handed them a large picture representing a large crowd of women in darkness, just entering the portals of an arch, which were inscribed, 'Liberty,' and upon which an eagle was perched. The gates were held open by Columbia and the Goddess of Justice. The foremost woman held in her hands a scroll, inscribed, 'The Fourteenth Amendment.' To the right were imps of darkness fleeing away, some with barrels of whiskey. On the left was pictured the Capitol of Washington, with men crowding its steps, cheering, &c. Streams of light flowed upon them, while, with the exception of this and the foreground, the picture was darkness intensified. The following lines appeared underneath:—

> "'We come, free America, five millions strong,
> In darkness and bondage for many years long,
> We've marched in deep silence, but now we unroll
> The Fourteenth Amendment, which gives us a soul.
> Glory, glory, hallelujuh, glory, &c.,
> As we go marching on.'
>

"NANNETTE B. GARDNER.[43]
"Detroit, Mich., June 30, 1871."

————

"With a great deal of esteem,

"Your friend,

JOHN R. FRENCH."

————

"Sojourner Truth lectured before the Pewamo Temperance Society last evening. She held the audience in breathless attention for one hour. May the Lord guide and protect her in her errands of mercy, and may her days be multiplied. One great desire of my heart has been gratified, which was to meet Sojourner and converse with her face to face.

"MRS. E. A. CHADDOCK,
"President Pewamo Temperance Society."

————

"Bristol, Conn., 1840.

"SISTER DEAN:—

"I send you this living messenger, as I believe her to be one that God loves. Ethiopia is stretching forth her hands unto God. You can see by this sister that God does, by his Spirit alone, teach his own children things to come. Please receive her, and she will tell you some new things. Let her tell her story without interruption, give close attention, and you will see that she has the leaven of truth, and that God helps her to see where but few can. She can not read or write, but the law is in her heart. Send her to brother Rice's, brother Clapp's, and where she can do most good.

"From your brother in looking for the speedy coming of Christ,

HENRY L. BRADLEY."

"May the God of truth sojourn with you through this world, and then give you an abundant entrance into mansions prepared for you in Heaven.

"**T. B. WELCH.**
"Vineland, N. J., Dec. 25, 1869."

"Hopedale, Mass., July 28, 1870.

"Faithful mother in Israel,
Raised up to bless thy people,
Fearless for God's righteousness,
Witness for Truth's almightiness,
Scourge of scornful oppression,
Shamer of vain profession,
Tender nurse of feebleness,
Helper of sad neediness,
Friend of all humanity,
And practical Christianity,
Wondrous age of thy sojournment,
Passing strange thy life's concernment,
Stranger than the tales of fiction,
Full of woe and benediction,
But crowned with rich fruition,
May thy Heavenly Father bless thee,
And guardian angels oft caress thee,
Till all thy toils are ended,

And thy spirit has ascended,
To be with Jesus mansioned,
Among his countless ransomed.

"ADIN BALLOU,
"LUCY H. BALLOU."[44]

"Sojourner Truth is the most marvelous person we have ever had the pleasure of meeting. May God spare her, to see her heart's desire accomplished.

"MRS. L. H. PEARCE."

"Vineland, Jan. 4, 1870.

"The Lord and good angels have blest you and your work, and will bless you in that better world where I hope to meet Sojourner Truth.

JOHN GAGE."

"Niles, Mich., Oct. 9, 1873.

"This neighborhood has been favored with the presence of Sojourner Truth among us. She dined yesterday at S. A. Gardiner's, took tea with Mrs. Henry Moore, and spent the night at M. F. Reed's. The Lord has blessed us with this angel in disguise, which has made our hearts very glad. May he bless her most abundantly.

MRS. H. MOORE."

"West Medway, Dec. 21st, 1870.

"DEAR AUNTY SOJOURNER TRUTH:—

"We intended to ride down to see you before you left Dr. Gale's, but shall not be able, for Mr. Ray has been to Woonsocket twice this week, and the rest of the week he is so much engaged that we cannot come. I am rather disappointed, for I wanted to see your dear face once more. Mr. Ray wishes me to tell you that he saw brother Gilbert Haven on Monday, and he said that he had been looking for news from you for some time, but didn't know your whereabouts. When

Mr. Ray told him that you would spend Christmas with him, 'God willing,' he said, 'That's good. *Now we'll have a big time.*' Mr. Haven is anticipating your visit with a great deal of pleasure, and I know you will have a nice time. We are all well. Our circle met this week, P. M. and there were many kind inquiries for you. I am sorry you could not have stayed longer with us. May God bless you. I feel that the conversations we had, did me a great deal of good, particularly the relation of your experience on Sunday evening after meeting.

"Yours in Christian love,

JUSTINA B. RAY."

"*Philadelphia, May 9, 1870.*

"MRS. TITUS:—

"We were made glad last evening by the return of our old friend, Sojourner, from Washington, where she has been for two months. She looks very well and bright, and is in her very best spirits as you will see by the following statement:—

"She has received from the government, through the influence of Gen. Howard, three hundred and ninety dollars, being fifteen dollars per month for twenty-six months. She has collected other funds to the amount of four hundred and fifty dollars, for which I send my check payable to your order, which you will please to pay to William Merritt on acc't of her mortgage, and get him to send the receipt to me with a statement of her accounts.

"She has lived to see her people delivered, and we may all rejoice with her.

"Yours truly,

"HENRY T. CHILD, M. D.
"*634 Race St.*"

"*Florence, Mass., March 8, 1871.*

"SOJOURNER TRUTH:—

"*Dear Friend*—Mr. Hunt informs me to-day that Mr. Wheedon, Methodist minister in Northampton, will appoint a meeting for you in his church, next week Tuesday evening, and will himself cause notice thereof to be given next Sunday in all the churches in town, or in such of them as will give the notice. Mr. Hunt will also have the notice in the *Free Press* printed next Friday, and in the *Gazette* printed next week, Tuesday. Now if you will inform me on what evening next week you wish to have a meeting in Florence, I will also have notice given here next Sunday, by the Methodists, the Congregationalists, and in our meeting. Will also have the notice given in the *Free Press* of next Friday (if I get your reply in season), and in the *Gazette* of next week, Tuesday. You will be welcome to the use of our hall next week, either Wednesday, Thursday, or Friday evening. Please send me word to-morrow, if you can, which evening you will occupy. If not to-morrow, send word the next day, and oblige,

"Yours truly,

SAMUEL L. HILL."

"On Saturday, Jan. 1st, 1870, our house received a new baptism, through Sojourner Truth, whose voice is continually praising God for the blessings bestowed upon her, and never murmuring because of hardships endured. She has been a wonderful teacher to me. I thank my God that I have met Sojourner Truth.

"PORTIA GAGE."

"Washington, April 10, 1867.

"ISAAC POST, ESQ.:—

"*Dear Sir*—Inclosed find a post-office money order for $20, which is intended for Sojourner Truth, it being the amount due her from the New York Freedmen's Commission for December last. Please assure her of my regards, and that we shall be glad to see her when she returns.

"Yours truly,

A. E. NEWTON,

"Sup't of Schools, &c."

"Sojourner Truth has been very acceptably received by the people of Vineland, and I trust that the many earnest words she has uttered, both in public and private, for the cause of woman and the abolition of the death penalty, will be like seed cast upon good ground.

"**Deborah L. Butler.**
"Jan. 17, 1870."

Sojourner was most cordially and hospitably entertained whilst in Lawrence, Kansas, by a family of the name of Simpson, bankers in that place.

The following testimonials of their respect are transcribed from her "Book of Life":—

"May your future, Sojourner, be ever brighter than your faith.

W. A. Simpson."

"I wish you the same, Sojourner.

"**Laura B. Simpson.**"

"**Sojourner:**—
"May our faith be like thine, and our duty as well done.

Kate L. Simpson."

"The Lord bless you, Sojourner, and may your immortal crown be studded with many stars.

"**Hannah P. Simpson.**"

"The Lord bless you, sister Sojourner. I believe you are endued by the Spirit of the Lord in your efforts for the elevation of your race.

"**Samuel Simpson.**
"Lawrence, Kansas, Dec. 1, 1871."

"Peterborough, N. Y., Dec. 11, 1868.

"**My Dear Sojourner Truth:**—

"I cannot let you go without telling you on paper how highly we have prized your visit to us. We have enjoyed your wit and powers of description, we have been instructed by your wisdom, and we have welcomed your religion. I trust that this is not your last visit to Peterborough, and that the good Lord and Father will spare you to come again to us. Wherever you shall go, there will, I trust, be good friends to receive you, to bless you, and to be blessed by you. I know that wherever you go you will be useful, for the head and heart that you carry with you are continually doing good.

"With much love to you from my dear wife and myself, your friend,

Gerritt Smith."

———————

"**Sojourner Truth:**—

"With weary hand, yet steadfast will,
   In old age as in youth,
Thy Master found thee, sowing still
   The good seed of his truth.

"**Rev. E. Marble.**
"Schoolcraft, Mich. Conference."

———————

"**Friend Sojourner:**—

"It would be folly in me to ask the Great Spirit to bless that which he has already so abundantly blessed. Why should I invoke him to shower blessings upon thy head, or strew thy pathway with flowers? Do not all these jewels naturally belong to and sparkle around the footprints of those who, like you, go about doing their Master's business? 'Tis not race, profession, or position, but knowing the right and doing it, which shall entitle an individual to a safe passport to the home of the angels.

"**Warren Samson.**
"Hammonton, N. J., 1870."

"Toledo, Ohio, Jan. 12, 1866.

"Sister Sojourner:—

"I have received my commission to return to Washington and Richmond as soon as I can possibly get ready, *i. e.*, collect about $300 more to go with. I want to be ready the latter part of next week. Oh, how I want to know how you are getting along. I have not been to Battle Creek, and hardly think I can reach it; but I have written them and hope they will send money and clothes by me to you. I cannot set precise date, but may, in a week or ten days, see Washington.

"Our Home is getting along finely. The colored people of Adrian placed $40 in my hands to buy a cow for the little folks at the Home. I have bought a good cow for them, which gives eleven quarts of milk per day, and Mr. Don gave them another, so they are nicely provided for. The colored people also gave us a Christmas donation for the Haviland Home, valued at $113.84, mostly in provisions and clothing, with some money to purchase hens for the Home.

"I must close with earnest desire for your prosperity in all things.

"Yours for the poor and needy,

"Laura S. Haviland."

"Washington, March 18, 1874.

"Dear, Blessed Sojourner Truth:—

"I must address you from the heart, mother of love and truth as you are. I am blest and thankful that I have held your hand in mine, been greeted by you, and heard your voice, which, longer years than I have known, has been lifted up throughout the land against oppression and sin, say to me, 'I know your soul!' Blessed words! Cheering me on my path and to be proved thrice blessed in the spirit world, where you and I will learn the deep import of your greeting, 'I know your soul.' God grant me strength also to 'be faithful unto the end,' even as you have been.

"When Christ the Lord makes up his jewels, you then exalted will receive the crown eternal, and clothed in white rise upward in joy unspeakable and full of glory. Thanks be unto God who giveth us the victory. Reverently and lovingly,

"Your child and sister,

"JENNIE LEYS."

———————

"Pawtucket, Nov. 10, 1870.

"DEAR SOJOURNER:—

"I hope there yet may be found ten righteous people to save us this way. At any rate, perhaps you'll help us to hunt them up when you come. There is a nice little hall here which the temperance people occupy only Wednesday evenings. In applying for it, I found old friends of yours who knew you in Bensonville, and it was at once tendered to you in your behalf, free of any expense whatever.

"Yours in haste,

J. ADAMS."

———————

"Benzonia, Mich., Nov. 8, 1864.

"DEAR MOTHER, SOJOURNER TRUTH:—

"We have received your 'shadow' all right—very beautiful. We esteem it very much. May God bless you and make you very useful, and prepare you for your higher life, and rest, and glory. To day we suppose Father Abraham is again elected. May God bless him and give him all needed wisdom and grace.

"We all unite in much love to you.

"Yours for the good cause,

"GEORGE THOMPSON."

———————

"From the Lion's Den, Mount Glendel."

"He who feedeth the ravens, careth for thee, true Sojourner, and blesses all thy labors of love abundantly. Go on proclaiming glad tidings. Preach the true gospel, and curse the follies and sins of this world.

"Your Old Lion S,

DOLLIE LION."

"*Schuylkill, Chester Co., Pa.*
"*April 5, 1863.*

"To Sojourner Truth:—

"*Dear Sister*—I saw, this morning, in the *Anti-slavery Standard*, an extract from a letter written by Mrs. Stickney to our mutual friend, 'Uncle' Joseph Dugdale. I was glad to learn that you are among kind friends. Although my sympathies were moved at the thought of your poverty and bodily afflictions, yet it was not with feelings of sorrow or regret. I rather rejoiced that your needs should have been the medium through which I learned your whereabouts, and that you still breathe in the atmosphere of truth, and feel an interest in the welfare of your race and all mankind. That notice will unquestionably bring you all needed temporal help as far as pecuniary aid can supply your wants. I will inclose a mite in this letter for you. It would be more only that I feel assured it will not be needed, as, no doubt, hundreds will feel glad of the opportunity of contributing to your needs.

"Let us bless and praise God for his manifold goodness. God's goodness is none the less displayed in his abused mercies turned into curses by a wicked people than in the fruition of divine joy by his obedient children. May his spirit in such fullness as thy vessel can contain and enjoy, ever be with thee. With fond Christian affection,

"Farewell.

Isaac Price."

"*Peterborough, May 4, 1869.*

"My Dear Sojourner:—

"I was very glad to receive a letter from you, but sorry to learn that you are suffering from indisposition. I hope you will soon be well enough to go to Brooklyn and call here on your way. We very often talk of the pleasant visit we had from you, and when I am alone I frequently recall the words you spoke to us and feel refreshed and strengthened by them. I send you ten dollars, for food and fire as far as it will go. Wish it were more, but it must suffice now.

"God bless you always, and keep you in his own peace.

In much love,

"Ann C. Smith."

"Alexandria, May 3, 1866.

"SOJOURNER TRUTH:—

"*Dear Friend*—The bearer of this note is desirous of going North and taking thence his family, consisting of wife and daughter. I have known him since my stay here, and recommend him to your consideration. If anything can be done as regards transportation, &c., it will be thankfully received by him.

Very respectfully, your obedient servant,

"A. W. TUCKER,
"*A. A. Surgeon, U. S. A.*"

———

"Glad to see our dear co-laborer, Sojourner Truth, again.

LUCRETIA MOTT.
"*Road Side, Philadelphia, Eleventh Month, 1869.*"

———

"Ever yours,
HENRY WILSON,[45]
"*Senator, Mass.*
"*April 20, 1870.*"

———

"This is my first interview with Abraham Lincoln's 'Aunty' Sojourner Truth. A pleasant season.

"GEORGE TRUMAN.
"*Philadelphia, Eleventh Month, 1869.*"

———

"I hope, dear Sojourner, that you will be enfranchised before you leave us for the better land.

"Your true friend,
"ELIZABETH CADY STANTON.[46]
"*New York, May 4, 1870.*"

———

"Very truly yours,
"MARY A. DODGE—GAIL HAMILTON."

"My friend, Sojourner Truth, the friend of the human race—God bless you.

"**Jacob Walton.**
"Adrian, Mich., 1871."

————

"Your brother in the hope of glory,
"**B. Sunderland,**
"Pres. Minister, Wash, D. C."

————

"May God bless and guide you!
"**Anne G. Phillips.**
"Aug. 1."

————

"Your true friend and co-worker,
"**Lucy N. Coleman.**
"Syracuse, N. Y."

————

"Your old young friend,
W. F. Morgan.
"Leavenworth, Kan."

————

"**S. C. Pomeroy,**[47]
Senator, Kan.
"April 20, 1870."

————

"**J. M. Thayer,**
Senator, Neb.
"April 20, 1870."

————

'**A. McDonald, Arkansas.**"

————

"Most sincerely your friend,
"**George W. Julian.**"[48]

"Henry E. Benson,
Lawrence, Kansas."

—————

"Jacob M. Howard,[49]
Michigan Senator."

—————

"T. M. Morrell,
Illinois Senator."

"Yours truly,
J. W. Patterson."

—————

"J. M. Bowen,
Mayor of Washington."

—————

"George E. Spencer,
Senator, Ala."

—————

"D. D. Pratt,
U. S. Senator, Ind."

—————

"H. R. Revels,
Senator, Miss., Colored."

—————

"J. S. Adams,
Louisiana."

—————

"Z. Chandler,
Mich."

—————

"R. E. Fenton,
N. Y."

—————

"Jas. S. Fowler,
Senator, Tenn."

Visits Western New York.

"We met Sojourner at Angola Station, stopped at Joseph Linton's to dinner, then took her to Alonzo Hawley's, a few rods distant, where she spent the night. The next afternoon Mrs. Hawley brought her to our house. Sunday, the 6th, called a meeting for her at Hemlock Hall, where, at 10 o'clock A.M. she addressed an appreciative audience of four hundred people. Wednesday morning we carried her to George W. Taylor's, distant six miles. The afternoon of the same day, Mr. Taylor and wife carried her five miles farther into the town of Collins, to the comfortable home of Isaac and Lydia Allen, aged people like herself, who extended to her a hearty welcome. In the evening she spoke to a good audience in the Rosenburgh school-house near by. The following day, Thursday, was spent by Sojourner with the family of Mrs. Cook, who are relatives of the Allens. The next night, Mr. Cook took her four miles, to Collins Center. There she addressed a large audience in the new Free Church, and felt that her labors were not in vain. Returned with Mr. Cook to the house of Isaac Allen.

"Friday night, Mr. Allen and wife went with her to Mr. Rosenburgh's, who took her to Gowanda, where she addressed an intensely interested audience. Saturday she was conveyed to G. W. Taylor's, and Sunday brought to Kerr's Corners, to the home of Lewis Baldwin, where she remained until the 14th, and then spoke to a large gathering in the Methodist Church. After the meeting she came home with us once more.

"She seems very quiet and happy here, and we are enjoying a feast which we may never be privileged to enjoy again. It is a blessing to be with her and receive her experience from her own lips. Wednesday night, James Varney carried her to Bront Center, where was assembled an appreciative audience in the new Methodist Church. On Friday night, the school-house in Pontiac was filled with people eager to listen to her teachings. Since that time she has been very quiet until the 22d, when she accompanied us to a political pic-nic at Hemlock Hall, where was convened an audience of probably three thousand people to listen to able speakers. I have endeavored in a hurried manner to write a little diary for Sojourner, to show to such of her friends as are anxious to know where she has been and what has been her success.

"PHEBE MERRITT VARNEY."

"James Varney conveyed Sojourner Truth to our house fourth day, the 23d of ninth month, 1868, where she remained till the following sixth day, when we carried her to the house of our son-in-law, P. Paxton, where she remained till seventh day evening, when she went to Potter's Corners to attend a large republican meeting in which she made a few remarks. This caused such enthusiasm among the people that it opened the way for a very large meeting the next evening. The large hall was nearly filled with an attentive audience, which she addressed for more than an hour, in her usually impressive and sarcastic manner, much to the satisfaction of the majority present. From thence, she went home with Alfred Moore and wife, with whom she spent several days, to the edification of the neighboring people who came to see her. In conclusion, we rejoice in the opportunity of becoming partially acquainted with Sojourner Truth. May she yet survive long to combat in her peculiar and impressive manner the errors with which this nation is enthralled.

ISAAC BAKER.
"East Hamburg, Erie Co., N. Y."

"On the 29th of ninth month, 1868, J. B. C. Eddy went to Harry Abbot's after Sojourner Truth to attend a meeting held in Dr. Dolin's neighborhood, which was very well attended, and to good satisfaction to those in favor of liberty. On the first day of tenth month, she held a meeting at Griffin's Mills, in the lecture room, speaking to a good and attentive audience, telling them many truths. Friend Sandford took up a collection for her. I can say on our part that her company has been very acceptable, and I hope she may live to have her wishes gratified in seeing Grant sit in the presidential chair.

"J. B. C. EDDY."

"On Monday, Oct. 19, 1868, Sojourner Truth, being in Courtland village, was sent for by C. P. Grosvenor, and brought to Mr. Granville's.

Tuesday eve she addressed a crowded assembly in the Methodist Church with good effect. She had been several days at Courtland, and lectured to a multitude, having her home at the house of the younger Dr. Goodyear, who was happy to have her company and make her acquaintance. Here she was visited by many ladies and gentlemen.

CYRUS P. GROSVENOR.
"McGranville, N. Y."

Meeting in New Lisbon.

"Sojourner Truth interested an audience in New Lisbon, Ohio, at the Methodist Episcopal Church, for nearly an hour, talking of slavery in this country, and the suffering and injustice inseparable from it. If earnestness is eloquence, she has a just claim to that appellation; for she makes some powerful appeals, which cannot but strike a chord of sympathy in every human heart.

"She sang the following original song at the close of the meeting:—

> "I am pleading for my people—
> A poor, down-trodden race,
> Who dwell in freedom's boasted land,
> With no abiding place.
>
> "I am pleading that my people
> May have their rights astored [restored];
> For they have long been toiling,
> And yet had no reward.
>
> "They are forced the crops to culture,
> But not for them they yield,
> Although both late and early
> They labor in the field.
>
> "Whilst I bear upon my body
> The scars of many a gash,
> I am pleading for my people
> Who groan beneath the lash.

"I am pleading for the mothers
Who gaze in wild despair
Upon the hated auction-block,
And see their children there.

"I feel for those in bondage—
Well may I feel for them;
I know how fiendish hearts can be
That sell their fellow-men.

"Yet those oppressors steeped in guilt—
I still would have them live;
For I have learned of Jesus
To suffer and forgive.

"I want no carnal weapons,
No enginery of death;
For I love not to hear the sound
Of war's tempestuous breath.

"I do not ask you to engage
In death and bloody strife,
I do not dare insult my God
By asking for their life.

"But while your kindest sympathies
To foreign lands do roam,
I would ask you to remember
Your own oppressed at home.

"I plead with you to sympathize
With sighs and groans and scars,
And note how base the tyranny
Beneath the stripes and stars."

Tobacco Victory—The Branded Hand.

The habit of smoking was contracted by Sojourner in early youth. Not many years since, whilst traveling in Iowa, a gentleman asked her if she believed the Bible, to which she readily assented. Her friend said, "The Bible tells us that 'no unclean thing can enter the kingdom of Heaven.' Now what can be more filthy than the breath of a smoker?" "Yes, child," she answered, "but when I goes to Heaven I spects to leave my breff behind me." But as time passed on she became convinced that the habit was wrong. She had not courage to chide people for using spirituous liquors while indulging in the use of tobacco, herself. Accordingly she discontinued the habit. She was told it would affect her health. She said, "I'll quit if I die." She did quit and *lived!*

"Rochester, Jan. 11, 1869.

"Dear Friend Sojourner:—

"The announcement in the *Anti-slavery Standard* of thy having laid aside the pipe, is receiving considerable attention. I received a letter from Dr. Trask, of Fitchburg, Mass., who rejoices greatly over thy grand and triumphant effort, and says, 'It ought to be proclaimed far and near to strengthen others to cast aside the abomination.'

"Also a letter has just come to me from our old and highly esteemed friend, Jonathan Walker, the original of 'The Branded Hand.'[50] Thou wilt probably remember him. He was captain of a small vessel running from New York to the Gulf States. He secreted several slaves and brought them to the free States, was taken and imprisoned, and the letters S S branded on his right hand, signifying slave stealer; but in our vernacular we should interpret it slave savior. This vessel with its entire cargo was confiscated, and he lay in a filthy jail in Florida for several months.

"Amy Post."

"Muskegon, Mich., Jan. 1, 1869.

"My Dear Aged and Venerated Friend:—

"Your earnest and effectual devotion, for so long a time, to the cause of human redemption, has, from my first knowledge of your missionary services to the present time, impressed me (as well as many others) with the warmest fraternal regard for your welfare and usefulness. When I saw it announced by Amy Post, in the *Anti-slavery Standard*, that you had abandoned the pipe at your advanced age, I could form no other conclusion than that you had done it under the influence of the keenest moral and religious sensibilities.

'I have known ministers and many professors of religion, as well as other good people, who tried hard and long to abandon the use of tobacco, yet made a failure, and confessed that they could not conquer the habit. I distinctly remember, also, the tedious and desperate struggle I had to emancipate myself from twenty years' slavery to the foul weed. Considering the effect its long use has upon the nervous system, I could hardly suppose you could have achieved so great a victory at your age without a break-down; nor do I look upon so heroic an act as much short of a miracle. May the example of such self-sacrifice in you, indeed stimulate and encourage (as Amy says) 'others to do likewise,' is the earnest desire of your

"Sincere friend,

"JONATHAN WALKER."

"P. S. I am not sure, but I think I met you twenty-five years ago at Bronsonville, North Hanston, Mass., soon after my return from imprisonment in Florida.

J. W."

The heroic deeds of Jonathan Walker have rendered his name immortal; and our prince of song has paid them a just and noble tribute in the exquisite poem entitled, "The Branded Hand," from which the following is an extract:—

"Why, that brand is highest honor! than its traces never yet
On old armorial hatchments was a prouder blazon set;
And thy unborn generations, as they tread our rocky strand,
Shall tell with pride the story of their father's branded hand!

"Then lift that manly right hand, bold ploughman of the wave!
Its branded palm shall prophesy, 'Salvation to the Slave.'

Hold up its fire-wrought language, that whoso reads may feel
His heart swell strong within him, his sinews change to steel.

"Hold it up before our sunshine, up against our northern air.
Ho! men of Massachusetts, for the love of God, look there!
Take it henceforth for your standard—like the Bruce's heart
    of yore,
In the dark strife closing round ye, let that hand be seen before!

"And the tyrants of the slave-land shall tremble at that sign,
When it points its finger southward along the Puritan line:
Woe to the State-gorged leeches, and the church's locust band,
When they look from slavery's ramparts on the coming of
    that hand."

Sojourner Truth's Age.

Sojourner is often asked her age. She is as ignorant of its date as is the fossil found in the limestone rock, or the polished pebble upon the sea-shore, which has been scoured by the waves ever since the sea was born.

It was the diabolical scheme of those dealers in human flesh to so stultify the brain of the slave that it might become incapable of reason, reflection, or memory. The slave child followed the condition of its mother, and seldom had any knowledge of father, or date of birth. They were Pompey or Cuffee, Dinah or Chloe, as the case might be, having no permanent second name, but taking the surname of the master; consequently they received a new cognomen with each new owner.

Sojourner counts her years from the time she was emancipated—says she began to live then. She thinks it is what we accomplish that makes life long or short, and says that some have been on earth scores of years, yet die in infancy.

The following account is well authenticated:—

The act of 1817 in the State of New York emancipated all slaves of the age of 40 years. From this time all became free as fast as they arrived at the age of 25 years, till 1827, when all were free. Sojourner became free in 1817. This statement is corroborated by an old gentleman by the name of Miller, who was brought up in the vicinity of Sojourner's birthplace. He recently died in Green Co., Wisconsin.

Her Parentage.

Mrs. Stowe was mistaken in regard to Sojourner's ancestry. Her mother's parents came from the Coast of Guinea, but her paternal grandmother was a Mohawk squaw. The "whoop" Sojourner gave in the horse-car at Washington was probably a legacy from her Mohawk ancestor.

Extent of Her Labors.

Sojourner Truth has traveled and lectured in the following States:—
New York, Massachusetts, New Jersey, Maine, Pennsylvania, Michigan, Wisconsin, Minnesota, Ohio, Illinois, Missouri, Indiana, Iowa, Kansas, Connecticut, Vermont, New Hampshire, Rhode Island, Delaware, Maryland, Virginia, and the District of Columbia.

Anecdotes.

SOJOURNER TRUTH AT ABINGTON.

About 20 years ago Sojourner attended a grove-meeting at Abington, Mass., to celebrate negro emancipation in the West Indies. Many of the old line abolitionists were there,—Pillsbury, Garrison, Phillips, Stephen and Abby Foster, Henry C. Wright, Charles Lenox Rimond, and a host of others.[51] Two fugitives from southern slavery, who were traveling over the underground railroad to Canada, stopped off a train to enjoy a day with friends before going to that "cold but happy land." They sat upon the platform with the speakers. One, a very large man, was squeezed into a coat much too small for him. The other, a diminutive man, wore a coat of such ample proportions that it hung in folds about his liliputian form. But as these garments had been given them by employees on the underground express, and were the first of the kind they had ever owned, the *fit* did not appear to disturb them, judging by the pleased look upon their faces. The contrast between their present condition and what might have been, had they been overtaken in their flight and dragged back into slavery, filled them with bliss. They were comparatively happy.

These coat collars were nicer than the iron collars which might now have been on their necks; and the cuffs, softer than the iron cuffs which they knew the captured fugitive was made to wear. The voice of blood-hounds baying in the distance, was superseded by kindly human voices. Traveling toward the North Star by night, they had hidden in dark caves and underbrush during the day, avoiding the light of the sun. Now, streams of golden sunlight flowed around them. Surely, they were receiving "beauty for ashes and the oil of joy for mourning."

One of them arose, and in a brief manner expressed his appreciation of this mighty change, and his deep gratitude to the people of Massachusetts for their kindness and generosity. At the close of his remarks, which were received with applause, Mr. Garrison said, "Sojourner Truth will now address you in her peculiar manner, and Wendell Phillips will follow." Sojourner began by improvising a song, commencing, "Hail! ye abolitionists." Her voice was both sweet and powerful, and as her notes floated away through the tree-tops, reaching the outermost circle of that vast multitude, it elicited cheer after cheer. She then made some spicy remarks, occasionally referring to her fugitive brethren on the platform beside her. At the close of her address, in which by witty sallies and pathetic appeals, she had moved the audience to laughter and tears, she looked about the assemblage and said, "I will now close, for he that cometh after me is greater than I," and took her seat. Mr. Phillips came forward holding a paper in his hand containing notes of Sojourner's speech, which he used as texts for a powerful and eloquent appeal in behalf of human freedom. Sojourner says, "I was utterly astonished to hear him say, 'Well has Sojourner said so and so'; and I said to myself, Lord, did I say that? How differently it sounded coming from his lips! He dressed my poor, bare speech in such beautiful garments that I scarcely recognized it myself."

As Sojourner was returning to the home of Amy Post in Rochester, one evening, after having delivered a lecture in Corinthian Hall, a little policeman stepped up to her and demanded her name. She paused, struck her cane firmly upon the ground, drew herself up to her greatest hight, and in a loud, deep, voice deliberately answered *"I am that I am."* The frightened policeman vanished, and she concluded her walk without further questioning.

———

During the war, Sojourner met one of her democratic friends, who asked her, "What business are you now following?" She quickly replied, "Years ago, when I lived in the city of New York, my occupation was scouring brass door knobs; but *now* I go about scouring copperheads."

———

At a temperance meeting in one of the towns of Kansas, Sojourner, whilst addressing the audience, was much annoyed by frequent expectorations of tobacco juice upon the flour. Pausing and contemplating the pools of liquid filth, with a look of disgust upon her face, she remarked that it *had been* the custom for her Methodist brethren to kneel in the house of God during prayers, and asked how they could kneel upon *these* floors? Said she, speaking with emphasis, "If Jesus was here he would scourge you from this place."

———

Previous to the war, Sojourner held a series of meetings in northern Ohio. She sometimes made very strong points in the course of her speech, which she knew hit the apologist of slavery pretty hard. At the close of one of these meetings, a man came up to her and said, "Old woman, do you think that your talk about slavery does any good? Do you suppose people care what you say?" "Why," continued he, "I don't care any more for your talk than I do for the bite of a flea." "Perhaps not," she responded, "but, the Lord willing, I'll keep you scratching."

———

Sojourner was invited to speak at a meeting in Florence, Mass. She had just returned from a fatiguing trip, and not having thought of anything in particular to say, arose and said, "Children, I have come here to-night like the rest of you to hear what I have got to say."

Wendell Phillips was one of her audience. Soon after this he was invited to address a lyceum, and being unprepared for the occasion, as he thought, began by saying, "I shall have to tell you as my friend Sojourner Truth told an audience under similar circumstances, I have come here like the rest of you to hear what I have to say."

**AUTOGRAPHS OF DISTINGUISHED PERSONS,
WHO HAVE BEFRIENDED SOJOURNER TRUTH BY
WORDS OF SYMPATHY AND MATERIAL AID.**

Wm. Lloyd Garrison.

A. Lincoln

Parker Pillsbury,

Gilbert Haven

Susan B. Anthony

Calvin Fairbank.

Wendell Phillips

H B Stowe

Charles Sumner

Lucretia Mott.

L. Maria Child.

Geo Thompson

Gerrit Smith

Jonathan Parker

J. S. Griffing

Sam'l J. May

O. O. Howard.

Rowland Johnson

Lydia Mott

Amy Post

Notes on the Autographs.

In Sojourner's correspondence are found names of such weight and power that it seemed fitting to have them engraven for her "Book of Life." Here are names that are indelibly stamped upon the pages of their country's history, and inseparably connected with it—names which will reverberate adown the centuries, and the echoes be caught by the generations in the coming time—"immortal names that were not born to die," but which are synonyms of all that is most exalted in human life and character—names of men and women, the luster of whose lives shed a light on humanity's page, pure and sparkling as the shimmer of a white wing flashing through the yellow sunlight—names of those who manifested their love to God by tender compassion for the lowliest of his children.

The name of one who was dragged through the streets of a populous city with a halter about his neck,* will be remembered when that city which permitted the outrage, would be forgotten but for the immortality attained through his sublime heroism. Boston with its moving atoms will fade away, but the waves of progress received an impetus from the breath of this true devotee of freedom which will help to cleanse and purify the streams of life till they are engulfed in the ocean of eternity.

The name of one is written who only "awaited the opportunity to enfranchise millions."

I read the name of one who traveled many winters among the hills of New England, braving its snow drifts and piercing winds, to preach the gospel of freedom to those whose hearts were harder than the granite rocks over which he toiled, and chillier than the snows and breath of winter. Abandoning a situation of honor and profit, he consecrated his giant intellect, and the best years of his life, to a cause that brought neither honor nor profit, despised by mammon worshipers and all who seek the applause of such. Beyond

---

*Reference to abolitionist leader William Lloyd Garrison (see endnote 6 to the "Book of Life").

the turmoil of the present hour, when its noise and uproar have died away, the refined and polished future will render his verdict. He can afford to wait. The present never knows its saviors; retrospection clears the vision.

The influence of another, who labors with deep earnestness in the Master's vineyard, confined to no locality, knowing neither North nor South, but imparting his loving spirit to all races and conditions of society, will be felt upon the tide of civilization whilst its waves break upon the shores of time.

Here is the name of a noble woman who has gone up Calvary bearing the cross, and gained the mount of ascension with bleeding feet; who has labored for the rights of her race and for the rights of her sex, braving the scorn and obloquy of conservatism. Bold iconoclast! endure a little longer. "The hour for your ideas has not yet struck."

One, languishing twelve years in prison, found compensation for his sufferings in the words of the divine Master, "Sick and in prison ye ministered unto me."

One of these, a world-renowned orator, said, "The age of reading men has come. The age of thinking men has come. The age of the masses has come."

One of Sojourner's friends, by her genius in the delineation of character, opened the world's eyes to perceive that irresponsible power vested in a Legree was a dangerous thing, and that Uncle Toms and Topsies were human beings after all.

Another inscribes this formula in Sojourner's "Book of Life": "Equality of rights is the first of rights."

A woman whose four-score years are so replete with good words and deeds that the name falls like a benediction upon the listening ear, has taught her sex that old age need not be desolate, but may be fragrant as a garden of roses. White hairs, like a saint's aureole, encircle her brow. We involuntarily bow our hearts in worship when the honored name of Lucretia Mott is pronounced.

Another is the name of Lydia Maria Child,[52] the key note of whose useful life and brilliant intellect has ever been attuned to freedom's cause.

One crossed and recrossed the Atlantic, to blend his efforts with the little band of reformers which eventually slew the giant, Slavery, with a pebble of truth, and demolished his castle, the corner stone of which was lies, and its superstructure the bleeding hearts of crushed humanity. Landing upon our shores he was pursued by the hooting mob,* as if the Plutonian regions had been emptied at his heels.

G. S.,† meaning "Great Soul," gave farms to poor blacks and whites, carrying out Sojourner's idea of encouraging industry, and making wild lands a source of revenue to the government. In Congress he said, "Truth lives and reigns forever. In proportion as we obey the truth, are we able to discern the truth." If all that is wrong within us was made right, not only would our darkness give place to a cloudless light, but like the angel of the Apocalypse we should "stand in the sun."

Another could bear the torture of the branding iron rather than be false to his convictions of duty.‡

Josephine S. Griffing labored for years to ameliorate the condition of the black race, and in her system were sown, by overwork, the seeds of consumption which bore speedy fruit.

Another in the sacred desk ever insisted that humanity was of all things under heaven the most sacred. A marble bust of this good

---

*Reference to English abolitionist George Elijah Thompson (see endnote 1 to the "Book of Life").
†Reference to abolitionist Gerrit Smith (see endnote 29 to the "Book of Life").
‡Reference to Captain Jonathan Walker (see endnote 50 to the "Book of Life").

man adorns the city of Syracuse, and a friend writing of it says, "It is eminently fitting that one of the purest of the once proscribed abolitionists should now be thus publicly honored."

Another, who holds a high position under the government, is Sojourner's friend, and unites his efforts with hers to promote the welfare of the race which has been so mercilessly tossed about by our Ship of State. He encourages her to persevere in her efforts to obtain a grant of land for the freedmen, and lends his influence to the cause.

And last but not least are those royal souls who sheltered and comforted the flying fugitive, who fed and clothed him, who warmed him by the sacred fires of their own domestic hearthstones. The money they have so freely given to the poor and needy, is out at an interest whose profits are beyond the power of arithmetic to calculate. Their names are engraven upon human hearts as with a pen of fire; and to them will the beatitude apply, "Blessed are the pure in heart, for they shall see God."

A MEMORIAL CHAPTER.

IN MEMORIAM.

———

SOJOURNER TRUTH,

BORN,

IN ULSTER COUNTY, STATE OF NEW YORK,

SOMETIME IN THE EIGHTEENTH CENTURY.

———

DIED,

IN THE CITY OF BATTLE CREEK, MICHIGAN,

NOVEMBER 26, 1883.

———

"And I heard a voice from heaven saying unto me, Write, Blessed are the dead which die in the Lord from henceforth; yea, saith the Spirit, that they may rest from their labors; and their works do follow them."

Memorial Sonnet.

SOJOURNER TRUTH, NOV. 26, 1883.

As some tall pine upon a mountain-side
   That o'er its fellows rears its lofty head,
One that a century's tempests hath defied,
   Yet falls at last beneath the weight of years;
So now thy mortal form lies cold and dead,
   After long sojourn in this vale of tears.
Oh, mighty were the burdens thou didst bear;
   But when from thine own limbs the shackles fell,
Thou didst take up the burdens of thy race,
   And thou didst wander, homeless, far and wide,
The story of their woes and wrongs to tell;
   Now mayest thou rest from all thy toil and care;
May angel hands prepare for thee a place
   In the eternal mansions. Brave, true friend, farewell.

"Behold, I come quickly, and my reward is with me to give to every man according as his work shall be."

A few months after Sojourner's emancipation, in 1817, she attended a religious meeting for the first time in her life. In those days, black people were not allowed to enter a house of worship, unless they occupied a corner known as the "negro pew." This meeting was held in a private house, and Sojourner, fearing to enter, stood outside, peering in at the open window. The speaker was a Circuit Rider, by the name of Ferriss. He took the above quotation as his text. Sojourner says this was the first text of Scripture she had ever heard, and it seemed that every word of it was engraven upon her soul. Also, at this meeting, she for the first time heard the hymn commencing, "There is a holy city." Mr. Ferriss first read the hymn, and then lined it for the singers. From hearing it thus read and repeated, Sojourner kept it all in her memory, and frequently sang it in her own meetings, telling where she learned it.

Death of Sojourner Truth.

SOJOURNER TRUTH passed to the higher life at three o'clock A. M., November 26, 1883.

Her death was not unexpected either by herself or her friends. Her health had been failing for a year or more, and the last three months of her life was a period of intense suffering. Ulcers on both limbs were the immediate cause of her death. Skillful physicians took charge of her case, and gave her such attentions as loving children would give an honored parent. But life's forces were spent, and she bowed her venerable head to the inevitable.

> "With calm and patient trust I wait
> The slow and sure approach of fate;
> What may betide me where I go
> I know not, and I need not know.
> I know my Maker, kind and just;
> This is enough. I calmly trust."

She talked of death as an advance toward a higher life, and said: "When we are done with these old bodies, their aches and pains, we shall be as Gods."

The writer of this article called upon Sojourner early one morning a few weeks previous to her decease. She had passed a night of extreme wretchedness and anguish. But at sight of her visitor, a smile that cheered like dawn of day overspread her countenance, and she began to sing,—

> "It was early in the morning,
> It was early in the morning,
> Just at the break of day,
> When He rose, when He rose, when He rose,
> And went to heaven on a cloud."

While she sang in a sweet, low voice, the rapt expression of her face and the far-away look in her brilliant eyes would almost lead one to expect her translation, rather than death. In that supreme moment, Sojourner and death seemed to have nothing in common.

The Mussulmen have a fable about Moses, that when the hour of his departure was come, God sent the angel of death, who appeared before him and demanded his soul. Moses, cheerful and undaunted, greeted the angel with a friendly salutation, but questioned his right, nevertheless, to touch a soul that had had communion with God. The death-angel was baffled at such assurance, and knew not how to proceed, for death and Moses, it seemed, had nothing in common. Then the Lord, seeing the difficulty, deputed the Angel of Paradise to carry him an apple of Eden; and as Moses inhaled the immortal fragrance, his spirit went forth from him, and was borne upon the odors of Eden into the presence of the Lord.

Such is the Mussulman's parable, the meaning of which is this: The assurance which disputes the power of death is the human spirit's unconquerable faith in God—the faith

> "That life and death alike
> God's goodness underlies."

In the spring of 1877, Sojourner's eye-sight, which had been defective for many years, returned; or, as she expressed it, "The Lord put new glasses in the windows of her soul." From this time onward her eyes never grew dim or had a faded look, as is often the case in old age. A few days before her death, as she lay upon her couch with closed eyelids, her friend said: "Sojourner, can you look at me?" She slowly opened those wondrous orbs which seemed filled with spiritual and prophetic light; and as they rested upon the anxious, questioning face before her, they seemed to say, "Let not your heart be troubled." Earnestly gazing thus for a few moments, the lids slowly closed, to open on earth no more forever, but we will devoutly hope to reopen amid the enchanting beauties and glories of Paradise. She soon sank into a comatose state, from which she never rallied.

> "Her eyes were closed to things around,
> Her ears were dulled to common sound;
> And yet, far gleaming on her sight,
> I think she saw a surer light,
> And heard harmonious wavelets beat,
> Prelude of something strangely sweet."

Robed for the Grave.

Sojourner's body was robed for the grave in black nun's veiling, with white muslin cap and folded kerchief. Mrs. Montague placed a bunch of exquisite white flowers in her poor, maimed right hand. The floral emblems covering the casket were appropriate and beautiful—a cross, a sheaf of ripened grain, a sickle, and a crown. A basket of lovely flowers was sent by Miss Kimbal of Chicago, and another by the Band of Hope in our city.

Sojourner Truth was this day honored as none but the great are honored. As water, the symbol of truth, seeks and finds its level, becoming purified by its struggles through earthy conditions, so had Truth Sojourner, from the mud and slime of basest enslavement, sought and found her level among the purest and the best.

Funeral Services.

At two o'clock P. M., November 28, some of Sojourner's near friends met at her house, No. 10 College St. After a short interval, the procession formed, and moved to the Congregational and Presbyterian church, on Main St., where nearly one thousand people had assembled. Some of the more prominent citizens of Battle Creek acted as pall-bearers. The casket was placed in the vestibule of the church, and the lid removed.

A concourse of people, composed of all classes and creeds, passed reverently by the open coffin to take a farewell look of one whom in life they had so much honored.

The funeral address, by the Rev. Reed Stuart, was eloquent and impressive. His remarks were supplemented by a tribute to her worth from her antislavery friend, G. B. Stebbins, of Detroit, who was listened to with appreciation, as he spoke of the rare qualities of head and heart which he knew her to possess.

Earth to Earth.

A long procession followed the body of the departed to Oak Hill Cemetery, where an open grave was ready to receive its own. "Dust to dust; ashes to ashes." Friends gathered around, forming in little groups. For a few moments, "silence like a pall" seemed to envelop them. This short November day, now drawing to its close, was the perfect day of the season. The long line of carriages, the hearse with its black plumes, the people—all so motionless—the cloudless sky, the great round, red sun lying low in the horizon, all made up a whole of solemn but exquisite beauty. The casket was lowered to its resting-place, Mr. Stuart pronounced the benediction, and while the tender, loving words still lingered upon his lips, the glorious sun sank out of sight. And with the poet we could say,—

"Calmly, calmly lay her down;
She hath fought a noble fight,
She hath battled for the right,
She hath won the fadeless crown.

"Hoping, trusting, lay her down.
Many in the realms above
Look for her with eyes of love,
Wreathing her immortal crown."

Farewell.

As we left this spot so soon to become historic, the departing sun, as if unwilling to leave the earth in gloom, sent back messengers of crimson and golden clouds to soften his farewell to earth. Casting a purple glow on distant spires, hills, and tree-tops, our pathway still lay in his reflected light as we journeyed homeward.

Farewell, Sojourner, O friend, farewell. We trust thy pathway through the valley of the shadow of death was illumined by the smiles of messengers sent by thy "God who was not dead" (even in the darkest hours of thy earth-life), to conduct thee to thy everlasting home in the kingdom of the blessed and the forevermore; and as thou turnest thy gaze from the earth-life toward thy heavenly home, I seem to hear thee say,—

"Ah! the way is shining clearer
As I journey, ever nearer
To the everlasting home.

Comrades who await my landing,
Friends who round the throne are standing,
    I salute you, and I come."

Lines to Sojourner Truth.

I look in wonder on thy dusky face;
    I mark full well each most unclassic line;
But soon there shines through all the inner grace
    Of Christly *soul*—a light far more divine
Than that which springs from folly's couch supine.
    Thy magic eye, than beauty's orb more bright,
Doth straight appear; all outward looks resign
    Their charms, and, to the spirit's inner sight,
A bright, celestial beauty fills their place.
    Thy tongue, untaught, of princely power hath more
To move the heart and melt the stubborn will
    Than cultured art, still practiced o'er and o'er
With all the aids that learning can instill;
    It speaks a *higher truth*, from God's own store.

A. S. Dyckman.

Dispatches from Fred Douglass and Wendell Phillips.

The New York *Telegram* of Nov. 27, in noticing the death of Sojourner Truth, has the following dispatches from two of her distinguished co-laborers:—

Washington, Nov. 27.—In the death of Sojourner Truth, a marked figure has disappeared from the earth. Venerable for age, distinguished for insight into human nature, remarkable for independence and courageous self-assertion, devoted to the welfare of her race, she has been for the last forty years an object of respect and admiration to social reformers everywhere.

Frederick Douglass.

BOSTON, Nov. 27.—Sojourner Truth was a remarkable figure in the anti-slavery movement, almost the only speaker in it who had once been a slave in a Northern State. Her Meg Merrilles figure added much to the effect of her speech.[1] Her natural wit and happiness in retort I have hardly ever seen equaled. Her eloquence was at times marvelous. I once heard her describe the captain of a slave ship going up to judgment followed by his victims as they gathered from the depth of the sea, in a strain that reminded me of Clarence's dream in Shakespeare, and equaled it. The anecdotes of her ready wit and quick, striking replies are numberless. But the whole together give little idea of the rich, quaint, poetic, and often profound speech of a most remarkable person, who used to say to us, "You read books; God himself talks to me."

WENDELL PHILLIPS.

Editor Fortune's Views.

The *Telegram* also interviewed T. Thomas Fortune,[2] editor of the *Globe,* the organ of the colored people of New York, who said: "Some steps should be taken to celebrate the death of Sojourner Truth, as she was one of the prominent figures of the past, and as it recalls the scenes through which she passed, and by which the colored people of to-day have profited largely. I do not think the colored people of to-day can afford to forget the labors through which they went; and such events as the death of Sojourner Truth should serve to recall that period, and to impress upon them that, now we are free, eternal vigilance is the price of liberty. There are few among us to-day whose names bring back the horrors of the past; and while we had many noble white women who sacrificed their time and talents to the suppression of human slavery, Sojourner Truth stands out most conspicuously as the one woman of her race who did valiant battle. Although the name of Sojourner Truth is familiar to many people, not more than one colored person out of ten knows who she is. This is accounted for in part from the fact that her life-work was confined mostly to the North. Some action will probably be taken by the Rev. W. B. Derrick,[3] of Bethel church, and other prominent colored people of this city."

Sojourner Truth.

The following is an interesting talk with this famous colored woman, who was liberated from slavery as far back as 1817; together with reminiscences of her association with the great abolitionists:—

Accompanied by two gentlemen well known in this city, a reporter for *The Inter Ocean* called yesterday afternoon at No. 22 Fortieth street. "Is Sojourner Truth in?" was answered affirmatively, and soon the venerable and famous guest of the house advanced quite unsupported into the parlor. Who would have believed, except on irrefutable evidence, that the erect and rapidly approaching figure had been on this earth one hundred and three years? The tufts of hair that protruded from under the neat white cap were as black as the kind, strongly-outlined face, in which intelligence and force of character were written in every lineament. As the old lady welcomed her callers with great dignity, the eyes sparkled with a lustre surpassing that of even the brand-new alpaca dress. At the throat was a white linen neckcloth, and matching this were the cuffs and the cap,—a Quakerish livery, and exactly suited to the hard, practical sense and heroic record of the wonderful woman. There was no trace of car-trumpet, more than of spectacles, and the robust and even stentorian voice would have surprised a basso profundo. Dropping back into a straight-backed chair, the ancient negress looked amused and pleased at the involuntary evidences of surprise at her appearance, and the bland smile discovered even rows of teeth harmonizing with the white of the eyes, "False? Yes," she afterward said, "And the only thing false about me." The hands, like the chin and face generally, were smooth and even plump, and but for a few deep lines on the forehead, the appearance, as well as the whole demeanor of the centenarian, was as of one less than half her age. Such marvelous preservation is certainly a phenomenon of the day; and the subsequent revelations were easily credited, that along with the gradual restoration of the color of the hair, which is still ridged here and there as with snow, have come back second sight and hearing. "I have well started on my second century of life," she smilingly said in the course of the conversation, "and God, blessed be his holy name, is putting new glass in the windows of the soul. Alleluia!"

"And this is Sojourner Truth," said a gentleman of the party, beginning the interview.

"Yes, and a great sojourner I have been these many years," the lady said, smiling.

"It is not a fact that you are over a hundred years old?"

"Well, I know of no contemporary to summon as a witness who could now tell the story. It is well settled, however, that I was over forty when I was freed from slavery, in 1817."

"But how young you look!"

"Everybody says I look younger than I did twenty years ago. My hair was as white as wool then, and my eyes almost gone."

"And you feel young, don't you, auntie?"

"Well, chile, let me tell you. It is the mind that makes the body. If I had no mind, I would be withered up. But the mind is the thing; new ideas, new thoughts bring a new mind and renew the whole system. I have lived to become a wonder to men and to my own self. I was paralyzed four years ago—this whole right side, clear up to the top of my head. It closed this eye, and it is rather weak now. On the limb the flesh fell out, or became gangrened, and two or three women fainted away to see it. But they doctored it like they would a horse, and I came up, although some gave me up, and I was even published for dead. This was when I was in Kalamazoo, where I had gone to hold a meeting. An old friend, whom I knew in Northampton, Mass., where I once lived, was telling of my death, and what I had done, and how I had traveled all over, and the good I had done, and now I was to rest in heaven. I hope he has only anticipated. And I really thought to myself the Lord wanted me to die while my name was up. I felt quite sad, almost, that I had not died while my name was up; but the Lord has been good; he has given me business to do, and has moved me to do it."

"You are now on your way to Kansas?"

"Yes, I am going out there to see the colored people; but I must stop and hold meetings to pay my way from Battle Creek and back again. I have prayed so long that my people would go to Kansas, and that God would make straight the way before them. Yes, indeed! I think it is a good move for them. I believe as much in that move as I do in the moving of the children of Egypt going out to Canaan, just as much. It will also be a benefit to the South, to the ungodly people there. The blacks can never be much in the South. They cannot get up. As long as the whites have the reins in their hands, how can the colored people get up there? I tell you they can't do it, for there is nothing to let them up. But if they come here to the North, and get the Northern spirit in them, they will prosper, and returning down there, some of them will teach these poor whites. They will go down there, and these colored people will bring them out of Egyptian darkness into marvelous light. The white people cannot do it, but these will; before forty years, they will teach the slaveholders the truth that they never had and never knew of. God works in a mysterious way. In Battle Creek a tramp came along, and looking upon him, a colored man recognized his old master, and gave him assistance to help him on; gave him his breakfast and supper. I tried my best, right after the war, to have colored people go to Kansas and settle on homes. I traveled there myself for this purpose, hoping to get the government to give a home to those colored people who were in Washington, living there at government expense, paying people great sums to feed them, when the money might carry them out to Kansas lands and fix it so they could support themselves. I was there in Arlington after the war, and for three years I hoped to get the people away. General Howard and General Butler approved of my general recommendation, and I see that my going to Kansas, though for the time being a failure, has been approved by the Lord, who is finally taking my people there in such numbers. The movement means the regeneration, temporally and spiritually, of the American colored race, and I always knew the Lord would find some way. I said his holy purpose must be fulfilled, and now he has put into their hearts to go out there, and not to stay South and be abused and heathenized any longer. There will be, chile, a great glory come out of that. I don't expect I will live to see it; but before this generation has passed away, there will be a grand change. This colored people is going to be a people. Do you think God has had them robbed and scourged all the days of their life for nothing?"

The old lady's voice had risen to a still higher note, and the closing sentences were pronounced with solemn gestures, including a slight swaying to and fro of the body and shaking of the head.

"It is well known, Auntie," said the reporter, "what an active interest you took in the war."

"Yes, chile; and I couldn't help going to see our God-given president. I had never spoken to one before. I had seen a number of presidents afar off in the city of New York, riding through, but I had never taken a president by the hand, to say, 'How do you do?' So I thought I would have an introduction to Mr. Lincoln, and it was a blessed introduction. He wanted me to see to the colored people. Terrible times! I told him that I had made up my mind to see him before the four years were up. 'I never heard of you,' I said, 'before you were put in for president;' and he said, 'Well, I have heard of you years and years before I ever thought of being president.' 'You are something like Daniel cast in the lion's den, and I don't know but the lions may tear you.' And he looked down on me, and said, 'They have not done it yet.' But they did do it. [A movement of the handkerchief toward the eyes.] I said: 'I thank God that you have been spared, for you are the best president that ever took the seat.' 'Oh, no,' he said; and he mentioned a number, Washington, and two or three others; I don't remember their names. 'Oh,' said I, 'they never did anything for us; they may have been good to others, but they neglected to do anything for my race.' Washington has a good name, but his name didn't reach to us. I knew well one of his slaves."

"Washington's slaves?"

"Yes, chile; Washington's slave. Her name was Mary Washington. We were intimate friends, but she died fifty years ago. So the president wanted me to see to the colored people at Arlington Heights and Mason's Island, where they came running in and died like cattle. They were driven in there, and the truth has never been given as it was. They would take and drive them in barns, and set fire and burn them up. Our boys would take some of the children, and taking them on their backs, would get them away from the rebels. This is the truth as they told it, and I suppose it's gospel. They certainly looked as though they had gone through fire and water. Oh, it was distressing, and the Marylanders are the most gross, low, savage, unfeeling set that ever was given birth, and treated my people worse than beasts. I don't say that all Maryland was so; but she didn't go out of the Union, and so made the colored people think she was going to help them, and then treacherously sent them to agonies."

"You have known yourself what the miseries of a slave are?"

"Indeed, yes, chile. I was sold from my parents when I was about eight or nine years old, as near as I can say, and cruel, cruel masters I had. There was nobody to tell me anything; I was just like a heathen. I was bred and born, if I was born at all, in the State of New York, among the Low Dutch people. They were very close and ignorant, and so, naturally, to this day I can neither read nor write. I knew God, but I didn't know Jesus Christ. I thought he was like Bonaparte or Washington, who were all the talk then. My mother, when I was sold from her, she used to set down and weep as if her heart would break; and I used to go and talk to her and ask what was the matter. And she said: 'Oh, matter enough, chile. Look up at the stars, and moon that shine on your brothers and sisters far away.' You see if anybody was sold twenty miles away, it was almost out of the world to the poor mother, who probably never would see them more. I asked who made the sun and stars. 'God;' and she said I must ask him to make my master and mistress kind. It is just as clear when she told me, as if I heard it from her now. That run in my mind, and I used to tell God what my master and mistress told me, and begged him that he would make my cruel master and mistress good. And I kept asking God, and at last I said, 'God, I don't think you can do it. O God, make them dead;' for I thought that all who died were killed by God. When I said that, my conscience burnt me. Isn't it singular, a heathen to have a conscience? But I nursed mine, and God talked to me the same as he still does. He came to me as a telegraph, like a dispatch to the brain, and thereby hangs the explanation of my name."

"Indeed! how did you come by it?"

"I will tell you; it has never been truly given before. Well, the Lord gave it to me. It came to me just like a telegraph dispatch to the brain; and God made my brain."

"Didn't your mother call you by that name?" said one of the visiting gentlemen.

"My mother? Oh, no, chile; I didn't get that name till I had been freed in 1817, along with all other New York slaves, and had been in New York City for some years. I wanted to be good when I got

there, and also to get some money. I had found out that I was a poor
sinner, and it was a greater proof to me than ever to find out how
people may be misers with all their religion. I thought I would work
and put some money in a savings bank. Well, I lived with the best
people in the city; and though I was only careful of my earnings, it
came to me that I had robbed the poor. My industry had doubtless
kept some poor wretches from paying work. I felt it, and I said,
'Lord, I will give all back that ever I have taken away.' I wanted to
give everything away, and I cried, 'Lord, what wilt thou have me to
do?' And it came to me, 'Go out of the city.' And I said, 'I will go—
just go.' And that night—it was night—I said, 'Lord, whither shall
I go?' And the voice came to me just as plain as my own now, 'Go
East.' And I just put a change of clothes into a pillow-case, and
started. All the money I had with me was twenty-five cents, given
to me by a good man at prayer-meeting. My outstanding moneys,
which I had meant to put in the savings bank, I never thought of
any more. And just as I was taking leave of Mrs. Whiting, where I
had such a pleasant home, it came to me that I must have a new
home, and I said, 'The Lord is going to give me a new home, Mrs.
Whiting, and I am going away.' 'Where are you going?' 'Going
East.' 'What does that mean?' 'The Lord has directed me to go East,
and leave this city at once.' 'Belle, you are crazy.' 'No, I a'n't.' And she
said to her husband, 'Why, Belle's crazy.' Said he, 'I guess not.' 'But
I tell you she is; she says she 's going to have a new name, too. Don't
that look crazy?' 'Oh, no,' he said, and urged me to have breakfast.
But I would not stay, and I went down to the boat and over to
Brooklyn, just a landing place then. I paid my fare out of the
twenty-five cents, and started on afoot with my pillow-case. As I
started, it came to me that the name was Sojourner. 'There,' said I
to my self, 'the name has come' [laughter]; and I walked on about
four miles. Then I felt a little hungry, and a Quaker lady gave me a
drink of water, asking me my name. I said, 'My name is Sojourner.'
I can see her now. 'What is thy name?' said she. Said I, 'Sojourner.'
'Where does thee get such a name as that?' Said I, 'The Lord has
given it to me.' 'Thee gave it to thyself, didn't thee,' said she, 'and not
the Lord? Has that been thy name long?' Said I, 'No.' 'What was thy
name?' 'Belle.' 'Belle what?' 'Whatever my master's name was.'
'Well, thee says thy name is Sojourner?' 'Yes.' 'Sojourner what?'

Well, I confessed I hadn't thought of that; and thereupon she picked that name to pieces, and made it look so different that I said, 'It don't seem to be such a name after all.' But I said I must go, and replied pettishly that I couldn't tell where my friends were until I got there. And so I plodded on over the sandy road, and was very hot and miserable. And in my wretchedness I said, 'O God, give me a name with a handle to it. Oh that I had a name with a handle to it!' And it came to me in that moment, dear chile, like a voice, just as true as God is true, 'Sojourner *Truth.*' And I leaped for joy—Sojourner Truth! 'Why,' said I, 'thank you, God; that is a good name. Thou art my last master, and thy name is Truth; and Truth shall be my abiding name till I die.' I had before had five other masters; and at the age of over forty, and the mother of five children, I was liberated."

"Well, you went East?"

"Yes, chile, and very soon found myself at Northampton, talking religion and abolition all the way wherever they would hear me. At Northampton I worked under Sam Hill, one of the best anti-slavery men in that abolition community. I was with them heart and soul for anything concerning human right, and my belief is in me yet, and can't get out. George Benson, brother-in-law of William Lloyd Garrison, was one of them. What good times we had! If any were infidels, I wish the world were full of such infidels. Religion without humanity is a poor human stuff. They built me a house in Florence. I was there about seven years ago, and they still call it by my name. Sam Hill built that house for me, and I paid him for it. Then I sold that house and bought one in Michigan, five miles from Battle Creek, where old friends of mine from Ulster County, N. Y., had removed, and wanted me to follow."

"When did you remove to Battle Creek?"

"Twenty years ago. I have near me my three daughters."

"You of course were a conductor on the underground railway, so to speak."

"Yes, indeed, chile. Though I came out of the Empire State, I had a warm heart for every Ethiopian in the land, and it almost broke over their woes. I lectured in New York under the auspices of the Tappans, and talked all through the East. I have spoken in favor of the slave in twenty-two States, including Indiana, another maugre section of this country."

"You knew Mr. Garrison?"

"Knew him! I should think I did. And I knew Theo. Parker, the so-called great infidel. I knew John G. Whittier[4]—in fact, I knew all the good people in the anti-slavery movement. I have sat on the platform with John G. Whittier. One time we had a great meeting a little out of Boston, and Garrison was there, and all the anti-slavery people. And there were two ex-slaves there, just arrived, who had put on the clothes just prepared for them. One was fat; the other was very lean. And the one that was fat had his clothes very tight on him, and I never laughed so in my life as when Garrison said, 'Here are two who have come to us, that we have to befriend. One has been a hostler, and the other has been a cook; I guess you can tell which has been the cook. Oh, I thought we would burst up, he was so bursting fat, you know. There were a thousand friends there, and I was selling songs; for I always had something to pay my way with. Nobody paid me, for I was a free agent, to go and come when I pleased. I would sell the songs for five and ten cents apiece, and that time some hesitated, asking, 'What tune do you sing it to?' and I didn't know. So Garrison said, 'Now, Sojourner, you go on the plat-form and make a speech, and you will sell your songs like anything.' Garrison sold a good many of my little songs for me, always. So I went up there, and Garrison called for order. Said he, 'It is time to begin.' And the people came and sat down on the boards, and some stood. 'Now,' said he, 'Sojourner Truth will address you in her own peculiar way, and Wendell Phillips will follow.' Well, I thought to myself that I didn't care about his following; but I thought, 'I can do one thing that he can't do.' I had some home-made songs—I used to make many songs. 'I will sing that to begin with, and that will stand a good chance.' So I said I had a home-made song that I wanted to sing. So I sung one; and if I skipped a part, nobody was the wiser. I sung this—I've carried it in memory ever since."

Saying which, the old lady broke out into a pathetic song, sung in a not unpleasant, though quivering, voice, probably the only solo ever given in Chicago by one of her years. "When my voice was good and strong," she said, "I could make that roar." Here it is:

"Whilst I bear upon my body
   The scars of many a gash,
I am pleading for my people,
   Who groan beneath the lash.

"I am pleading for the mothers
   Who gaze in wild despair
Upon the hated auction block,
   And see their children there.

"I am pleading for my people,
   A poor, down-trodden race,
Who dwell in freedom's boasted land,
   With no abiding place.

"Yet those oppressors, steeped in guilt—
   I still would have them live;
For I have learned of Jesus
   To suffer and forgive."

"After I got through, how the people did clap; and then Wendell Phillips got up, and everything I had said he took hold of. And he had a little paper in his hand, and said, 'Well may Sojourner Truth say so and so;' and if he had not said that, I would not have known that I had said anything; and he dressed it up so, and made it so fine, that I was glad I spoke fust, instead of sorry."

"Did you know Lucretia Mott?"

"Oh, very well. I was where she was, in Rochester, a year ago in July. She is not as old as I am, but she is all broke down. And she said, as much as seven or eight years ago, 'Why, Sojourner, how is it that I am so wrinkled, and your face is just as smooth as can be?' 'Well,' said I, 'I have two skins; I have a white skin under, and a black one to cover it.'"

"You have heard Fred Douglass often?"

"Oh, yes; I saw him in July."

"Your eyesight is good?"

"Oh, yes; I can see you as good as ever I could, I suppose. I did wear spectacles, when ironing, for thirty or forty years, but I don't want any now."

"Do you feel you are growing old?"

"Yes, chile; I used to be like a lash of a whip, just as strong. I used to manage as much as the strongest man. I had one child sold into slavery in Alabama, but he was recovered, it not being lawful."

In closing, the lady said she had been a Methodist till that church outgrew her; it had changed, and not she. She then preached quite a sermon, and very energetically, against the worldliness of professing Christians, and insisted that they should obey the command to "come out and be separate."

Sojourner will leave for Kansas in a day or two.

Sojourner's Favorite Song.

We are going home; we have visions bright
Of that holy land, that world of light
Where the long, dark night of sin is past,
And the morning of eternity has come at last;
Where the weary saints no more shall roam,
But dwell in a sunny and peaceful home;
Where the brow celestial gems shall crown,
And waves of bliss are dashing 'round.

CHORUS: Oh, that beautiful home! oh, that beautiful world!

We are going home; we soon shall be
Where the sky is clear, and the soil is free;
Where the victors' song floats over the plains,
And the seraphs' anthem blends with the strains;
Where the sun rolls down his brilliant flood,
And beams on a world all fair and good;
And the stars that shone on nature's dome
Will sparkle and dance o'er the spirits' home.

CHORUS.

The tears and sighs which here were given,
Exchanged for the glad songs of heaven;
The beauteous forms that sing and shine,
Are guarded well by a hand divine.
Pure love and friendship joined,
Are waving above that princely band;
And the glory of God, like a molten sea,
Shall bathe that immortal company.

CHORUS.

The ransomed throng, the sea of bliss,
The holy city of gorgeousness,
The verdant earth, the angel choir,
The flowers that never winter wear,
The conqueror's song—it sounds afar;
'Tis wafted on ambrosial air.
Through endless years, we then shall prove
The depths of a Saviour's matchless love.

CHORUS.

ENDNOTES

Narrative of Sojourner Truth

1. (p. 6) *"She often speaks of T. W. Higginson and Frances D. Gage—thinks 'dey are appointed of God'"*: Thomas Wentworth Higginson (1823–1911) was a prominent abolitionist writer and a colonel in the Union Army in the Civil War, during which he commanded the first black regiment in the U.S. armed forces. Gage (1808–1884) was an abolitionist and a suffragist. She authored one of the best-known essays of her time on Truth, "Reminiscences of Sojourner Truth," which includes Truth's famous speech, "A'rn't (Ain't) I a Woman?" (see pp. 99–101), which was republished in *The History of Woman Suffrage*, vol. 1, edited by Elizabeth Cady Stanton et al., New York: Fowler and Wells, 1881.

2. (p. 9) *She was the daughter of James and Betsey, slaves of one Colonel Ardinburgh, Hurley, Ulster County, New York:* Colonel Johannis Hardenbergh was a member of the Low Dutch community. "Low Dutch" refers to both migrants to New York from Holland and the dialect they developed.

3. (p. 26) *a mere farce, a mock marriage, unrecognized by any civil law:* Olive Gilbert apparently was unaware that New York State legally recognized marriages between slaves, unlike the law in southern states.

4. (p. 31) *Slaves have sometimes been severely punished for adding their master's name to their own:* Olive Gilbert is making reference to the illegitimate and unrecognized bi- and multi-racial offspring of white masters, who were often prohibited from carrying their father's names, despite their lineage.

5. (p. 32) *he had sold her child to a Dr. Gedney, who took him with him as far as New York City. . . . who took him to his own home in Alabama. This illegal and fraudulent transaction:* New York State law prohibited the sale of slaves to other states. This prohibition was enacted to ensure that those slated for emancipation under New York's legislatively approved process of gradual emancipation would actually be freed, rather than remain enslaved elsewhere.

6. (p. 46) *Frederick Douglass:* One of the most prominent African-American abolitionists of his time, Douglass (1818?–1895) authored the celebrated *Narrative of the Life of Frederick Douglass, an American Slave, Written by Himself*, which established him as the father of African-American literature.

7. (p. 54) *Two years passed before Isabella knew what character Peter was establishing for himself . . . passing under the assumed name of Peter Williams:* The Rev. Peter

Williams, Jr. (1780–1840), an ordained Episcopal priest, was the founder and first pastor of St. Philips African Church, whose congregation included many of New York City's most prominent African Americans. Peter Williams, Sr. (1749–1823), was a businessman and a founder of the African Methodist Episcopal Zion Church; chartered in 1801, it was the first African-American church in New York.

8. (p. 58) *she was gradually drawn into the 'kingdom' set up by the prophet Matthias:* Robert Matthews, a Scotsman from New Jersey, led the cult-like charismatic Pentecostal group called the Kingdom of Matthias, to which Truth belonged. The organization ended in disgrace in 1835 with allegations that Matthias had murdered a wealthy member of the group and committed sexual improprieties.

9. (p. 70) *Those who are curious to know what there transpired. . . . she happily escaped the contamination that surrounded her,—assiduously endeavoring to discharge all her duties in a becoming manner:* The Folgers, members of the Kingdom of Matthias, accused Truth of attempting to poison them. Truth was tried and found not guilty; she then sued the Folgers for slander and won.

"Book of Life"

1. (p. 98) *she left her home in Northampton, Mass., for a lecturing tour in Western New York, accompanied by the Hon. George Thompson of England:* George Elijah Thompson (1804–1878) was an activist against slavery and indenture in the British colonies. At the request of William Lloyd Garrison (see note 6, below) and others, he came to address antislavery audiences in the United States in 1834. He returned in 1851 and again during the Civil War. He was met with great hostility, and his life was frequently threatened by pro-slavery mobs.

2. (p. 99) *"An abolition affair!" 'Woman's rights and niggers!' 'We told you so!' 'Go it, old darkey!'":* It was a common concern of abolitionists and suffragists that by blending the concerns of the two constituencies they might weaken the persuasive force of their arguments.

3. (p. 100) *She spoke in deep tones . . . "'Well, chilern, whar dar is so much racket dar must be something out o' kilter'":* This poor approximation of southern African American dialect is nothing like how Truth—a New Yorker and native Dutch speaker—would have spoken. Gage was using popular racist conventions to depict Truth's blackness through speech, without concern for its accuracy.

4. (p. 101) *Parker Pillsbury was speaker, and criticized freely the conduct of the churches regarding slavery:* Pillsbury (1809–1898) was a Congregationalist minister whose clerical license was revoked for his outspoken critique of the church's complicity with slavery. He went on to become an abolitionist orator, author, and editor with Elizabeth Cady Stanton, of *Revolution*, a weekly women's suffrage periodical.

5. (p. 102) *Marius Robinson, of Salem, Ohio, editor of the* Anti-Slavery Bugle, *whose*

clarion notes never faltered in freedom's cause, was her friend and co-laborer: Rev.
Marius R. Robinson (1806–1878) was an itinerant lecturer for the American
Anti-Slavery Society in Ohio (1836–1839) and later an editor of the *Anti-
Slavery Bugle* (1851–1861) in Salem, Ohio.

6. (p. 103) *W. L. Garrison:* One of the most important and uncompromising abolitionists, William Lloyd Garrison (1805–1879) established the antislavery
newspaper *The Liberator* with the slogan "Our country is the world—our
countrymen are mankind." He also founded the New England Anti-Slavery
Society and helped organize the American Anti-Slavery Society. After emancipation, he focused his energies on temperance and women's suffrage.

7. (p. 103) *H. B. Stowe:* Harriet Beecher Stowe (1811–1896) was the celebrated
author of *Uncle Tom's Cabin* and other novels, as well as books of nonfiction.
Stowe was a reformer, as well as one of the forerunners of late-nineteenth-
century literary realism.

8. (p. 104) *Sojourner told them that her breasts had suckled many a white babe, to the
exclusion of her own offspring:* It seems unlikely that Truth would have been a
wet nurse for white babies, as that practice was relatively unusual in the North.
It is more likely that Truth was taking some poetic license here, and using her
powerful voice to communicate the condition of many southern black women.

9. (p. 106) *Mrs. Griffing:* Josephine White Griffing (1814–1872) was an anti-
slavery activist and a women's rights advocate. Her home in Litchfield, Ohio,
was a stop on the Underground Railroad. She worked for the Western Anti-
Slavery Society, was a founder of the Ohio Woman's Rights Association, and
lectured frequently on both subjects. After emancipation, she advocated the
creation of the Freedmen's Bureau and helped run several of its employment
offices in the North.

10. (p. 109) *"The graphic sketch of her by the author of 'Uncle Tom's Cabin'":* Stowe's
essay "Sojourner Truth: The Libyan Sibyl" was a celebrated depiction of Truth,
though it was full of racist imagery and factual errors. For instance, Stowe
states that Truth has died (see p. 125), though she was alive at the time Stowe
was writing. She also portrayed Truth as speaking in a stereotype of southern
black dialect, as did Frances Gage (see note 3, above).

11. (p. 114) *Dr. Beecher:* Henry Ward Beecher (1813–1887) was the brother of
Harriet Beecher Stowe and an influential preacher who opposed slavery and
advocated suffrage for women.

12. (p. 124) *Wendell Phillips:* A Harvard-trained lawyer, Phillips (1811–1884) was
converted to the abolitionist cause by William Lloyd Garrison. He went on to
become the American Anti-Slavery Society's most popular speaker and served
as its president after Garrison resigned in 1865. He also authored numerous
essays and pamphlets decrying slavery.

13. (p. 126) *he showed me the clay model of the Libyan Sibyl:* The designation "Libyan
Sibyl" likely has its origins in a detail by the same name in Michelangelo's Sis-

tine Ceiling. The detail portrays the strong, almost masculine, physique and elaborately braided hair of a female seer.

14. (p. 130) *"The president was seated at his desk. . . . He then arose, gave me his hand, made a bow, and said, 'I am pleased to see you'":* Abolitionist Lucy N. Colman recounts in her memoirs that Elizabeth Keckley, Mary Todd Lincoln's dressmaker, described this meeting far less favorably. However, Truth had reason to allow the mythology of her encounter with the President to stand, for the sake of the morale of the newly emancipated African Americans.

15. (p. 134) *Soon after the Freedman's Bureau was established, Sojourner was appointed to assist in the hospital:* The U.S. Bureau of Refugees, Freedmen, and Abandoned Lands (1865–1872) was established by Congress in the aftermath of the Civil War as an agency providing training, resources, and teachers to assist the newly freed. The bureau also provided medical services through its hospitals and distributed rations. However, it failed to provide the economic redistribution or political transformation necessary to ensure African Americans their full rights after the end of this period.

16. (p. 137) *Mrs. Laura Haviland:* Haviland (1808–1898) was an abolitionist who helped form the first antislavery society, and first Underground Railroad station, in Michigan. The town of Haviland, Kansas, is named for her, in honor of her work on behalf of the freed people who relocated there to escape the backlash against Reconstruction in the South.

17. (p. 143) *Gen. Howard:* General Oliver Otis Howard (1830–1909) served in the Union Army during the Civil War and afterward headed the Freedmen's Bureau. Howard University, in Washington, D.C., one of the nation's preeminent historically black universities, which he helped to found, is named after him.

18. (p. 145) *"We, the undersigned, therefore earnestly request your honorable body to set apart for them a portion of the public land in the West":* Truth sought to secure a place for African Americans in the new settlements in the West. She was likely inspired by the reservations that were being established for American Indians and the homestead movement. Benjamin "Pap" Singleton (1809–1892) called for a movement of African Americans from the southern states to Kansas in the 1870s. A massive exodus took place in 1879, motivated by resettlement activists like Singleton and growing southern violence against African Americans.

19. (p. 153) *Rev. Gilbert Haven:* Haven (1821–1880) was a Methodist Episcopal bishop who supported the freed people's aspirations to education by helping to establish Clark Atlanta University.

20. (p. 153) *Rev. L. A. Grimes:* Leonard Grimes was a prominent black abolitionist and pastor of the Twelfth Baptist Church in Boston.

21. (p. 153) *William Wells Brown, M. D.:* Brown (c.1814–1884) escaped from slavery in Kentucky and became a conductor on the Underground Railroad, as well as a highly regarded lecturer on the antislavery circuit. He is believed to be the

first African American to publish a novel, a travel book, and a play; he also authored several historical books as well as a popular autobiography.

22. (p. 158) *Mrs. Lucy Stone:* Stone (1818–1893) was an abolitionist, a lecturer on women's suffrage, and a founder of the American Woman Suffrage Association. She was controversial for maintaining her maiden name after marriage.

23. (p. 158) *Mrs. Livermore:* Mary Ashton Rice Livermore (1820–1905) was a noted author and organizer on behalf of women's suffrage and rights. She was a founding member of the American Woman Suffrage Association.

24. (p. 159) *Mrs. Paulina W. Davis:* A feminist and social reformer, Paulina Kellogg Wright Davis (1813–1876) organized the first National Woman's Rights Convention and established *The Una*, the first women's suffrage paper owned and operated by a woman.

25. (p. 160) *Rev. Norwood Damon:* Damon (1816–1884) was a spiritualist lecturer and reformer.

26. (p. 162) *Elijah F. Pennypacker:* Elijah Funk Pennypacker (1802–1888) was an abolitionist and a manager of the Underground Railroad in Pennsylvania.

27. (p. 168) *"The principal points touched were . . . the inconsistent relations assumed by Greeley:"* Horace Greeley (1811–1872) was a radical Republican who initially supported full equality for the freed people but eventually sought to restore relations with the South and disavow Reconstruction. Here reference is made to his 1872 challenge of Grant for the presidency. He was roundly defeated, winning only six states.

28. (p. 169) *"The book in question contains scores on scores of names. . . . Foremost in the list is Lucretia Mott's":* An outspoken leader of the women's rights and antislavery movements, Mott (1793–1880) was known for her oratorical gifts. She was one of the cofounders of the first women's rights convention in the United States, held at Seneca Falls, New York, in 1848.

29. (pp. 169–170) *There are letters from Gerritt Smith . . . Theodore Tilton":* Philanthropist Gerrit Smith (1797–1874) lectured on and gave generously to the causes of abolition, temperance, and women's rights. A reformer who spoke eloquently for women's rights and abolition and wrote poetry and essays, Tilton (1835–1907) today is best known for suing Henry Ward Beecher for criminal indecency with his wife, Elizabeth Tilton.

30. (p. 180) *Rowland Johnson:* One of the first abolitionists, Johnson (1816–1886) was a member of the Society of Friends and participated in a number of charitable organizations.

31. (p. 186) *Amy Post:* Amy Kirby Post (1802–1889) and her husband, Isaac Post, (1798–1872) were Quaker abolitionists and advocates of women's rights, spiritualism, and temperance. Their Rochester home was a stop on the Underground Railroad. Amy was a close friend of Harriet Jacobs (1813–1897), author of *Incidents in the Life of a Slave Girl*, and wrote the postscript to the book under a pseudonym.

32. (p. 187) *Oliver Johnson:* Johnson (1809–1889) was an abolitionist and reformer.

33. (p. 188) *Samuel J. May:* Samuel Joseph May (1797–1871) was a Harvard-educated antislavery Unitarian minister who was among the first clergymen to advocate suffrage for women. His Syracuse home was a stop on the Underground Railroad; he also supported temperance and penal reform. He served as principal of the Normal School for girls in Lexington, Massachusetts.

34. (p. 189) *Samuel L. Hill:* Hill (born 1808) was the spiritual and financial leader of the Northampton Association of Education and Industry, the egalitarian society where Sojourner Truth found a home.

35. (p. 190) *C. A. F. Stebbins . . . Giles B. Stebbins:* Catherine A. Fish Stebbins (born 1823) was the wife of Giles Badger Stebbins (1817–1900), a prominent antislavery lecturer, and later a spiritualist and supporter of suffrage for women.

36. (p. 192) *Joseph A. Dugdale:* A member of the temperance, peace, and abolitionist movements, Dugdale (1810–1896) was one of a number of abolitionists whose activism resulted in his alienation from the Quaker community.

37. (p. 193) *Byron M. Smith:* Smith was a Kansas land agent who worked with Truth as she pursued the goal of settlement in the western states.

38. (p. 195) *Rachel C. Mather:* Following the Civil War, Mather, a native of Boston, founded and was principal of the Mather Industrial School for African Americans in Beaufort, South Carolina.

39. (p. 200) *"After he left, my friends told me that that gentleman was Mayor Bowen":* Sayles J. Bowen (1813–1896) was mayor of Washington, D.C., from 1868 to 1870.

40. (p. 202) *Josephine S. Griffing:* In this letter, Griffing (see note 9, above) is referring to Truth's work finding employment in northern states for African Americans who had gone to Washington, D.C., in the years following the Civil War.

41. (p. 206) *Charles Sumner:* Sumner (1811–1874), a lawyer from Boston who became a political radical after reading the work of Lydia Maria Child (see note 52, below), was in the vanguard of many reform movements. He helped form the Free Soil Party, challenged school segregation in Boston, and was elected to Congress, where he was the Senate's leading opponent of slavery. After emancipation, as a Radical Republican, he was a fierce advocate of the first Civil Rights Bill in 1866. He remained frustrated by public figures, in particular President Grant, who did not sufficiently advocate rights for African Americans.

42. (p. 207) *Susan B. Anthony:* The most famous of the early feminists, Anthony (1820–1906) advocated for women's property rights in land and labor and pushed for the University of Rochester to admit women. She founded the first women's temperance organization and was a supporter of the antislavery cause.

43. (p. 210) *Nannette B. Gardner:* In 1871, Nannette Brown Ellingwood Gardner (1828–1900) became one of the first two women to vote in a Michigan city or state election. It would be almost fifty years before another woman would be allowed to vote in the state.

44. (p. 212) *Adin Ballou:* Ballou (1803–1890) was founder of the utopian community at Hopedale, Massachusetts, and a leading nineteenth-century exponent of pacifism and Christian socialism, as well as a supporter of abolition and temperance. Lucy Hunt Ballou (1810–1891) was his second wife.

45. (p. 220) *Henry Wilson:* A senator from Massachusetts, Wilson (1812–1875) served as the eighteenth vice president of the United States, under President Ulysses S. Grant.

46. (p. 220) *Elizabeth Cady Stanton:* Stanton (1815–1902) was an abolitionist and architect of the 1848 Seneca Falls Convention on women's suffrage. She remained a leader of the women's rights movement for the rest of her life. Stanton was the cousin of Gerrit Smith (see note 29, above), another reformer with whom Truth interacted.

47. (p. 221) *S. C. Pomeroy:* Samuel Clarke Pomeroy (1816–1891) was a Republican senator from Kansas and an agent of the New England Emigrant Aid Company, an institution dedicated to the abolitionist settlement of the Kansas Territory and its admittance to the Union as a free state.

48. (p. 221) *George W. Julian:* An Indiana congressman from the Free Soil Party, George Washington Julian (1817–1899) stood for women's suffrage and against slavery and corporate growth.

49. (p. 222) *Jacob M. Howard:* Jacob Merritt Howard (1805–1871) was a Michigan representative to the U.S. House of Representatives and, later, to the U.S. Senate; while in the Senate, he drafted the first clause of the Thirteenth Amendment to the Constitution, which reads: "All persons born or naturalized in the United States, and subject to the jurisdiction thereof, are citizens of the United States and of the state wherein they reside."

50. (p. 227) *"Jonathan Walker, the original of 'The Branded Hand'":* Captain Jonathan Walker (1799–1878) was captured in 1844 aiding runaway slaves trying to escape to the Bahamas and was punished with imprisonment and by having his left hand branded with the initials "S.S.," for "slave stealer." He was deemed a martyr of the antislavery cause and memorialized by John Greenleaf Whittier (see note 4 to "A Memorial Chapter," below) in the poem "The Branded Hand," in which "S.S." is said to stand for "Slave Savior." After his release, Walker traveled, lecturing on his ordeal and exhibiting his hand, which he called the coat of arms of the United States.

51. (p. 230) *Many of the old line abolitionists were there . . . Charles Lenox Rimond, and a host of others:* Charles Lenox Remond (1810–1878) was born of free blacks in Massachusetts. He was the first African-American lecturer for the Anti-Slavery Society and is believed to be the first black public abolitionist lecturer in the United States. Like Frederick Douglass, he traveled abroad to lecture; together Remond and Douglass advocated that blacks abandon churches that would not allow them full membership.

52. (p. 239) *Lydia Maria Child:* A novelist, editor, journalist, and scholar, Lydia Maria Francis Child (1802–1880) was also a radical abolitionist and an advocate of American Indian rights. Today, though, she is mainly remembered as the author of the Thanksgiving poem "Over the River and Through the Woods."

"A Memorial Chapter"

1. (p. 252) *Her Meg Merrilles figure added much to the effect of her speech:* Meg Merrilies is a character in Sir Walter Scott's novel *Guy Mannering;* she also appears in John Keats's poem "Meg Merrilies." She is described as an exotic sorceress or Amazon, tall, masculine, and unusual—similar to the way Sojourner Truth was described.

2. (p. 252) *T. Thomas Fortune:* Timothy Thomas Fortune (1856–1928) was one of the most prominent black journalists during the period of the rapid growth and rise of the black press in the late nineteenth century. A leading advocate for African-American civil and political rights, he was a key founder of the Afro-American League, a forerunner of the National Association for the Advancement of Colored People (NAACP), and he worked with such luminaries as Booker T. Washington and W. E. B. Du Bois.

3. (p. 252) *Rev. W. B. Derrick:* Derrick (born 1843) was a bishop of the African-American Episcopal church, and president of the board of directors of Payne Theological Seminary, at that time part of Wilberforce University, the oldest private black university in the United States.

4. (p. 260) *John G. Whittier:* John Greenleaf Whittier (1807–1892), the self-educated and distinguished poet and abolitionist, served in the Massachusetts legislature, and advocated a number of humanitarian causes.

INSPIRED BY
NARRATIVE OF SOJOURNER TRUTH

Sojourner Truth's life has inspired generations of ordinary Americans, without regard to gender, class, or race. Her accomplishments have also motivated artists in many fields to immortalize her in their work.

"The Libyan Sibyl"

Sculptor William Wetmore Story (1819–1895), son of antislavery U.S. Supreme Court Justice Joseph Story, was a friend of essayist and poet Ralph Waldo Emerson and one of the first artists to be inspired by Sojourner Truth. In her 1863 essay "Sojourner Truth, the Libyan Sibyl" (included in the "Book of Life" portion of this volume), Harriet Beecher Stowe (1811–1896) recounts a conversation with Story: When visiting him in Rome, Stowe learned that Story had "begun to turn to Egypt in search of a type of art which should represent a larger and more vigorous development of nature than the cold elegance of Greek lines." For Story, African-influenced art was the next frontier. Stowe told Story about the life of Sojourner Truth, and two years later, after completing his sculpture "Cleopatra," the artist called on Stowe and "requested me to come and repeat to him the history of Sojourner Truth, saying that the conception had never left him. I did so; and a day or two after, he showed me the clay model of the Libyan Sibyl" (p. 126). In classical mythology, a sibyl is a prophetess; Story saw Truth as a contemporary prophetess, though Truth downplayed the tribute. Her "Book of Life" records, "She would never listen to Mrs. Stowe's 'Libyan Sibyl'. 'Oh!' she would say, 'I don't want to hear about that old symbol; read me something that is going on now, something about this great war'"

(p. 128). Story's "The Libyan Sibyl" is now part of the permanent collection of the Metropolitan Museum of Art in New York City.

Theater about Sojourner Truth

A number of dramatizations of Truth's life appeared in the twentieth century. In 1948 "Sojourner Truth," by noted poet and playwright Katherine Garrison Chapin (later Biddle; 1890–1977), opened in New York and was praised for its strong characterization of the title character. The musical "Miss Truth," by Broadway veteran Glory Van Scott, played as part of the Newport Jazz Festival in 1972. The *New York Times* reported, "It broke all of the rules of cool professionalism to lay its heart and—literally—hands on an audience." Intended for middle-school audiences, Sandra Fenichel Asher's play "A Woman Called Truth" was published in 1993. It begins: "My name? Which one is that, I wonder. Oh, I've had a bunch of them in my day. And a bunch of days for each of them. Yes, indeed, I've lived a life, I have."

Truth, *by Jacqueline Sheehan*

Novelist Jacqueline Sheehan published her debut work *Truth*, a fictionalized life of Sojourner Truth, in 2003. The robust and striking account describes the extremes of horror and hope that Truth experienced. Sheehan's novel attempts to humanize its title character by exploding the legend of a faultless, omnipotent public figure and replacing it with a flesh-and-blood woman. Sheehan, a psychologist, spent five years researching the novel, drawing upon her professional training to describe in convincing detail how Truth's religion drove her incredible social activism. While remaining relatively true to life, the first-person narrative allows Sheehan to capture Truth's incendiary voice, thereby underscoring the orator's enormous personality. The first page reads, "Mau Mau said every child is born a different way. Some are born by water, some by lightning, some by blizzards, and some squeeze in through the cracks in the wall. You never know until the baby arrives." As for Truth? "I rode to earth on the backside of a comet."

COMMENTS & QUESTIONS

In this section, we aim to provide the reader with an array of perspectives on the text, as well as questions that challenge those perspectives. The commentary has been culled from sources as diverse as reviews contemporaneous with the work, letters written by the author, literary criticism of later generations, and appreciations written throughout the work's history. Following the commentary, a series of questions seeks to filter Narrative of Sojourner Truth *through a variety of points of view and bring about a richer understanding of this enduring work.*

Comments

G. W. P.

'Sojourner Truth,' a negro woman, formerly a slave in the State of New York, made some acceptable remarks, in her peculiar manner. This woman, who can neither read nor write, will often speak with an ability which surprises the educated and refined. She possesses a mind of rare power, and often, in the course of short speeches, will throw out gems of thought. But the truly Christian spirit which pervades all she says, endears her to all who know her. Though she has suffered all the ills of slavery, she forgives all who have wronged her most freely. She said her home should be open to the man who held her as a slave, and who had so much wronged her. She would feed him and take care of him if he was hungry and poor. 'O friends,' said she, 'pity the poor slaveholder, and pray for him. It troubles me more than anything else, what will become of the poor slaveholder, in all his guilt and all his impenitence. God will take care of the poor trampled slave, but where will the slaveholder be when eternity begins?'

Sojourner has attended several of these conventions, for the purpose of selling her most interesting Narrative, and all who become acquainted with her esteem her most highly.

—from *The Liberator* (April 4, 1851)

NEW YORK TRIBUNE

Mrs. Sojourner Truth, a colored woman, and a slave until emancipated by this State in 1828, delivered a very interesting discourse last evening at the First Congregational Church in Sixth st., between 3d and 4th avs. . . .

She had been robbed of education—her rights; robbed of her children, her father, mother, sister and brother; yet she lived; and not only lived, but God lived in her. (Applause) Why was her race despised? What had they done that they should be hated? She frequently asked this question, but never had received any answer. Was it because they were black? They had not made themselves black; and if they had done anything wrong why not let them know, that they might repent of that wrong. It had been said that the colored people were careless, and regardless of their rights and liberties; and this was partly true, though she hoped for better things in future. And why had they been careless and unheard? It was indeed hard that their oppressors should bind them hand and foot, and ask them why did they not run. . . .

She deprecated the people who were satisfied with their enslaved lot, and as a colored woman, she wanted *all* the rights she was entitled to. Her address occupied a considerable time, and at its conclusion an interesting narrative of hers was handed round, and several copies sold for her benefit. She intends to hold other meetings in New York and bids fair to excite considerable interest and popularity.

—September 7, 1853

HARRIET CARTER

The secret of [Sojourner Truth's] fascinating power lay in her distinct personality. Her incisive mind from its very lack of education, was also untrammeled by the necessarily attendant train of imparted ideas, and so sought and grasped truths in its own original way. Her nature was impulsive, and overflowing with affection,—in the first days of her Christian experience she thanked God that He had given her so much love in her heart that "she couldn't help lovin' even de white folks." Enthusiasm, perseverance, the courage of her convictions, and true self-respect, were marked traits which helped to win her great success.

No more unique character ever stamped its impression upon the history of any age. As geologists discover now and then in fossil remains certain rare and peculiar specimens which, far surpassing all others of the same class, exhibit the highest development possible under the once existing conditions of their formation, so students of history will find in the records of Sojourner Truth a phenomenal production of the days of slavery.

—from *The Chautauquan* (May 1887)

ANGELA Y. DAVIS
"Ain't I a Woman?"—the refrain of the speech Sojourner Truth delivered at an 1851 women's convention in Akron, Ohio—remains one of the most frequently quoted slogans of the nineteenth-century women's movement.

—from *Women, Race, & Class* (1981)

ERLENE STETSON AND LINDA DAVID
The woman who boarded the Fulton Street ferry early in the morning on the first day of June 1843 had chosen for herself a name that resonated with the pain of an oppressed people dwelling for many generations in a strange land. Within the Old Testament context the sojourner was the non-Hebrew stranger who lived among the Hebrews. During part of their own history, the Hebrews had lived as sojourners among the Egyptians, with some rights and duties; afterward they had been enslaved: "My people went down aforetime into Egypt to sojourn there; and the Assyrians oppressed them without cause" (Isaiah 53:4).

—from *Glorying in Tribulation:*
The Lifework of Sojourner Truth (1994)

NELL IRVIN PAINTER
To this day, the *Narrative of Sojourner Truth* remains outside the canon of ex-slave narratives. It ends, not with an indictment, but with the Christian forgiveness of a slaveholder.

—from *Sojourner Truth: A Life, a Symbol* (1996)

Questions

1. Does the Christian component of Sojourner Truth's thought enhance, weaken, or distract from the political and moral components of her thought? After all, many serious Christians of Truth's time argued that slavery was compatible with Christianity.

2. Leaving aside the fact that someone other than Sojourner Truth did the actual writing of her *Narrative*, can you make out a distinct personality behind the prose? What do you think Truth would be like at a relaxed social gathering? Could she engage in idle chitchat, tell a joke, innocently flirt? Would she be easy to like?

3. What are Truth's greatest virtues? Courage? Intelligence? Determination? Religious faith? Or something else?

4. Is reading Sojourner Truth now, in the twenty-first century, still inspirational? Are her message and her example still applicable? Is there some area of public life in which we would do well to emulate her spirit? If so, in what area? If Truth lived today, would she still be a political activist, or would she be a satisfied American?

FOR FURTHER READING

Biography

Bernard, Jacqueline. *Journey Toward Freedom: The Story of Sojourner Truth.* New York: W. W. Norton, 1967.

Ortiz, Victoria. *Sojourner Truth, a Self-Made Woman.* New York: J. B. Lippincott, 1974.

Painter, Nell Irvin. *Sojourner Truth: A Life, A Symbol.* New York: W. W. Norton, 1996. The best biography of Truth.

Stetson, Erlene, and Linda David. *Glorying in Tribulation: The Life-work of Sojourner Truth.* East Lansing: Michigan State University Press, 1994.

Criticism

Accomando, Christina. "Demanding a Voice Among the Pettifoggers: Sojourner Truth as Legal Actor." *Melus* 28 (Spring 2003).

Fitch, Suzanne Pullon, and Roseann M. Mandziuk. *Sojourner Truth as Orator: Wit, Story, and Song.* Westport, CT: Greenwood Press, 1997.

Humez, Jean M. "Reading the *Narrative of Sojourner Truth* as Collaborative Text." *Frontiers: A Journal of Women's Studies* 16:1 (1996), pp. 29–52.

Joseph, Gloria I. "Sojourner Truth: Archetypal Black Feminist." In *Wild Women in the Whirlwind: Afra-American Culture and the Contemporary Literary Renaissance,* edited by Joanne M. Braxton and Andrée Nicola McLaughlin. New Brunswick, NJ: Rutgers University Press, 1990, pp. 35–47.

Lipscomb, Drema R. "Sojourner Truth: A Practical Public Discourse." In *Reclaiming Rhetorica: Women in the Rhetorical Tradi-*

tion, edited by Andrea A. Lunsford. Pittsburgh, PA: University of Pittsburgh Press, 1995, pp. 227–245.

Mabee, Carleton, with Susan Mabee Newhouse. *Sojourner Truth— Slave, Prophet, Legend.* New York: New York University Press, 1993.

Mandziuk, Roseann M. "Commemorating Sojourner Truth: Negotiating the Politics of Race and Gender in the Spaces of Public Memory." *Western Journal of Communication* (June 2003).

Sánchez-Eppler, Karen. "Ain't I a Symbol?" *American Quarterly* 50:1 (March 1998), pp. 149–157.

Historical Context

Andrews, William L., ed. *Sisters of the Spirit: Three Black Women's Autobiographies of the Nineteenth Century.* Bloomington: Indiana University Press, 1986.

Campbell, Karlyn K. "Style and Content in the Rhetoric of Early Afro-American Feminists." *Quarterly Journal of Speech* 72:4 (November 1986), pp. 434–445.

Cone, James H. *A Black Theology of Liberation.* Maryknoll, NY: Orbis, 1986.

Fauset, Arthur Huff. *Black Gods of the Metropolis: Negro Religious Cults of the Urban North.* Philadelphia: University of Pennsylvania Press, 1944.

Johnson, Paul E., and Sean Wilentz. *The Kingdom of Matthias.* New York: Oxford University Press, 1994.

Quarles, Benjamin. *Black Abolitionists.* London: Oxford University Press, 1969.

White, Shane. *Somewhat More Independent: The End of Slavery in New York City, 1770–1810.* Athens: University of Georgia Press, 1991.

Yellin, Jean Fagan. *Women and Sisters: The Anti-Slavery Feminists in American Culture.* New Haven, CT: Yale University Press, 1989.

(continued)

Middlemarch	George Eliot	1-59308-023-9	$8.95
Moby-Dick	Herman Melville	1-59308-018-2	$9.95
Moll Flanders	Daniel Defoe	1-59308-216-9	$5.95
The Moonstone	Wilkie Collins	1-59308-322-X	$7.95
My Ántonia	Willa Cather	1-59308-202-9	$5.95
My Bondage and My Freedom	Frederick Douglass	1-59308-301-7	$6.95
Nana	Émile Zola	1-59308-292-4	$6.95
Narrative of Sojourner Truth		1-59308-293-2	$6.95
Narrative of the Life of Frederick Douglass, an American Slave		1-59308-041-7	$4.95
Nicholas Nickleby	Charles Dickens	1-59308-300-9	$8.95
Night and Day	Virginia Woolf	1-59308-212-6	$7.95
Northanger Abbey	Jane Austen	1-59308-264-9	$5.95
Nostromo	Joseph Conrad	1-59308-193-6	$7.95
O Pioneers!	Willa Cather	1-59308-205-3	$5.95
The Odyssey	Homer	1-59308-009-3	$5.95
Oliver Twist	Charles Dickens	1-59308-206-1	$6.95
The Origin of Species	Charles Darwin	1-59308-077-8	$7.95
Paradise Lost	John Milton	1-59308-095-6	$7.95
Père Goriot	Honoré de Balzac	1-59308-285-1	$7.95
Persuasion	Jane Austen	1-59308-130-8	$5.95
Peter Pan	J. M. Barrie	1-59308-213-4	$4.95
The Picture of Dorian Gray	Oscar Wilde	1-59308-025-5	$4.95
The Pilgrim's Progress	John Bunyan	1-59308-254-1	$7.95
Poetics and Rhetoric	Aristotle	1-59308-307-6	$9.95
The Portrait of a Lady	Henry James	1-59308-096-4	$7.95
A Portrait of the Artist as a Young Man and Dubliners	James Joyce	1-59308-031-X	$6.95
The Possessed	Fyodor Dostoevsky	1-59308-250-9	$9.95
Pride and Prejudice	Jane Austen	1-59308-201-0	$5.95
The Prince and Other Writings	Niccolò Machiavelli	1-59308-060-3	$5.95
The Prince and the Pauper	Mark Twain	1-59308-218-5	$4.95
Pudd'nhead Wilson and Those Extraordinary Twins	Mark Twain	1-59308-255-X	$5.95
The Purgatorio	Dante Alighieri	1-59308-219-3	$7.95
Pygmalion and Three Other Plays	George Bernard Shaw	1-59308-078-6	$7.95
The Red and the Black	Stendhal	1-59308-286-X	$7.95
The Red Badge of Courage and Selected Short Fiction	Stephen Crane	1-59308-119-7	$4.95
Republic	Plato	1-59308-097-2	$6.95
The Return of the Native	Thomas Hardy	1-59308-220-7	$7.95
Robinson Crusoe	Daniel Defoe	1-59308-360-2	$5.95
A Room with a View	E. M. Forster	1-59308-288-6	$5.95
Sailing Alone Around the World	Joshua Slocum	1-59308-303-3	$6.95
Scaramouche	Rafael Sabatini	1-59308-242-8	$6.95
The Scarlet Letter	Nathaniel Hawthorne	1-59308-207-X	$4.95
The Scarlet Pimpernel	Baroness Orczy	1-59308-234-7	$5.95
The Secret Garden	Frances Hodgson Burnett	1-59308-277-0	$5.95
Selected Stories of O. Henry		1-59308-042-5	$5.95
Sense and Sensibility	Jane Austen	1-59308-125-1	$5.95
Sentimental Education	Gustave Flaubert	1-59308-306-8	$6.95
Silas Marner and Two Short Stories	George Eliot	1-59308-251-7	$6.95

(continued)

Sister Carrie	Theodore Dreiser	1-59308-226-6	$7.95
Six Plays by Henrik Ibsen		1-59308-061-1	$8.95
Sons and Lovers	D. H. Lawrence	1-59308-013-1	$7.95
The Souls of Black Folk	W. E. B. Du Bois	1-59308-014-X	$5.95
The Strange Case of Dr. Jekyll and Mr. Hyde and Other Stories	Robert Louis Stevenson	1-59308-131-6	$4.95
Swann's Way	Marcel Proust	1-59308-295-9	$8.95
A Tale of Two Cities	Charles Dickens	1-59308-138-3	$5.95
Tao Te Ching	Lao Tzu	1-59308-256-8	$5.95
Tess of d'Urbervilles	Thomas Hardy	1-59308-228-2	$7.95
This Side of Paradise	F. Scott Fitzgerald	1-59308-243-6	$6.95
Three Lives	Gertrude Stein	1-59308-320-3	$6.95
The Three Musketeers	Alexandre Dumas	1-59308-148-0	$8.95
Thus Spoke Zarathustra	Friedrich Nietzsche	1-59308-278-9	$7.95
Tom Jones	Henry Fielding	1-59308-070-0	$8.95
Treasure Island	Robert Louis Stevenson	1-59308-247-9	$4.95
The Turn of the Screw, The Aspern Papers and Two Stories	Henry James	1-59308-043-3	$5.95
Twenty Thousand Leagues Under the Sea	Jules Verne	1-59308-302-5	$5.95
Uncle Tom's Cabin	Harriet Beecher Stowe	1-59308-121-9	$7.95
Utopia	Sir Thomas More	1-59308-244-4	$5.95
Vanity Fair	William Makepeace Thackeray	1-59308-071-9	$7.95
The Varieties of Religious Experience	William James	1-59308-072-7	$7.95
Villette	Charlotte Brontë	1-59308-316-5	$7.95
The Virginian	Owen Wister	1-59308-236-3	$7.95
The Voyage Out	Virginia Woolf	1-59308-229-0	$6.95
Walden and Civil Disobedience	Henry David Thoreau	1-59308-208-8	$5.95
War and Peace	Leo Tolstoy	1-59308-073-5	$12.95
Ward No. 6 and Other Stories	Anton Chekhov	1-59308-003-4	$7.95
The Waste Land and Other Poems	T. S. Eliot	1-59308-279-7	$4.95
The Way We Live Now	Anthony Trollope	1-59308-304-1	$9.95
The Wind in the Willows	Kenneth Grahame	1-59308-265-7	$4.95
The Wings of the Dove	Henry James	1-59308-296-7	$7.95
Wives and Daughters	Elizabeth Gaskell	1-59308-257-6	$7.95
The Woman in White	Wilkie Collins	1-59308-280-0	$7.95
Women in Love	D. H. Lawrence	1-59308-258-4	$8.95
The Wonderful Wizard of Oz	L. Frank Baum	1-59308-221-5	$6.95
Wuthering Heights	Emily Brontë	1-59308-128-6	$5.95